GW01368439

2

The Teenage *Poems*

and what I've learned since 2

madhuri

M PRESS

Copyright 2022 I.Z.K. Akin

No part of this book may be reproduced or transmitted in any form or by any means without express written permission of the publisher.

ISBN 978-1-7396395-2-5

Some of these poems first appeared in *Hanging Loose* magazine and/or in *Impassioned Cows by Moonlight*, by Katy Akin, published by Hanging Loose Press, New York, 1974.

Some appeared in the UC Riverside annual poetry collection.

Patriotic Lovesong to Joe first appeared in *Transatlantic Review*.

Some names have been changed to protect privacy.

Cover and Interior Design / Layout: Peggy Sands, Indigo Disegno

www.madhurijewel.com

FB pages: Madhuri Z K Akin Poetry

Mistakes on the Path

Metaphysical Therapy Arts

This is Volume 2 of *The Teenage Poems
and What I've Learned Since.*
It's called *Hitchhiking, the Caravan, and Beyond.*
To preserve the continuity of the adventure, the two
volumes are meant to go together.

Hitchhiking and the Caravan

June – August 1970

My sister and I hitchhiked away from Riverside in late June, with $10 between us, a pile of food stamps, and a note from our mother to show to any policeman who might challenge us, saying that we were traveling with her approval. We made it easily to San Francisco – everybody was going to San Francisco – where we stayed with some vague acquaintance, a blond kinky-haired guy named Art who tried it on with my fifteen-year-old sister, and was roundly rebuffed, I'm happy to say. Meanwhile I met another David while I was out dancing – this one a dark-eyed, slouchy sophisticate of twenty-seven with pale, pitted skin and wonderful moves. (He said, "It's all in the spine, it's all in the spine." I was very impressed.) As usual in this new time of my life I'd told him I didn't want sex, but to be friends – for our conversation was good – and he'd agreed, and then a couple of days later, at Art's house while Art was away, pushed me backwards down onto a bed anyway. Not really expertly, not at first…

It was all kind of strange and dislocative, to be seduced in broad daylight on a bare mattress on the floor, after I'd said No. (In those days the world belonged to young men – clueless, shuffling, bold – and so niceties like clean sheets and blankets had been dispensed with.) A few days later I spent the night with him, in a big old house he shared with several others.

From David's Window

Fists fall open
Thighs release
Down in the park
trees bang and twine
to the sad knowing of the wind
I am more still
I dance by hearing
the edge of wind
My hair drooping
in front of the window
My cheek on rocking night.

What I've learned since: I write, and wrote, from moments which pull me into mystery. But something has changed: Osho gave me permission for simple joy; cleaned out the brushy detritus from the landscape to make a place for simple joy. It is okay to dance wildly, and okay to droop watchfully; and okay to shout hallelujah. I needed a bit more reinforcement for the latter, and now I have it.

But it's not about choosing; it's about embracing it all – and often, all in the same moment. This poem feels like that to me – and makes me feel like standing up and waving my arms above my head in strong celebration! ...So, right now, I just did.

On the Bus

Look at her
composed as a hand.
Who would guess
what lovemaking she has inside?
Look at the ripples of her hair.

It's all there.
In the blink of a night she twined
polar bear sinews, thighs
around her lover;
waterfountains,
battleships in her eyes.

At first
he had the hands of a gentle naturalist
overturning a log.
A mosquito died, the blinds turned once.
his hips quickened.
He had python arms,
the tongue
of a gargoyle in love,

      hair a wild treetop in the mad pull
      for gravity —

      in her undone quicksand of surprise
      their two tongues juttered, butting;
      lips met like two halves of night –

      gone. Unflexed,
      hair naped,
      she leans her huge
      and oft-stroked eyes
      to the glittered bay.

Quickly David's peculiarly bitter taste (caused by smoking, drinking wine, and whatever else he took, I guess) and Mr-Uber-Cool litheness, plus frank vulnerability, got to me, and I was hooked. My sister and I had a program, though: to keep on hitching, up to Ferndale, then across the country, at least to Colorado, and climb Storm King Mountain with a friend of mine who'd invited us. And so it was known that I would be taking off again soon.
This poem is a celebration of a good night.

What I've learned since: When we are young, and then when we are mature; when the sap of life runs hot in our veins and pheromones come off us like cinnamon and vanilla smells from a bakery – it is extremely important to live all that love-and-sex stuff. Live it well, badly, wildly, raucously, greedily, serenely; but *live* it. You do not, do *not* want to become a dirty old man or a dirty old lady later. You really don't – you will be in shamed torment, and people will shrink from you, and you'll dress ridiculously, and die, I am told, with lust on your lips and in your loins, instead of gratefulness.
Instead, if you plunge in with all four feet and give up your prim propriety and your careful calculations, and just immerse yourself in all that love is and, we hope, all that it can be – though you make an idiot of yourself a thousand times, and get your heart broken, and curse and gnash your teeth and sob for a week, and then bounce back to love again, quite soon, really – if you can answer

Katy and David making love

ll and meet her running – you will *live*, and you will age with
ing grace. You'll become wise, and serenely objective, and deeply compassionate; and, best of all, you will develop a really broad sense of humor – for everything to do with mating *is* bizarre! Here we are, mammal angels, so frequently utterly bewildered, and love bewilders us further, and in so doing makes a bridge to an unseen destination. A strange bridge, but inescapable; I won't say the only bridge either (though I don't truly know another); but not to be despised. I recommend it – and, if you can add Tantra (and by Tantra I do not mean soft-core porn dressed up with incense! I mean the frank, demanding, structured, utterly sober practice of bringing the Witness to relationship and sex) to the mix, you're home free.

Her Jacket

Francesca
forgive me,
I am being dashed on the crags of my company,
belonging to sidewalk fog.
I dug your jacket out of the back room,
Francesca,
and I am glad to have it belted on me,
a rope to a mountainclimber.
Your leaf skin
joins me now. I need the way your jacket
sleeves my body in the fog.
I am flushed
with the memory of your thin arms inside it,
Francesca,
the nights you wore it
safe with pocketed hands.

My sister and I fled Art's and went to some other strange person's house while that person was away – a friend had steered us to it.

One foggy evening we were going out with David, and of course I had no warm jacket, since I came from the South; so I opened a cupboard and found a brown suede one and happily belted it round my waist. (Mark Twain once said, "The coldest winter I ever spent was a summer in San Francisco.") David criticized me sharply for borrowing a garment without permission. But in my youth I had not such a clear sense of people's possessions and how they might prize them – not at all. The world was a huge strange place and perhaps I couldn't bear the boundaries in it – for they might exclude me in some final way. Perhaps I just shut them out. (And of course in my childhood everybody's everything was everywhere, and if you found something lying around you mucked about with it if you felt like it, regardless, and then left it where it lay when you were done.) And I had little conception of how people labor for their possessions and are invested in and identified with them. My friends and I shared our clothes; we were Communists of a sort. I must have had some sort of sense though because I did not *take the jacket away* with me, but only borrowed it.

What I've learned since: Someone once told me, "It's okay to borrow something if you know that the person would have said yes if you'd asked them." Hmmm. I'm not sure – but anyway, there it was; and no harm done. If I'd left a copy of the poem in the jacket pocket (and I can't imagine that I wouldn't have) that would fall under the "write-something-beguiling-and-thus-get-away-with-things" strategy that has worked so well in my life. I don't think you can really make a rule about these things, except that of course stealing the jacket would have been altogether wrong. Borrowing, when you are cold – that's something else.

I did notice that when my seventeen-year-old grand-niece visited me when I lived in a big fine house in Missouri – fifteen years ago now- she was similarly clueless about boundaries regarding possessions. She simply raided my sock drawer and wore my socks without asking; and ended up taking *one* of them (!) away with her when she left. She draped her clothes about the house as if the house was all hers, and ate anything she pleased from the fridge without asking – no kombucha was safe from her. She did try very hard to please me when I pointed things out to her (which I did in as generous, friendly, and creative a way as I could, explaining how someone's labor has gone into their acquisition – making an example of a particular embroidered Indian pillowcase she'd gotten a stain on, and explaining how that pillowcase came to be in my life: the sessions I'd done, the leagues I'd traveled, the thought I'd put into the purchase, then the later posting of the thing in a box to the West, and the money that had cost and how I'd worked for it, as well as how the women or children who had made the item had worked, in whatever difficult conditions, moment by moment; and so on; how the beauty of the thing was important to me, how each item in the house represented the labor of work, of choice, of care, of carrying – a thing she was apt to scorn, having not yet labored.) But maybe the young just are Communists, and that's okay. They grow out of it, and that *might* be a pity – I don't feel qualified to say.

After the San Francisco sojourn of this poem, when I lived in London, I was cold so much that, later, when I could afford it and clothes became so much more generally available, I made it a policy to have a superabundance of jackets and coats: velvet, faux fur, quilted, puffy, corduroy, etc etc; and plenty of sweaters and thick cotton tights too.

What I've learned since: It's good to have lots of coats (we'll hear more about coats, or rather their lack, later). You never know where you'll find yourself. And you can lend them to chilly guests.

The Stomach

I
on the body

the most vulnerable place
is the stomach.
it tightens in crying,
swells over a baby's head.

In People's Park, Berkeley, June 1970

it is where food goes
it shifts before the storm
of soup and cherries and cheese
like a planet
expecting visitors, meteors.
it accommodates, this stomach does,
and is a natural patting place
for the hand.

II

the stomach in lovemaking.
this is something I know little about.
I expect it ripples before the chasm
like a horse's muscles
giving the neigh.

As I've said, I was fascinated with my belly, as young girls often are. It was a somewhat beleaguered one, what with wheat bloat, and having by this time been stuffed and starved quite a lot. It was regarded with fear: would it stick out and make me look bad? Fashion and ballet training told me it should be *completely flat*. Often it hid constipation.

I had bad opinions of the poor thing, which was only doing its best with what I gave it. It was my bugaboo, my *bête noire*. Poor innocent thing.

What I've learned since: The second chakra of the woman is a power place. And, like most power places, it is designed to stick out. (Women in the 14th century used to pad theirs to get the effect!) This swelling is echoed in the aura: we women have huge, erectile feeling-auras! They rise and fall depending on what's happening in the moment. They never lie, the way the mind routinely does.

Women's second chakras can be encouraged! They can swell mightily with delicious sensation! This is great! Only when this is allowed is the woman potentially ready for sex. And it can't be hurried – she has to *feel* what she feels.

Mostly that chakra is clogged with old anger though… that needs clearing first. Enter Dynamic meditation!

If the stomach is being held in, the woman can't really feel. I held mine in for years... until I was informed of the wheat allergy and stopped eating that stuff. This changed my life. Belly still lovingly rounded; but not preggie-size-by-evening any more.

It is wonderful to explore this region, physically and metaphysically. Hiding two inches below the navel and deeper in is the *hara* – the word is Japanese and means "the place of birth and death." All chakras arise from here and go back to here: it is the primeval Emptiness. Our true center.

There are lots of nice guts in here too which benefit by being listened to, so it's nice to visit them sometimes and let them speak to you. I'm not exactly talking about the rumblings of hunger; more the responsive registering of whether the gut feels it likes something or not – a situation, direction, person. Ye olde 'gut-feeling'.

Any organ has something to say – for we store in our bodies everything we are and everything we fight or have fought; everything that's happened to us, and all the inconvenient things we really felt but dared not show. There are beautiful techniques for freeing these truths from our flesh and letting us see them again. I recommend this as a pursuit! Bioenergetics – Healing Journey – my own Self-Healing – Voice Dialogue – and on and on. Wonderful! If your belly – or any voice in it – gets to tell you how it really feels... you are free. Free from carrying dark poo you could not get shut of because you didn't exactly know it was there.

"the stomach in lovemaking..." must be allowed to fully function as a present, wild feeling-power. The man must learn to hold space for this, and the woman not to dump undigested emotion on him. When all is clear and flowing, hers can fit into his and bloom there (I have experienced this – it is mysterious, helpless, wonderful), and both are fed with sensate, scary, voluptuous joy.

What I've also learned: When I finally at long last let go and began to trust my body (I was in my late twenties) and its rhythms, it turned out that it knew exactly how much to eat and when – I didn't need to mess things up by fussing and freaking out about it! Now it just stays the size it was meant to be – all by itself. And yes, it has a nice little mound.

nge and excitement, I found time to go on the bus
one of my Junior-High rebel-clique, who was living
sco with her boyfriend John, a musician older than
as away just then.

To Beth

Entering you
our wings slide together.
You are unplanned
as rips in leather, smoke in eyes.
You smell your own recent love
and gift me with your mouth.

Friend of years
I see everything of you
and turn over in some sleep
I didn't know I was in.

I breathe low.
Leaving you,
walking backwards up the sidewalk,
my cheeks are rough leather.
I want more.

A rich dirt forms on my eyelids
as the unburying hastens
and the smoke of us together
leads away again, curling, looking.

In those funky, shaggy, scraggy days, in San Francisco with its London weather; in and out of tall, narrow, neglected wooden houses – we were all busy about our Youth. And as kids everywhere do, we formed deep relationships with each other. This was of course during my thinness-obsessed years, when I found naturally-

Mary Beth, 1970

round girls attractive; though I couldn't quite say what I wanted with them (it was my own body being relaxed that I wanted). Beth was lush: satin-skinned, bosomy, sturdy-legged, with long silky light-brown hair and refined features. And she didn't seem worried about her curves. She was a lovely friend, and we had a great time discussing our men.

When I say "Entering you" I mean psychically, aurically; I mean, *being in her energy field*. I don't mean anything physical – if we kissed, it would have been chaste – but I took the risk to write about it the way it felt to me energetically, emotionally.

I did show her the poem, not a lot later; and her face lifted and crinkled inwards in worry! It's okay, Beth, it's okay – this was a different kind of intimacy than the grosser sort.

From the Zoo

we are the car-wrecks of elephants,
junkyard bears, rollerskate foxes
strewn in the alley.

The decorated primates
stroll among us,
feeding us
the ends of frostycones.
We wait behind spiked bracelets
on slumrock balconies
where coyotes pace in rags:

where the panther is a black pearl
on a sidewalk,
and ocelots are left sprinkled to the night.
We are the lion cub,
fierce from the moment of conception,
the Goodwill-box snowleopard
growling at a porcupine with dulled quills –

the egret's wings are newspaper
flapping from a scabbed head and twisting eye.
monkeys roam jittery beats
eating trampled salad,
demented, stabbed a million stabs
with boredom, scratching red asses,
grace scraped from them
like color from butterfly wings.
Our babies are soon thickened
with the hardness the air gives;
dying scalps, fur dead, tits wilted,
prehensile tails
losing their spring,
dying in spite of all the water
flushed onto us
from the washing of San Francisco's hands –

Our time beats different
Our flesh ripples
from the bruise within.
We trade tones
trade low discord
trade swipes and glances,
trade shattering teeth,
trade bones and teeth and cages.
The moon turns over turning otters,
over dark tapirs,
over the dream-booms
of Siberian tigers,
 the drums of the slum, the zoo.

David took me to the San Francisco Zoo shortly after we met. I don't know why exactly – I think it was his idea of a day out – but the place reminded me of Tijuana, only worse.

What I've learned since: In the 90's I went once to a zoo in Northern Norway – the furthest-north zoo in the world – which had no cages, just very large fenced-in areas in wild nature, far from any town. The creatures were not necessarily delighted, but they were not madhouse inmates like those San Francisco ones were. I didn't come away horrified; rather, intrigued by the glimpse, at some distance, a pair of wolverines with their intense, pointed ferocity; enchanted by the arctic foxes. But still... a zoo is a sad thing. Cities for humans are often zoo-like too. We do to ourselves what we do to them, our creature brothers.

It is my contention that humans are made to co-exist with, and daily view, wild creatures. That our murdering of animals so that we are seemingly here with only each other, dogs and cats, and a few brutalized farm animals, has impoverished us beyond all knowing. That our sanity actually depends on glimpsing wild beasties, plus stars, campfires, and each others' bodies nude; and by covering up these things or deleting them from our lives some primeval nourishment is denied us – an eye-food we actually *need*. Without it we are not really altogether here.

What I've learned since: In meditation one learns some empathy; it just happens. As we become more sensitive to ourselves (and Osho says, "Sensitivity is your birthright. Become more and more sensitive,") we naturally become more sensitive to everything and everyone around us. Then we will not want to hurt them.
This is our only hope.

on the journey

    my dress is ragged black and green.
    i wear the jewels of earthquaked people.
    there are crickets in my hair.

    i am late awake with a jittered candle
    near a cold ocean –
    i can hear it crashing in and out,
    hear the crickets

thrown from that bitter thunder
cry for it.
with the quick shrieks of stars.

this is what i came for.
i ran from a morningful of crows
to sit up late with my infections
to write of my rags, my rags.

My sister Serafina and I (born Susannah, called Sukey or Suze or Enchantress or any one of a number of loving nicknames; she decided she wanted to be called Serafina – so we mostly all obliged) hitchhiked up to Ferndale then, and stayed with a lesbian couple we knew who ran an artsy, earthy shop and lived in a rustic old house with pottery vases full of dried flowers in the windows, and had very short hair, and were kind. I sat up late one night and wrote this.

Surely I did wear rags; we all did. The "morningful of crows" I'd run from was Riverside. As for the infections: there was some sort of *discharge* going on, and a general itch and unease; and I didn't know the cause, and had no money to find out. So I endured. I think it was probably yeast, as I'd had two courses of antibiotics in the previous two years and nobody had told me what that does to your system.

What I've learned since: A spoonful of yogurt gently pressed up the vagina with the fingers is very helpful for this. So is a few drops of tea tree oil in warm water. Most important: take strong probiotics by mouth, best got from fridge section of health food shop. Stop eating sugar altogether.

What I've learned since: STDs love the way sex is so irresistible. Yeast infections can be caught by men, particularly under the foreskin, leading to misery – and then given back to you. Olive oil used as a lube encourages this!

It is necessary, not just desirable, to educate oneself about STDs. At least then you know what you're risking. Some will kill you, some will annoy you, some will annoy everybody you encounter, some ck you viciously at intervals all your life without killing you. st itch. Some make you infertile, some can give you cancer. Some give you disgusting little warts, some painful raw sores, some make you blind and bent and crazy and shuffling. Some muck with your blood cells, some attack your liver. Some just make you feel low and mean and oozy while they set about scarring your inner tubes and crevices. Some have wiped out entire populations.

What happy little beasties all these things are, in their own universes! I hope you don't get any of them; but chances are you will unless you're co-monogamous with someone else you met as a virgin. What can you do?

- Condoms can cause cystitis, since they increase pull and tear. This is still not a good reason to avoid them. To minimize this possibility, drink a lot of water before getting into bed. Use oodles of lube, pee within half an hour after sex, rinse pubic area after with warm water and lavender oil.
- Condoms don't necessarily block herpes. The virus is small enough to pass through the membrane. But they help. Herpes is contagious if it is broken out; almost but not quite broken out; and when the sores are healing. It can even be contagious when there are no sores or other signs (aching, grumpiness, flu-feelings). If you've got it, try to find a lover who has it too. There are more strains than yours and so you might get a new one as well, but it's still preferable to getting it when you don't have it, or giving it to someone who hasn't got it. Don't let a prospective lover convince you he or she "isn't scared of it." He/she isn't scared because he/she can't imagine what it is like to have it; and he/she is fueled by that reliable force, Lust. Have mercy on him/her – don't pass it on.
- Condoms can break. Use enough lube; and if things are getting very poundy, know that that is when things are getting dangerous. Slow down.
- Don't have sex with anybody who has a sore – even if that sore is beside the mouth. Oral herpes can cross over and become genital, and vice versa. Or it can attack the throat.
- Both partners must wash their hands before touching the other's genitals (and after!). Street-dirt introduced into

delicate membranes can cause infection. (I was in the hospital at the Ranch with a kidney infection after an adventure with a certain Brazilian with bedroom eyes.)
- or a woman, washing 'down there' with normal soap can cause unpleasant irritation. I am so grateful for Dr. Bronner's Castile soap, which comes in a bottle with a rather loony, verbose label. I like the lavender and rose formulas particularly. It's great for armpits too – utterly benign.

What I've learned since: Diseases like these are not fun. The medicines are not fun. At the age I am now I would absolutely *hate* to get trich or chlamydia or, god forbid, the clap – though when I was young I took these things in my (wayward) stride.
In my elder age, taking care of myself is a tender, nurturing, soft sort of thing, sensitive and listening. (And with plenty of brisk walks in all weathers too, just to keep things balanced and challenging and fresh.) When I was young it was a bashing, crashing sort of thing, about getting up and getting out and getting on and getting laid.
But all those diseases... *ugh.*

Ah – I still wear "the jewels of earthquaked people." I have wonderful lapis lazulis from the Himalayas, Afghanistan... I love ethnic, rich, colorful jewels. (And no, in case anyone is wondering: I don't think mining semi-precious stones causes earthquakes. Earthquakes come from much bigger forces, much deeper down!)

shifting

darkness struts her breasts against the house.
my lovers are in Reno and San Francisco
prowling with watchful eyebrows.
i am proud for their restlessness,
i have my own.
in Riverside a man sleeps.

we have torn apart like newspaper
in the morning;
and apart bloom, curl, fold back to trees.

i see my old house as a cage
and a man asleep there, breathing,
rhyming the print of my bark
against his flesh.

outside Reno i want there to be trees
for my lovers to walk through.
the short bones are restless in my toes.

What I've learned since: I still want there to be trees in deserts. The short bones are still restless in my toes (I have short toes), but less so. A different man now rhymes "the print of his bark

Fending off mosquitoes by putting our sleeping bags over our heads, in Wells, Nevada

against my flesh –" and beside him, his new wife sleeps. I must get over that man. Chris, my Missouri beloved, lost to me by my own adventurousness.

Lovers. They seem like a thing life needs to have in it – the word sounds sweet and frivolous and ardent and periodically attentive. I've scorned all the hopeful ones lately. Menopause rewrote my plot.

Recently I did a self-healing to unplug from that last love. The meager drip of nourishment within the cord to him was starving me. He has oh-so-gently-but-surely turned his molded, curve-muscled back.

It was a radiant healing. Perhaps it worked. (I have had a few heartache dreams since, though.) Perhaps now I want a man who will support me, hear my confidences, and otherwise keep out of sight – making his own breakfast in his own abode, and sometimes phoning just to tell me poems. A man with a boat, that tips and skims and sloshes under him in salty seas. Or a memory of tall mountains in his legs.

If he takes his boat into a sweetwater river, or even a rather murky barge-coasting one, I might come along. If he wants to climb a medium mountain, where you don't need ropes, I will be delighted.

night in Durango

people are sleeping.
cows eat through libraries of grass
moths die into the candle.
i eat my own hair
breathing hard
wax dripping hot like semen
on bare feet.
looking for more things to know
i climb a mountain
and dream an orgasm
while the grass eats softly of rain,

moths and mosquitoes
thrash for warmth
and i allow myself shelter.

My sister and I then hitchhiked to Durango, Colorado to climb 14,000 ft. Storm King Mountain with Ken, an old friend of mine, a folk-dancing partner from Redlands, near Riverside. But then we got a message that he had hurt his ankle and couldn't come. And so we climbed the peak anyway – with an eighteen-year-old fellow we'd met on the road. This was a wonderful, true adventure: a five-day trek, climb, and subsequent rescue (we'd run out of food) by a Methodist youth group out camping in the woods.

Standing atop Storm King as night fell, in my shorts, hiking boots, and suede Goodwill lady-gloves that stained my hands green when it rained – looking out over peaks, valleys, and forests deepening into dusk – was a teaching: "Now what? I've done this – what next?" said my mind. I saw that even a glorious accomplishment doesn't satisfy the mind.

Me, Serafina, and our friend Paul on top of Storm King Mountain, Colorado. 14,000 feet!

Once we got back to Durango, my sister and I sat on the shady courthouse lawn and demolished a half-gallon of chocolate chip ice-cream with two spoons! We were staying in some sort of crash pad, a wooden house, where we got into heated philosophical arguments with the young male inhabitants. We stayed for a few days there.

What I've learned since: I'm still a bit suspicious of shelter – owning or renting a dwelling asks so much of us. (Perhaps there is a Sadhu in me, or an ocelot.) And yet we do truly need it, I guess – so as not to die of exposure. In 2021, I live in a very comfortable flat in the beautiful Pennines, but am positively itching to up stakes and go a-wandering!

And a P.S.: Ken Thackwell, the young man who'd invited us to climb and then couldn't come… when we'd bumped into him in Berkeley he'd acted, I'd thought, strange – abstracted, introspected, not quite all there. Secretive, if affable. He was staying in some grungy place with a mattress on the floor. (We all slept on mattresses on floors of course.) I had adored him in those dancing years and was bewildered by the change; he was the lanky young man in a red Porsche who took me to Disneyland for my Junior High graduation, and kissed me till my mascara ran. I'm sure he came from a posh family, though he never said. So I googled him a few years ago, and found out he had died – cause not given. Ooosh!

questions late at night

what kind of creature am i?
i go into a mantis tremble;
my cheekbones, the shell of my nose
luminous.
i can't remember if i am pretty,
or even beautiful.

insects.
three spiders in a rock,
the old shadow of vines.
their legs are silent, they stay and die.
i don't know what i am
or how long a life lasts.
can my locust arms be desired?
no answers from the air tonight.

the black web of the window says,
"your face changes,
angle to angle,
like the pages of a text on insects.
you are as beautiful as something
that is not all bee, or all cricket."

have I lost my long curled tongue,
my passion-flower heart?
through how many wings
does a day last?

When we were kids, our father, a passionate entomologist, taught us about insects. We would spread out a sheet under a tree on a summer night, and Glen would shake the tree; the sheet would be covered in tiny creatures, and our father would display them to us in the beam of a flashlight, proudly, as if he himself had made them. He loved these complex, graceful little beings; and taught us to respect them. I was always surprised when other children were frightened, disgusted, or, above all, ignorant about them. Didn't they know a nice light-brown, bunch-legged Agelena spider was different than a black widow, and perfectly harmless?

And then, of course, as a teenager, I began to question myself from all directions – and insects got their legs into this querying too.

What I've learned since: I can't really love mosquitoes, fleas, cockroaches, ticks, or *poisonous* spiders, no matter what my father

after the mountain, she sits up late reading David's poem again.

Writing in the night after the mountain-climb. Durango, Colorado, August 1970

said. I've had dengue fever (otherwise known as bonebreak fever, for the way it makes you feel your bones are breaking, it hurts so much) in India! Several times! I've seen flat little bedbugs nesting in the corners of my mosquito net, and felt their itchy bites! I've seen fleas in a rented house pogo-sticking out of the carpet to amazing heights! And in Missouri I had for seven years to inspect my pajamas and my bed every night for brown recluse spiders! But, like many people, I adore bees – partly since the name Osho gave me means "Love that is sweet like honey." And partly because bees are furry world-saving little bundles of joy, possible stings notwithstanding.

What is a flower-garden without bees and butterflies – trees without birds – woods without deer – sea without fish – tide-pools without sea anemones and starfish?

Yes – we need to ask ourselves this – day by day.

About the questioning-who-I-am: Any life worth its salt will have plenty of this in it. There are so many answers, each of which dissolves, leaving more questioning. That questioning is Space: the best thing we have. And Space goes on being renewed too.

Any time we're lost: Be lost, open your arms, wait. Be happy with maps you love, but don't let them stop you. A map is two-dimensional; life has many more dimensions than that. Explore. Flounder. Question. Sit, too, and wait, and watch your breath, your thoughts, your energy. Seek, find, lose, seek again.

The question *Who am I?* is a shovel, digging down into the mother lode of Nothing but Presence.

To John

far up in the night
when you have just gone
out to the weeds to sleep –
i marvel that i am fond.

we sat all night writing
with moths blowing
ragged messengers at the windows.
the world tilts
the deck of a colored ship,
and I, looking for sea legs
come instead to this warm wood kitchen
an island in traveling,
a galley of china cups, baby powder,
teakettle and water pipes –
things that can be plumbed.

and now that you've gone out to sleep
the moments pass just the same.
it is the moths
blown in off the white-capped ocean
who say different things.

This was at the Durango house. The boys there were kindly and respectful and argumentative to us by turns. They did not importune us. I don't now remember John, but he must have lived in the back yard in a tent (back yards often held tents in those days). We must have been writing that evening... how lovely! The 'white-capped ocean' was far away, but coming –

What I've learned since: Hmmmm... nobody else has ever written with me all night... there was just that once! I don't know what that says about anything, but there it is!
If you are a traveler, a blank book to write in can be your land, your anchor; your purchase on the earth or in the sea.
And then, one day, sit yourself down somewhere and type it all up... or, even better, find a helper. Or, of course, take your laptop, and blog or type on the journey. Hand-scribbling is still my fave – quiet. Comfy. Much more intimate and soft.

The Caravan Poems

I. Lost Magic

It fled me, that tangled beehive.
turmoils of half-digested bees
stinging inside wrists,
making a mound of my belly,
blooming from toenails,
bejeweling my throat
with a diabolical hum –
it fled from either pole of my body
and I am a dry snakeskin
sitting cross-legged in Ohio,
listening for honey.

So. The plot thickens. My sister and I, hitchhiking East, were invited to a rock concert. This proved to be out on a brushy plain tilted towards the looming Rockies. BB King sang on a stage and colorful, flying-haired hippies strode about purposefully. I was 'discovered' in my 100-year-old white lacy dress (well, it looked Victorian, so we called it that) by a glowing, stoned-out-of-his-gizzard, extremely sophisticated Belgian professor I had noticed from the van as we drove in... a glamorous, bare-chested, swinging-haired, golden man in chamois bellbottoms. I was invited along on this caravan of music and dope, to dance at the concerts we put on... all across the country – and then to fly to England. (Someone later told me there were twenty-five tie-dyed teepees, fifteen painted school buses, and one hundred and fifty freaks. At the time, I didn't count.) My sister... Ah woe... was taken in by the Hog Farm commune, they went back to New Mexico, and our mother hitchhiked to rescue her; they two went on to New York together, having a memorable adventure my mother later wrote about lyrically – her account was published in a counter-culture magazine, *Black Bart*.

I felt sad about the separation – Jacques had phoned our mother, got it all set up – but it was *so sad*. I'm sorry, Sarita. (She wanted to study ballet and I didn't – and New York didn't appeal to me – so our paths were heading towards a divergence anyway. But still...)

The trip I was being offered was just too wonderful an opportunity to miss – how could I refuse? And Jacques had said that my sister, at fifteen, was too young to go. (I was to turn eighteen shortly.) Though, much later, he said he had subsequently discovered she *could* have gone. He *so* regretted not taking her!

I'm guessing this poem refers to Jacques having temporarily left the Caravan to go back to his work at UCLA; to rejoin us later in New York. I would have been abuzz with his warm, grown-up (sort of) energy; and might have felt its loss, and the loss of his support, and his buffering between me and the more working-class (doping-class) vibe of the bus-riders. I was abruptly cast in amongst them after having ridden privileged with Jacques in a chauffeured car, staying at motels and often eating in restaurants, and I felt it, rather.

My sister and Jaques: sis in braids, Jacques on far right. I'm behind the person in the foreground

learned since: Peace lies in exactly that cessation: ~~~ness afforded by my own lightweight presence, my ~~~ vulnerable presence. I will come to cherish this peace above all else, one day: my rest, my salvation, my simplicity, my bliss.

From a letter to my mother
Caravan, Thurs night, 1970

Ma Cherie Mama,
on the endless beginnings of the Midwestern plains, I sit of a balmy night in my improvised office and write to you. I'm sitting in a car with the door open so the light is on. It doesn't matter about the battery because it's a rented car and Warner Bros. pays.

...Tomorrow we do a concert for thousands of Boulder-Denverpeople with some famous bands and stuff too. I am fine – Serafina and I saw one another last night at the Hog Farm, a most high and wonderful place. A busload of hogfarmers who had been on the road for a while got all homesick and as they approached it finally, shrieked and screamed hollered with delight. Sukey cried in the firelight and everybody was moved. She has a nice Pisces boyfriend named Joseph. She made two superenormous applecrisps. Understandably she doesn't want to feel stuck there; I hope hope you get the dancing school arranged.

My beautiful Jacques bought for me an Indian necklace in Santa Fe. It is of turquoise and coral beads. He is older, he will not say how much. He is totally generous and open. He sits beside me now reading *The Crows*. One of the Frenchmen, Alain, wants some of my poetry to send somewhere in France. We turned on to some nitrous oxide (laughing gas) by the doctor bus a while ago, and then I danced on a platform in the warm wind. This letter will therefore sound funny.

After this we will go to Nebraska, and who knows where. We eat at restaurants all the time except I'm never hungry because all we do is ride in a car, except for at night...

Send all mail and bread to that Maryland address. And please, please send these things, or as many as possible (they are light):

1. my red silky-satiny long skirt with soft striped weave and elastic waist
2. my pink chiffon see-through blouse
3. my little velvet cap with bells
4. my pantaloons
5. tights: green or orange or blue or red

I need things to be elegant and crazy-strange in. Anything else you can send is cool... My boots shrank on the campfire so essentially I'm barefoot. I know! Send the green filmy short-cape and maybe those green shoes. And both my good strings of beads. I'll be sending home diary, etc after while. The things Serafina had planned for my birthday were so beautiful it broke my heart. I felt I didn't deserve it.

I'm making friends with people now, and getting into some palm-reading.

I'll keep in touch. We'll be in Maryland probably by the 24th, so send it on.

I love you very very much. Oh Mama to be turned loose in Europe! I can do it.

We sleep in teepees made of wonderfully tie-dyed canvas, we eat crunchy granola and vegetables and brown rice and ham cooked with oranges. Everyone is kept in immense supply of dope, cigarettes, beer and wine.

Tom Donahue, the producer, is fat and incredible. He buys all the Indian jewelry in Santa Fe and has a young wife from Riverside. Today a tragedy which was forseen *[sic]* by a French fortuneteller – one of the trucks fell over. The people got out and then it exploded, with incredible amounts of equipment burning up. I'm getting a French accent in my sleep. I haven't dreamed since I joined the Caravan – I don't need to!!...
love,
Katy Zelle Araminta

P.S. It's all wonderful. I love you. also send my knickers, either pair.

II. Watching the French Cameraman Christian Eating a Sandwich

walking behind the fire
Christian takes a mouthful
of the sandwich he holds.
It opens a little,
a soft book of cheese.
Christian's big bones
are grateful for this sandwich to burn.
Christian's eyes hold the scene –
camp-fire and caravan, blackness
like a ring of camels encircling all.
A rich bubble in me swells
for Christian, nourished, black-eyed
licking his fingers.

So, this was midway on that crazy caravan. Jacques wasn't there; the caravan continued across the plains towards the East Coast. I slept in teepees or tents, and ate around camp fires with everyone else. Christian was part of the French film crew – and here my eye rests on him for a few moments, and a poem is born, of simple gratefulness and looking-kindly-upon.

What I've learned since: Two seemingly contradictory things: and contradictions are just fine. Licked fingers can leave cold germs on surfaces that survive for two days! The best thing you can do, as well as washing your hands after licking them (if you are going to do it, which I don't any more) is wash them when you come in from outside. (And while you are outside, don't rub your eyes or touch your nose or mouth. I don't care how fussy you think I am. I just don't care. Your culture could judge me neurotic or merely careful… whatever! And hasn't history now borne me out?) This keeps all those germs out of your house.

And!!! It's useful to acknowledge blessings and goodnesses and moments of grace. So many things go right… the sun comes up, the sun goes down, food comes along, people are friendly, machines work, there's a place to sleep. So many *small* things go right. It's nice to say them to oneself, in the night, if one wakes up… *so* relaxing. And it's nice to let a poem catch one and sing a little blessing softly. What else are we here for? (Besides being aware of on what side of the temple door you left your shoes, and being aware of what you do with your hands – and feet and everything else!)

III. Boulder, Colorado

my good people
out on the land
peace running in us
like clouds through the day
the plains stretch forever
the sun puts out its hand
in a sky of work-shirt blue

hammering together
painting our buses
swaying through camp on gentle horses –
the days make a chain
twisted from the same soft weeds.
We are each different,
a circus on the plains
singing of bio-degradable
or brown rice   of peyote
of amplifiers   for those waving grasses
in our hands, those roads.

So, here the sense of community was welcome and strong. What held us together, though, was peculiar: movie money, money seeking profit; and yet, too, an ethos people discussed constantly, with lavish pepperings of the word "man," (not, for some reason, "woman" – maybe it takes too long to say?) To me the ethos was self-evident: peace, love, et al just seemed right and proper, along with floaty garments and as much hair everywhere as you could muster. But we thought (albeit a bit defensively) drugs were some sort of virtue and answer; and we didn't exactly comprehend what brings peace and love to the human being, really: enough awareness of ourselves that we become sufficiently un-mechanical to avoid becoming Xeroxes of our parents. Or, if we are to some large degree Xeroxes, that we *know it in every instance.*

It is awareness that releases love; one of the strange rules of physics that can perhaps only be explained by another hoary old word: 'truth'. What is true, resonant right now as-is: erupts in love; love from inside. We don't know why. Maybe they're the same thing, truth and love; though they often seem to have a little lapse of time in between.

Me among the teepees

Letter to my mother
en route, 1970

Dear lovemum,
last night as we were rocketing airily along in our bus, the *Lotus Bay*, with thunder and lightning ripping the sky, the bedspreads on the ceiling blowing as though we were under a balloon – I wrote you a long letter. To my dismay I find it is largely illegible. Here is the gist –

Everybody's talking about Europe. The hashish of Paris, the clothes of London. Nobody's coming back. I think secretly of December on the Mediterranean in Tunisia. Jacques says that winter in Europe is a bitch, but if I can stick it out maybe we'll meet... Departure: August 27, Washington D.C. The movie is rumored (and rumors are as plentiful as bodies on this trip) that the last scene of the movie is us floating down the Seine on a barge. I dare not even look forward to the time when we can talk endlessly – I want to get the marvels firmly established, like an English custard first.

I hope you go to live in S.F. ... – Mamalove before this adventure dropped about my shoulders I was having very specific longings about it.

...I met a chick here who has known David for ages, and has good good things to say (she's usually cynical; a Scorpio). Guess what mama, I'm a groupie. The bass player in Jethro Tull (famous rock group English).

Very very important: I NEED CLOTHES!!!

If you saw how the Elegant Ones dress you would know why. I have always been that elegant, it's just nobody appreciated it in Riverside. I would never have gotten to come if it hadn't been for a dress I was wearing and my dancing. In England I must be elegant, and I won't have the bread to buy stuff.

Guess what, Jacques gave me $20 for some shoes. I found some grey kneeboots, a perfect fit, in the droll and merry senior citizen's *[sic]* thrift shop in Yellow Springs Ohio (in the funky P.O. of which I now stand). They cost 25c, so I bought an Indian necklace for $1.50 and a bunch of other stuff too. I hope you've already sent that stuff I requested. I also need: that peach silk shawl & the

n. My heavy long green skirt. Brown clogs if possible… crepe mini-dress with weird unsleeves, a paisley print. ...ith my new boots!) Send all my whole tights. I'll have to scrounge a better luggage… I'd like the long dress and the red crepe shorts… and the red crepe jacket to go with the shorts… Oh! And my green lace see-through sleeveless dress with its green cape.

Guess what, Joni Mitchell played for us in Nebraska Mon. night.

Three horrible boring days of Midwest scenery, ugh! I need the pink silk skinny scarf to go with the pink crepe blouse and red satiny skirt you're sending. And that crepe blouse-dress, strapless with purple wisteria on it.

My caravan, at times a traveling small town. At times a conquering army. A pilgrimage. A big communal honeymoon…

Read any letters from David before forwarding, so you can tell me. Also to let you see his soul.

…Jacques is Aries. You would madly luff him – he's anywhere from 20-40, except he has a daughter 10, which pins it down…

Everybody is sick with stomach-blecccch. We have a house Dr. and a house psychiatrist. We eat steak, brown rice, vegies, crunchy granola, fruit, wine. Or go to uniformly horrible restaurants. (Someone commands grandly, barefoot and headbanded – "All the hippies go on one bill! We're in a movie caravan for Warner Bros!) Yes sir, yes sir! it makes them gallop.

…I have made many friends, and somehow it all seems inevitable.

…I sing your praises whenever appropriate.

Jacques says I (and Serafina) should be around very sophisticated people… I'll write longer novelish letters from across the ocean, when I feel safely there.

Maybe you could convert my foodstamps to cash illegally for the benefit of all. Also for dinner we have peyote buttons.

I wrote to Morris for addresses. Jacques works at the same place at UCLA that Jim Richard used to! *[Note: Jim Richard, a family friend, appears in a poem near the end of the book.]* I'll bet they know each other. I'm sending you a poem I wrote on a peaceful campfire evening in Boulder.

Oh, I'm so grubby, I'm going over to the motel and see if I can take a shower. We're doing a concert here Friday.

I rack my brains out trying to remember clothes I need. They are important. Also very much I need Khadine perfume, and can't seem to find it here. It goes with my kohl.

Look through the pictures I'm sending back. Love you love you. Keep writing, I crave it.

Love, Katy Araminta (Jacques whispers this in his French accent).

And to my sister

My love Serafina,
written in a bumpy bus on the way to Nebraska...

Jacques loves you. Trust him totally – he is whole love earth. He said for me to send you to him – don't feel funny about it, if you ever need anybody, you can go to him. I'll give you his address. He's in L.A. right now, but may rejoin the caravan later. He is Morris-style, Ricki-style. He is the kind of man who brings home beautiful lovers (male and female) for his chicks.

He talked about you a lot. He sees everything and is infinitely whole and real. We took some acid the day of the concert in Boulder. I have never had such a fantastic time in my life, and next day I felt mellow and loving – no bad shit. It is because everything is all right! Someday you will hear it all. On acid I managed to find a Moroccan gay chick named Fey. We were falling in love and making out on the grass and Jacques was there and every time I think about it I laugh, because she wanted to make love to me, but not with him there. Then she got all freaked and split because she had decided not to be gay anymore, and I was tempting her too much. It was incredible. I danced, wearing only a gypsy skirt and that white robe. Everything else had fallen off.

We're in the Midwest. It's all flat... We are to be in Jacques' inner circle. He gave me some kohl for my eyes. When I was on acid I missed you. Being on my own trip is damned good for me, my love – I hope it comes through with you. I can feel my clothes changing – more trappings. Write to me.

Later

...the caravan may travel around Europe playing music. Another rumor. Phil and Sharon gave me two addresses.

I love you, my sister, with an earthful of love. so many girls are cold bitches! I think of your warm strong body, your thick mass of hair, of walking with my arm around your waist. Often I stop and look at the sky and feel you, feel that you are alive somewhere. You are so beautiful! There are beautiful people in New York; a yoga teacher is on the caravan from there. I'll try to get her name for you... She would love you.

The caravan is supposed to leave today for Washington, D.C. Never go to Ohio, Nebraska, Illinois, Indiana, or anyplace like that. They are boring and ugly. Full of cornfields, nothing else. One of our chicks, a black one named Henry, got busted for cocaine, and they took her baby away and cut his hair. That was in Kearny, Nebraska.

There will be stories and stories for us to tell each other. Know this – love is, it is everything. It needs no hurry or rush or prodding or stifling.

Are you still virgin, my love? Jacques said it would be good if he were your first lover, because he is so gentle. He hopes to see you again. I would love to hear from you.

Later

...at this moment I am as happy as a river in the rain. Jacques and I are each other, and he takes care of me better than I know how to. At this moment my cunt is douched, medicated, baby powdered, and the hair clipped. And well loved. I had trichomonas ugh. I am in a motel near Yellow Springs, Ohio. This morning when I got up I went out running on the good earth. I am wearing my red minidress – it is good to me. I bought grey leather boots in a thrift store...

Out running, I picked a dressful of cornflowers, clover, snowflake flowers and geraniums. When I came back in I strewed them on the sleeping Alain *[Jacques' driver]* and Jacques. The only thing is, a big clump of them stuck in Alain's underarm, and he woke up...

We put on another show Friday in Antioch College. Everybody acided as always. I was lying on the grass with Kit, an incredible two-dimensional blond fellow with cosmic eyes. We were being each other in ecstasy. I was seeing myself in the black center of his topaz eyes. We were laughing. François, the director, was filming it, and Jacques was pissed because François thought he was filming Romeo and Juliet. Jacques and I became each other's devils, and we had to go into a teepee so nobody would see us scratch each other.

So you are going, you are going to New York! Mama said that when she talked to David on the phone he said that he had talked to Merc *[sic]* Cunningham, and he is very good and easy to talk to. When Mama told me the plan I was so happy! I wanted to tell everybody, except nobody knows you...

I had a horrible hassle with Tommy Donahue, the producer's son, when Jacques was in L.A. He kept wanting to ball me, ugh. Guess what, I'm a groupie, I made half-assed love with the Taurus bass player in Jethro Tull. Tommy made sure to report it to Jacques, which is funny because Jacques is infinitely loving...

IV. To Warner Bros.

we have come across the country,
but where have we come?
hypnotized by cornfields
balanced on the straight fingers of motels
wearing promises like medieval gauze,
our pirate crew
was asked to scrub decks of flesh,
hang sails on eyelashes.
we raised teepees with fisted shoulders,
hung pretty breasts over the campfire.

the bosses patted out ebony ships
and smiled with teeth made of records,
then smashed at our spirit
with nicotined thumbs.
now we are scrambled

into the dirty eggs of New York City.
We look up at the red sun, asking –
where do we park our old ships?
are we now to cross the turquoise sea?
we are armed with turquoise,
the deep dive of vaginal coral.
our brown skins float.

you didn't really want us,
Hollywood mythical bosses,
yet you give us a passage.
behind the doors
of cracked soggy hotels,
waiting for our plane to London,
we sharpen our teeth.

Of course it was fashionable to diss the bosses. I didn't really care about the bosses and would not have given them much thought at all had I not heard them being discussed at breakfast in the dreadful hotel-under-renovation we were housed at in New York (on the streets outside of which five of our lot were mugged in the few days we were there!) For me, New York seemed apocalyptic – bad air, crowding, decay, speed, hardness and hustling. Culture shock for a Californian! Very different too from our camping holiday across the country. The Caravan was a California spawn, and we took California with us; we weren't prepared for New York!

What I've learned since: It doesn't matter, it's all good, primates are intricately hierarchical and hierarchies are constantly changing, it doesn't matter, don't give energy to unnecessary concerns that aren't yours. (Unless you're made that way. I'm not.) I was along for the ride, and a glorious one it was, for it leapt with me over the sea, where I longed to go. Thank you, Warner Brothers.

Too Young For All This

Cataclysmic Jacquism – you
are forty-two
and I'm eighteen yesterday –
i don't necessarily believe in all this
ageism but
you gave me your cries in the night –
And yes you still can cry

i gave you fingernails in satin
Skin welts
Your raw white teeth
kept closing on my mouth
all night in New York
All day i look at you with many eyes
a bellied spider
i don't know why it hurts
my belly on your brown satin royal
i don't understand us
Jacques
It's just a little hot in here –

This properly belongs with the Caravan poems but somehow seems to need its own place.
Seventeen and *forty-two*? (You insisted the age difference didn't matter a bit.)
Ah, Jacques – I *do* love you and look very kindly on you – you are such a *warm* man – and I know you look back on that Caravan summer as the best in your life; to me this is *greatly* pitiful, but lord, I don't want to take it from you. I loved your soul too – as you felt that you loved mine. You were a mentor in the big world – and the posh world too – and you rescued me from hitchhiking stuck-in-America traipsing. And it was wonderful to be intimate with you. You were so fond, so thrilled, so exuberant. I can still feel honored, whilst feeling indignant. You'd missed some of your own youth, and I was it, I guess.
But oh, Jacques, how clueless you were about females! I know you

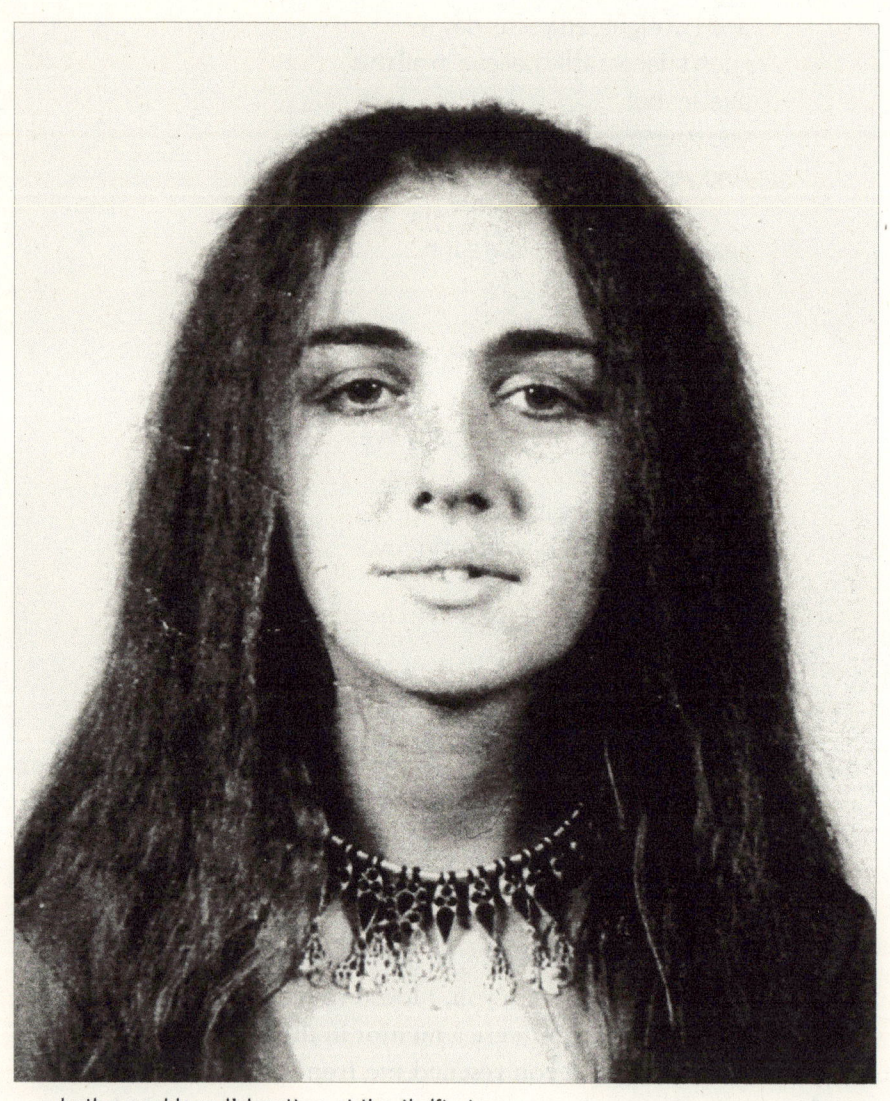

In the necklace I'd gotten at the thrift store

waited too long to get to know them – not by your own choice, your privileged upbringing was also poor in certain ways, your racing driver dad crashed at Le Mans when you were two, you had no siblings, and went to a boarding school – and then once you began with women, you tumbled headlong; detoured for a bit by a doleful marriage. And then you took root in sunny California, to bloom in all your purring, white-teethed charm. I did love you – do love you. It's impossible not to love you – I doubt anyone has ever been able to do it. But you hadn't a *clue!*
I wish I had that summer to do over again – I'd teach *you* a thing or two!
The vulnerability of female sexuality is *acute* – her ease in passion can't be taken for granted! – and all the patient, attentive technique in the world can't wake up a traumatized teenager. One who'd asked you not to go there; one who even had an unknown *infection*, and had told you so. You were so sweet about it, but still…
Is it really not possible to have a *dear* intimacy without trying to seal it in sex? Maybe we really are soul-mates from another life who had to spend time together; I can't rule it out. But your greater age gave you responsibility… responsibility I was just not capable of.
To really open to you I would have needed time, and proper courting, and some sort of provision for my warmth in winter (for I had no coat, and London was cold). And, quite frankly, you should have wanted to marry me (for you were not married then) – or set me up as mistress – to which I would have said No, for I had to move on. (I was, though I didn't know it, headed eventually to India.) But you should have asked me. You wanted too much, too fast, and then to set it aside while you went back to California.
My shy, halting, skittish eroticism in all this never had a chance. (Not to mention that… somehow non-violent little braided *whip* you carried in a diminutive leather case, which confused me utterly. Even the *suggestion* of pain has no place in a bed of love! felt I.)
And, you see, if you'd *questioned* me about my sexual response – and you may well have done – I could not tell you the truth exactly; I had nothing with which to compare my experience. I'd been raised Victorian. I thought I was lacking, in the modern new world of easy lust and connections. I might have lied, just to reassure you. Probably I did. And those "…fingernails in satin / skin welts…"

That was all an act – I can assure you – for I remember it well. Yes, some kind of energy moved, but it was yours, not mine; and I felt it through your body and thus through mine, but it was without pleasure, it was more like solemn earthquakes of random origin; and I expressed it through what I thought might look good in the movies-of-us.

And all the time I secretly wondered, "This doesn't feel good yet – I am *so intrinsically deficient!*"

Couldn't you feel our connection was a mismatch that way? Though poetically it was lovely? Couldn't you *feel?*

Oh Jacques – I tried to tell you some of this, in 2009 in Sausalito, when you lovingly prepared dinner for me despite being in recovery from a stroke. I thought we'd be able to talk like two self-revealing adults – but you became hurt and defensive, saying, "Oh – I thought you were *experienced.*" And that was that. Such a warm man – I held your hands and felt that abundant glow, and loved you just the same as always, with little spikes of regret in me for the communication that was not to be.

Your wife... oh yes, how she resented the other women in your life. She was caring for you in your illness, and still you beamed on others. I didn't find out you had left your body until a year after it had happened – by chance, on Facebook. Laryce didn't even send me an email: pretty, quiet Laryce, who intercepted all the letters I sent you, all my years in India. I mourned you, Jacques. I still mourn you – I would have loved to love you as two adults; celebrate the heart that was always our real connection.

Such a warm boy-man.

In polyester dress from the thrift store

London – Europe

August 1970 – August 1972

e flew over the sea... among a rollicking band of
rs. It was thrilling beyond belief!

From Letter to Mama and Serafina
England, a Sunday in August, 1970

My dear mum, my precious Serafina,
The paper sogs beneath the pen. A British night, colder than what we're used to. The caravan is lively and good here. Right now the Hog Farm movie is being shown over by the fires, and our band is rehearsing for tomorrow's show inside the kitchen tent. Everybody is optimistic all over again, because we're finally here... It is more wonderful to write to you than I can say – I have spent so much time lately just sitting, waiting – for food, for somebody, for entertainment, for news. Everybody does... I do not know, I do not know if I need suffering to create. Everything is so ...*comfortable*, and the least little individual thing I do surprises everybody. I am so hard on myself, and everybody, especially Jacques, is so easy on me! I'm just not sure which I need.

In departure lounge at JFK Airport. England ho!

...The caravan flew on Air India in three hunks. I was on the last day, so Jacques and I spent two days in New York City. We visited his model friend, who is a chocolate preying-mantis with butterfly eyes. We ate at the Riviera, a sidewalk cafe in Greenwich Village. We had steamed clams in their shells, and a pitcher of Sangria. What surprises you depends on what you're used to. I have outgrown the flabbergasted Akinchild, because it got meaningless. Not wholly, though... In the Village I felt very strongly the poetry that was spawned there. We bought things – we each got a tie-dyed Indian shirt from an old lady who sells them from a cart on a corner. Jacques bought a shoulder-bag that is made of goatskin, legs and all. He looks fantastic in the shirt, transparent electric blue, with the fringey bag and his hair gone all curly... I got some brown bellbottoms and some purple ones, which I'm wearing right now, that button up, and gold leather belt. I am so sick of the clothes that I brought that I could die. I gave the white anti-lust pants to the Hog Farm. Likewise my poor shrunken hikingboots.

The Hog Farm is in awe of absolutely nothing, and it was a trip to see them nursing babies in the Maharajah Lounge of Air India. Air India is a flying bureaucratic, leprous, bilious, pompous elephant. Your Katy is in awe of many things. Not of other people, but of the rewards of aspiration.

...The tents here keep burning up from candles.

...I called Victoria house from N.Y. airport, but nobody was there, so I called Date house and talked to Papa. I couldn't hear in the noise, and Glen didn't know what was going on (he told me to take care of Sukey), so it was horribly unsatisfactory. It felt weird to fly off with no contact with my bloodpeople. No harm though I guess; it is good for me to be on my own. And Jacques takes infinite care of me. Grass and mescaline and wine were going around on the flight, and we chuckled for hours about silly things and cosmic things. It's weird to have such a short night – we flew into the rising sun. The colors!!! The peace of clouds. Poems.

It is said that on the first flight the caravaners had to restrain the stewardesses from taking mescaline, and the pilot smoked dope. In the middle of the night they gave us a huge dinner of hot curry and all kinds of weird prepackaged goodies. Then, a couple of hours later when we got to sunrise, they gave us breakfast. It was distressing.

I slept in a tent here at camp all afternoon, and woke feeling sweet and deep and sad. Excited as I am with the world, also, my sweet mum, I am very afraid.

You must be having adventures too... It feels important that we keep our hand clasp established. I hope Fina is keeping diary too, so we can catch up someday. I feel a need to always be thorough with every moment. Unfortunately many moments droop their mouths open and say bleeeghh when you look at them.

There are two guys in the caravan who used to play at the Gasser, and know Jim. If you hear any more about Morris coming to Europe!! – I wrote him immediately when I got his letter.

...Mama, write to me any fantasies you have about England. I love how they talk! Everything is sort of staid and rounded and quaint and droll and subdued. "But there are many English realities," says Jacques. He was just here in July. He almost didn't come with me, but he's glad now that he did. He's taking me to Chelsea Tuesday or so.

In New York: my merry red-haired fashionplate Randy was knocked down by Puerto Rican junkies, and his suitcase full of his dope and favorite clothes was ripped off. The driver of the Lotus Bay, Mike, was pistol-whipped near the hotel, and his money stolen. Jacques lost his wallet in a cab. Credit cards, pilot and driver's licenses, $60, some acid.

We're going to sleep soon. They're showing Moby Dick, a Warner Bros. flick, on the screen. I will write to many people, now that I'm here... What is important are my people, my sparkling moments, my retreats, and my decorations.

I love you. I crave mail. I'll keep it coming to you if you'll do the same, or even if you don't. Love, Katy Araminta

P.S. I had a dream where a New Yorker was saying – "one of the things we do around here for recreation is to have nightmares." Jacques dug that...

Night Poem to Jack

I. Do you know how I cradle you,
brown bird,
across from me, feeding my blind young mouth?
In my yielding, brownbread fire?
You feed me
more than I knew I could take,
bird. Cloudhead. Blue light.
Do you know that I am burning
always to death?
I think that I am no thicker than a flame.

II. We make some black universe in our mouths
behind star teeth.
You tell me about the people
you carry water with, then come
and tip water over me cover me,
put your tongue in this little burner,
say goodnight,
and leave on the table
a pile of eggs
some broken by the stretching limbs
of amethysts

There are two possibilities here: one is that this poem shows how foolishly susceptible young girls are to the blandishments and philosophical B.S. of older bad-boy physics professors and the like. The other is that, regardless of age, it is wonderful for people with inquiring minds and open sensibilities and cosmic-adventurous streaks to get together with a bit of wine and explore each other's consciousness in a somewhat raucous yet respectful manner. But there is one thing that happened in all those inspirational evenings in London about which I still feel deeply indignant.

When the Medicine Ball Caravan left me in London with a return ticket to New York in my pocket and nothing else, I was not alone: Jacques was still with me. I had not wanted to be lovers – though I adored his innocent friendliness, and he was dauntingly impressive. But he'd gotten his way and I'd submitted in helpless, hopelessly-outclassed lostness to his careful, fond, unselfish lovemaking. He did not ejaculate; he looked into my eyes; he courted me; he did so many things right. He thought he was different from the boys who'd disillusioned me, and that he'd heal my wounds with his tender sexual adoration. He got some of that right – he *was* different – but the timing was wrong for me.

Anyway, here we were in London. We stayed with Jacques' friends, Jack and Judi Grodsky and their little blonde daughters, Tanya and Michelle, in a large flat in South Kensington. Everything was strange for me. The smells, the agedness of the buildings, the

Just arrived in London

accents, the air, the food. And England was so *cold!* My thin used-up clothes were hopeless for the climate!

Jacques was enormously caring, but he couldn't stay long – his job at UCLA called.

We two couples slept together in one huge bed. This felt to me weird and uneasy. Judi – poor long-suffering pretty blonde Judi, slim and straight with pale-pink lipstick and a quiet, tidy air – put up with these two middle-aged fellows cavorting around a clueless, snaggle-toothed little poet-girl, all over her house, for a week or more. She cared for the kids, made meals neatly, did the shopping, while her husband (who looked much like Alley Oop the cartoon caveman) smoked, drank, and held forth with great guffaws of laughter on subjects cosmic and arcane. Judi didn't join in with the discussions or the mescaline-taking – she was too busy being a real-life mum.

And then, as inevitable as heartbreak, and in keeping with the current fashion, one night we all lay down in the bed, Judi, with her period, turning away to the wall. And both Jacques and Jack in turn

Jack Grodsky, London 1970. Sketched during a cosmology discussion

selves up and penetrated me with their big grown-up-, and did whatever they do, not for very long and of ut any knowing of what this was like for me – and I was y, shocked, and ashamed to say how devastated I was.
Did they think I somehow *enjoyed* it? It was just a trial and a sorrow for me, an enduring, and a terrible embarrassment: more evidence of my great uncoolness, that I could not like what was obviously 'freedom'. Poor Judi snorted once in disgust and then tried to go to sleep. And I know those guys meant well – or something – but they were just *idiots*.

What I've learned since: This is not the way to make proper love to the sort of Goddess I am. That way would have been: cosmic discussion and adoration, fine. Then, I get my own room, nobody bothers me (though Jacques would have been allowed a cuddle and some confiding murmuring), and next day they will ask if I will read aloud any poems I've written. Ha ha!
My sympathies are entirely with Judi. In fact, not so long ago I hunted her down on FB and sent her a loving apology, via snail mail; plus the original of a portrait I drew of Jack at the time, and a poem I'd written for Tanya and Michelle. She replied most graciously, saying kind things about the young girl I had been; and my heart is still touched by this.
Jack was killed when his car, for unknown reasons, went off an ocean cliff in Big Sur in, I believe, the mid-90's.

What I've learned since: Welcome talented young girls into your house, if you wish. Mentor them. Don't expect wisdom from them – that's your job. And don't fuck them: "Keep your P in your pants," as I've heard a wise woman say. If that P bothers you overmuch, undertake the true, *meditative* study and practice of Tantra. And, if your wife is lying beside you, make sweet love to her instead. If she has her period, say nice things and cuddle her for a few minutes, then let her alone and mind your own business.
Separate bedrooms are a wonderful thing.

To T & M

Tanya is a silken balloon
of a little piglet.
Michelle is a silken balloon
of a little pony.
They are tied to the red chimney
by long colored threads
and spend the day
nibbling at sugar-clouds,
picking the feathers from clouds,
arguing with clouds
about hassles that are easy to solve.

The little silk Tanya
has cheeksful of daisies.
The little silk Michelle
watches the trees breathe
and remarks on how the leaves clap hands.
Mama reins them in for dinner
and they bob at the table.
Tanya eats a little earth, Michelle eats a little air;
Mama puts them to bed
where they make sleeping locomotor sounds
of little zoo-flowers
pushing up.

This was of course written at Jack and Judi's, where I cluttered up the place for weeks after Jacques left. They finally politely asked me to leave – and luckily David had just arrived from San Francisco.
The 'earth' and 'air' here refer of course to the little girls' astrological signs. Everyone was very into that then.

What I've learned since: Nothing, really... it was always going to be the case that I'd not have any kids of my own. Kids are like other people's cats (though I tend to get more involved with the cat) – nice to talk to for five minutes, and then really nice that someone else feeds them and takes them to the vet. But I look kindly on them – kids, cats – and have a great theoretical interest in kids being allowed to grow up as themselves (which almost never happens – if it ever does happen at all. Perhaps kittens get to?)

But when I look back at this poem – I feel happy that I had the space to look tenderly on these little ones.

From Letter to Mama and Serafina
London, 1970

Saturday
My poppies, my looking-backward flowers –

> Tonight Sal *[from the caravan's house band, Stone Ground – friend of Jacques']* is playing guitar and I am building ladders of lists of things to do to make to learn. I am writing poems and drawing pictures. Sal is singing
> > *I got everything I need*
> > *Since I became this woman's joy*
>
> and your Katy is melting inside knowing that she can catch no more of an edge to things than she has within, and oh the edges she feels! Deirdre is on some opium to soothe her cough. She sits in brown velvet with her twisted face and a cigarette smoking between her fingers. I was all down today, and Judi held me, and I felt at least human, if not all I want to be. I don't want a clubbed soul, and all jagged edges must be reunited sometimes, or it is tragedy. Your Katy is a tragic un-princess.
>
> This room contains beautiful women who have built and grown on their lives. Deirdre, who modeled when she was 15-16. Judi, so thin, in deep rich blue-purple silk. Maria, Spanish, who talks with an English accent about lace and chiffon and pastel and silk and velvet and crepe. Deirdre is patching a patchwork.
>
> I am going to read poetry Monday night at a coffeehouse called The Troubadour. Sal sings –
> > *I won't be through till I'm happy,*
> > *and that's when you're happy too!*

It rained all day. Judi and I almost went crazy. I'm sending poems. I dream of warm southern Spain, of rolling with a sun-filled body. You will get erotic-dream letters until David gets here. I dream of sensation, and yet I am speedy and put it off and won't relax into it.

I sewed black crepe stars on the ass of my plaid little shorts. I wear them with grey tights and grey boots. There are nine people here, endeavoring or not endeavoring, as each is disposed. I made stroganoff with green noodles tonight, and everybody loved it...

...Today was a zenith of bleakness, and i almost thought of home, but who knows, anyplace, anyplace. (Judi says you need depression to be cleansed.) I went up on the roof today. Mary Poppins, chimneys, a beautiful sunset. Cathedral and museum spires, millions of chimneys...

Sunday –
It began sunny, but the clouds moved in. I'm lying on the bed with Jack and Sal, getting all mellow and onto an English noon. People are not expected to be productive anymore, Jacques says, but this person is happier if she does stuff. We're taking the kids outing today. They bounce on the beds in the morning and we admire them, just as you used to do with us...

Later
...We all went and visited some good people across London, had tea and cheesecake, and Jack and I got lost in the *Encyclopedia of the Supernatural*. I got all mellowed out, witched in, feathered and bejeweled inside. London, London, that's where I am, riding in two-story buses in the rain, looking at lanes of quaint houses, blooming our umbrellas in the doorways.

Last night I dreamed that a woman came out of the Underground leading another woman on a leash. So I wrote to Jacques today too.
Love love Katy Araminta

Saturday Afternoon

Slide open this drawerful of violets.
and find lumpy wax dolls.
That is me.

Turn one over.
a devil grins unexpected diamonds.
The second has no hands.
The third is fashioned like a tree.

A fourth is heavy with perfume.
A fifth is one hard eye
too hot, and too cold, to touch.
The thirteenth coils, hisses
a riverful of snakes.

Stroke them, one by one
and watch the cocoons
melt and crack like burned skin.
Watch the butterflies
the tight, unbaked eyelashes
the lip-red poppies
begin to emerge,
hear the raking fingernail sound
of those that prefer to stay dark.

Close the drawer.
Replace the suitcaseful of hair
that hides the knobs.
Go into the front room
and stroke the clock, or watch the rain,
or whatever it is we do.

What I've learned since: Human beings are composed of layers. There's the surface: what we do, what we present to others, what we know of ourselves (usually not very much, as it happens). There's the subconscious; full of power, archetypes, unlived energies. If we venture

there we might encounter these energies as symbols, as in dreams. There is in life the possibility, indeed I'd say the mandate, to re-enter those energies in meditation and allow them to bloom. This will then open the space below the subconscious – where the deepest primal and primeval directives are stored: the cave-man district, I'd call it.
Visiting this locale, re-embodying those essential energies of survival, sex, hunting, being hunted, shelter-seeking, and so on – is very freeing. But this too is part of the unconscious – and so deeper than *that* is found the beauty, the joy abundant, the free ground of Being connecting us to everything, while still being most reverently our own. It's vast, explosive, blissful, transcendent. It's Beyond. (This layer actually permeates everything, all layers; but we are often not aware of it. Glimpses give us a sense of meaning and the preciousness of life. We can call it the super-conscious.)
When I wrote this poem I had no idea of the symbologies I was adopting; they just came to me. I didn't question them. I was rapt with the music and the melancholy of what was emerging. But I did have a sad perception that something rich and thick was waiting in those drawers, and that I had no idea how to access it; and that accessing it was very important. (What I only partially understood too was that a lot of this material doesn't even belong to us... it comes from our parents, and their parents, and our surroundings. It moves through us... and by our becoming conscious of it, that much more liberation has occurred, cosmos-wide.)
And so I needed help.
I had just over three years to wait – until I met a man whose very presence sprang the trap. Who also had the gift of a multitude of techniques and devices. This is rare! So rare! (And he had a spectacular sense of humor too!)
There is silence beyond the images... between them also; within their very cells. That silence he served up too, first, last, and always.

What I've learned since: Do your homework. Get help. Unpick your own seams. You will be rewarded with continual astonishment – a lifetime of miracle. Is that not a worthy road to ramble/blunder/coast upon?

Origins

Moths have always burnt orbits around our house
it is a buoy covered with moth-droppings,
sinking, but always there. Inside
my father eats what he likes
beans and cornbread,
what she raised him on.
His mother, a black cloth spider, is dead.
"We do not eat fish," she said.
"The fish is akin to the sarpent."
My mother always said
she would rather be shot
than fix dinner in the kitchen, where jam
stuck to the chairs, grease to the walls, soup
cans lay in the corners. It was dark.
I cannot write for them.

Not for my mother, climbing
the ladder to her shack
the inside of her head
a pear with brown wrinkles, never still
and somehow precious to my breasts.
Not for my father, who in his change of life
(he is crawling back, shivering,
into diapers)
said something about her grounded wings.
He is made of glass and sand,
horribly life-size.
Their parents
still comb their hair with hard fingers.
There is a hand on my mother's bottom,
saying –
"Don't let him pump his filth into you!"
My father can only strain inside the glass
worse than voiceless.
Money rattles in his pockets, his words run
on, dying crabs scuttling scuttling.

My mother reads psychiatric journals
and no, I cannot write for them.

When I climb the hills at evening
I am tangled in everything I see.
There is the city, down below the granite.
The light is still there
at my parents' house,
I see it through the elm leaves.
He is looking for his false teeth,
lost among cigarette ashes.
She is standing on the balcony
beside boxed Scientific Americans,
watching the jacaranda's colors
fade into the night.
They are both crying.

I must climb up the hill
and turn myself, a sea anemone,
blooming into quick orgasm
while it is still high tide, alone.

This poem still moves me quite terribly – for it describes exactly the mood around my parents when they were separating. A teenager suddenly sees her mother and father as people separate from herself – and sees their feet of clay and ashes. It was like that – just like that – in that beaten-up old house, with its unfinished outbuildings – one, at the very back of the back yard, was called The Summerhouse, though it was always summer; and the house had no walls, but was just a framed structure set on a concrete slab. It had three storeys, and for a while our mother slept in a bed on the second storey, where she could be alone. So this is "climbing the ladder to her shack."
(Behind the structure was a fence and behind that was marvelous jungle – a well-to-do family, the Kietches, had half a block with an overgrown circular drive, a big wooden house with glossy floors and a piano, and a wild thicket of oak, and other tall trees, and trumpet vine, and god knows what – all the glorious vegetation

Virginia Harvey, age 16, Berkeley, California

of a California that has barely survived now, in hidden pockets. The Kietches lived in a different world than we did.)

I regret the last stanza rather, because it can be misunderstood. Somehow even then I knew that welling-up of one's own energy skyward – which happens in meditation – can result in orgasm-like phenomena, where energy spills through the body and out the top of the head, and all is well. So although this line sounds masturbatory, and, I suppose, why shouldn't it – that wasn't my meaning. I meant in some way to reclaim my own nature – and sex is not the substance of it. In fact I don't like that word *orgasm* – it is clinical and yet rather creepily onomatopoetic – like a fish flapping in death throes. And too intimately shoving its staring eyes into one's private moments. I'll ponder a different word here...

What I've learned since: Finding out who we are and in what way we are not our parents is probably the most difficult work we ever do – because along the way we must meet all the pain that was in our childhood house, and it seems to have no end. But that very feeling of 'no end' – is a signal that intensity is here; and intensity, rightly allowed and observed, leads to breakthrough.

It is churlish too, to ask life to deliver us once and for all from our parents' hold. We must be ready for a long slog – for they are in our moments and our days. Embrace them – find out what they really wanted, what they really didn't want – then declare ourselves – all within our meditation. Every little bit is a big slice of freedom – for only in finally allowing our parents their unhappinesses without trying to rescue them, without trying to parent them – do we give them the responsibility – no matter how helpless we *know* they are – to be free to grow into their true natures. No need to interfere the whole time, with unconscious behaviors full of attempted rescue and compensation.

I'm saying this; but do I really *know* it? For when I see the line, "They are both crying –" my heart and middle come out and gasp and look about themselves lost as a kicked dog.

I can only observe this... try not to take up the imaginary sword that would supposedly, in the mind of my unconscious, help me to do battle on their behalf, thus ignoring my own life-stream. I can try not to suppress *nor* to coddle the pain; and I can try to trust my

Illustration in handmade book, London 1970

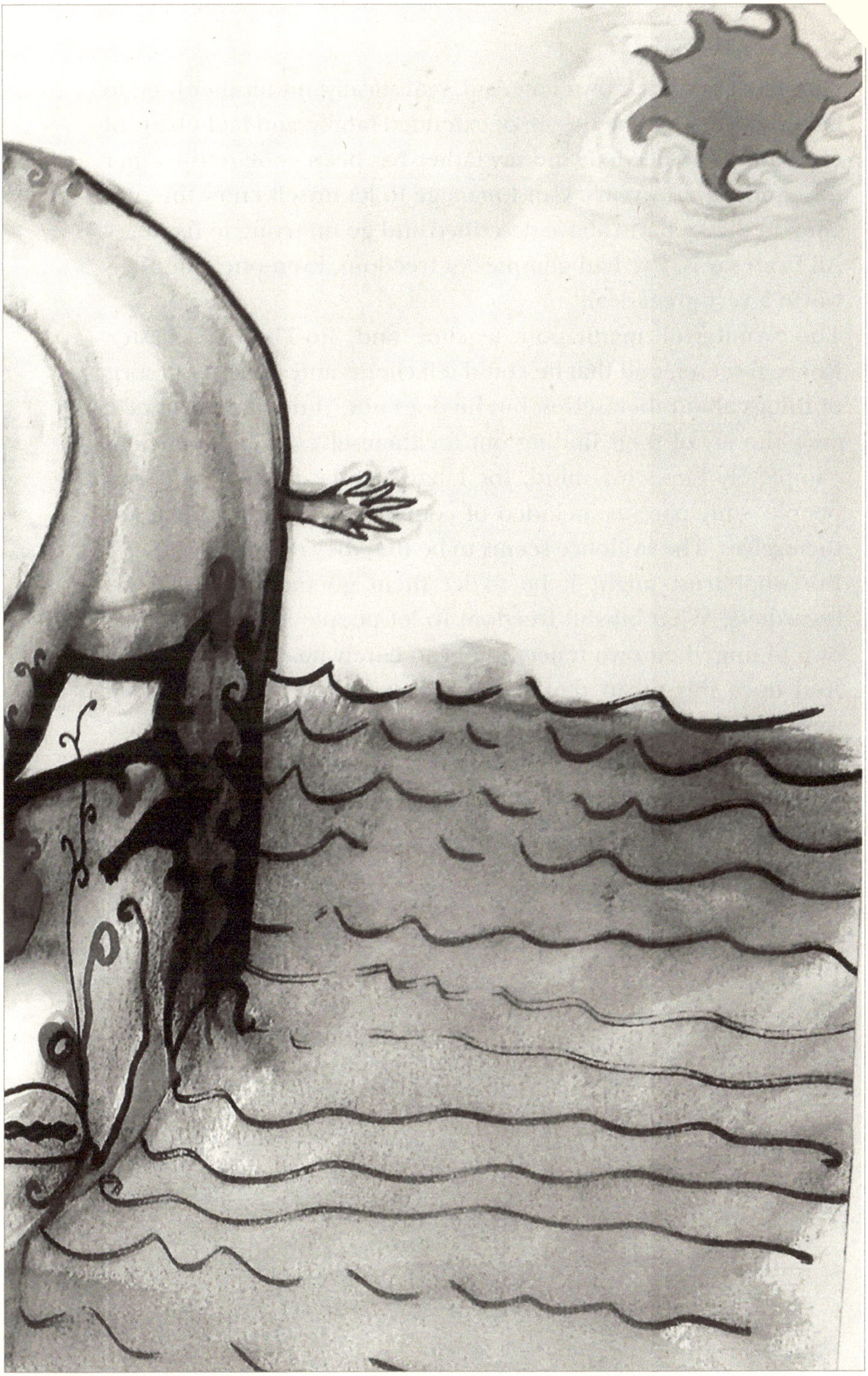

o find their own way. And, realistically: my mother lived to
-nine, in the bosom of extended family, and had plenty of
everything she needed; and my father has been gone to the ether
for almost twenty years. Can I manage to let myself know this, not
cling to the scenario above-described and go on trying to fix it?

All I can say is, I've had glimpses of freedom. Even one glimpse is
worth a very great deal.

The wonderful meditation teacher and Ito-Thermie master,
Kohrogi-sensei, said that he could tell clients and students all sorts
of things about themselves; but he does not. "I don't want to take
away the joy of their finding out for themselves." This statement
completely blows my mind, for I have to see that I don't trust
people – my parents included of course – to find out things for
themselves. The evidence seems to be that they don't!

But what trust might it be to let them go on their own way
regardless! What blissful freedom to let people be, to have their
own timing, their own trajectory! I can barely imagine it.

And does this mean that I don't trust myself to find my own
way? Something to ponder... And still, I know from experience
that only things I discover for myself have worth and depth and
meaning to me. Only they are transformative. The presence of a
Buddha is incredibly helpful – but it is helpful as a catalyst for my
own exploration.

Just his presence gives me trust; just his presence.

London Untitled

David.
be undead.
David. the leaves are falling,
and it is time
to walk in the graveyard with me
halfway around the world.
David,
i am tired of waiting.

> England is mulling into fall,
> and without you, it is too beautiful to bear.
> Myths echo myths
> hugging talking low all night
> the dry leaves of our voices
> breaking, finally, into wet winter
> cry with me
> for there is much to cry about
> Fall, and i have made so many hardships
> while you were gone.

Jacques had gone and I was still at Jack and Judi's, with my welcome wearing thin. David was due to fly in soon, whereupon we would go to a hotel for a night or two and then take off on our adventure. Meanwhile I walked London for hours, exploring – but not reveling, for I was cold. And I was puzzled, and hungry for something I could not name. I thought sometimes that it was love, and it *was* partly that; I thought that it was ambition – and certainly I was ready to direct my energies, in some effective manner, towards their natural gifts – and it would also have been lovely to study, to be taught. But such was not my fate then. All I could do was write... And I was overwhelmed by culture gap! For London and California are worlds apart, and were much more so then. My whole system felt disturbed. The language was odd, the coins confusing, the ancient houses blank and energetically shuttered to me. I had no money for shopping, so could only wander and stare in shop windows.

What I've learned since: David had emphasized the notion that we all have 'life-myths' we are acting out. I didn't in the least understand what he meant, but the word 'myths' got into my poems anyway.

So the first lesson is: Don't use in your writing phrases you don't understand or resonate with, just because someone you have a crush on uses them. You steal your own authenticity and your own voice, and that is not good. This goes too for 'made many hardships' – someone had told me, "We create our own lives," so I was trying that idea on – but really didn't know what it meant.

But I used it here anyway. (Ultimately it means: We're responsible for our own universe in that it is our eyes it's being seen through. It doesn't mean that willpower will suffice to alter life to fit our ideas. A common misconception I call the American-Nike-Just-Do-It-Religion.)

Second: Love the person in you who did that. She is young and needs your tender parenting, acceptance, and understanding.

And: "It is too beautiful to bear"…Mysterious, how beauty breaks our hearts unless we share it. And yet… that solitary heartbreak is one of the most wonderful things there is – for one can write it. And even if one can't *really* write it… one can try. And the trying is sublime.

And: Romantic love satisfies something – not everything. Love plus consciousness does better.
Yet even then… to the extent that we are each irrevocably alone, it comes down to Me plus Beauty.
The muse is the intermittent lover.
That's what writing is for – the bridge between I and beauty – helplessness and power. Beauty and sorrow. Beauty and the impossibility of expressing it.

I looked at this poem again in 2006 after many years of its having hid in my mother's attic. I was startled, because I'd recently discovered on Google that David had died in 1996, of colon cancer, in San Francisco. (His brother Carl told me later that David had been surrounded by his beloved wife, daughters, brother, and friends, and that people were streaming in to see him, until finally one day David said, "Can I have some space? I'm trying to *die* in here!") I have often felt since that I would have loved to meet with him again after we had both grown up, and see if we could really talk. It would have been juicy: for we did have real chemistry, and there was the potential for challenging and interesting sharing.

Winter: for Children and Spiders

When the ice-blown wind comes
down on London
Desire's candle gives my hat shadow.
The backs of knees especially
need my tongue,
toes need my tongue between them
and young legs need my drum.

The wind builds a beast of rattling segments
poison teeth
centipede lust, a hundred
feet worth, a hundred spiders' worth
of bursting eggs –
The wind makes an ice web
The candle makes poison.

Blue consciousness
The one, the big one,
the one with spiders in it, the child one,
the blind one
The lusting October consciousness
enters my limp fox-skin
makes my killed eyes bleed
on passing children,
their exquisite knees, their ragged hair
my waking winter in their sweat-lined sleeping hands.

"**Makes my** killed eyes bleed..." What *is* loss of innocence, really? Here I am longing to have innocence back again; childhood instead of spiderhood.

These are not the spiders of my actual childhood, sanctioned by my father, beauteous constructions; they are pain and sinister hopelessness; an archetypal, collective spider view. (Easy to adopt despite my pro-spider training.)

How did this spiderhood happen to me? I was desirous – as humans are – and this was, for me, all linked in with the energy of creativity. I want because I want to *make* something – love, cookies, a delightful outfit, a relating. Each energy of desire and/or creativity wanted to expand, to dance, to get colorful, receive a divine energy, to break boundaries, to own itself. And I was in this cold place with nothing but a notebook, a pen, and some magic markers. (Though I have to say, I did my best while I was there; made one of my artisanal hand-bound, illustrated poetry books. I have it still.)

And I was, as I walked about the cold city with its littered sidewalks and earthy markets, channeling the underbelly of the British psyche – though I barely knew it. All those spiders. All that buggery and pedophilia. All that frustration and congealed rage.

There was the usual mundane evil about, frigid in the autumn chill, and it penetrated me, and I regarded its foreign mystery and let its words trickle from my tongue.

What I've learned since: If I find myself in a place with strange energy, I can leave; or, if I suspect I might have some karmic link to it – something is pushing my buttons – I can enter the energy deeply and dance it wildly until it has told me what it *really* is – for it will be something innocent, underneath; even if it is the animal innocence of the caveman murdering to defend his cave.

What I've learned since: If you're blessed/cursed with a never-ending creativity, you can play with it everywhere, anywhere, somehow; but it is really nice and fun and luxurious to have things to play with: art supplies, *clothes, shoes,* cloth, places in which to dance. So I give these things to myself now.

What I've learned since: Meditation first owns, expresses, then dilutes the concentration of these cataclysmic images from the unconscious, then lights them up, then transforms them, then glows with joy at the alchemized vapors in their lovely colors.

When I typed this poem up after not having looked at it for forty-two years, I was a bit dismayed at its darkness. *Moi? This* dark? What's all this about *children?* My greatest interest in the word is in the context of excavating my own inner child and protecting and caring for her. There is nothing of the grandmother about me, or the pedophile either. Where did all this *come* from? Yes, I had been channeling the whole dark past of orphans and street-kids in that city; cold and hungry and exploited; perhaps in a past life I was one (I think so). But was there something more immediately personal too? So, I just tried a little trick I have: I imagined a frame around the scene – the young girl on the city street, in her ragged dress and thin synthetic boots, cut through by the wind; trees blowing behind her. Then, I tap the top of the frame with a wand, and ask, "What's really going on?"

I am shown that this girl really needed true Tantra and healing – to take her abused and infected yoni, love and heal it, find out its true energies and proclivities, its divine nature; to release from it the rough and stupid uses made of it by ignorant men. Take its pain and disappointment and show it how to clear itself, then honor itself with true observance. *That* would be innocence, that healing; all else is the detritus she's already gathered; and the subterranean lusts of this vast metropolis.

It was she, that vulva, who had been seized upon and masticated – by idiots with disappointed expressions, as if, for their purposes, I was not really adequate. We were all idiots in those days, hopping upon each other like toads. All that febrile lust, quick, stupid, and as shallow as we could make it with our slack-jawed obtuseness. And, at least for me, not even truly lustful. Until my poor yoni and all its systems could be healed, real libido would have been much better served by a glorious shopping trip! But it was not to be.

What I've learned since: seek ye first the Queendom of the Goddess, and all else will be added unto ye.

On Gloucester Road

On Gloucester Road
evil rain slid off me,
making my hair hang in wet tendrils.
My eyes were mouths.
Somebody spoke behind me –

"Witch!"
titling me, and the title ran off like evil rain.
I heard my name called twice,
turned, a knife unclasping in my chest.
The hatred of my body makes me weak.

Orange leaves fell, a dry rain.
The hatred of my body makes me weak.
If I had a road of orange cloth
I would paint words on it, and drown it in the sea.

On Gloucester Road
a black cat sat in the window
of a butcher's shop.
Recognized me, said nothing.
The shop was closed, and all the orange meat
had gone elsewhere with its October blood.

I was still waiting for David to fly in with his younger brother Carl (their parents had commissioned David to take Carl on a Grand Tour, and gave him $1,000 to cover costs). Just a piece of luck, that the man I'd fallen for in San Francisco was coming to Europe anyway! But meanwhile I wandered, aware of hauntings – some of which were rooted in me, in my sugar addiction, dieting attempts, and related neuroses. I had no money save $60 from my father every month, which would not have covered food, let alone a warm coat, rubber boots, a scarf, umbrella, and so on. I remember buying ribbons and needles and thread, so I could add another patch to my terrible orange granny-dress.

I had been into a big shop only a handful of times up to then – twice with my mother when she'd sold a story, and a few times with Taffy when her mother was outfitting her for school (and I would weep silently in heartbroken envy of their purchases, terrified someone would notice). So I was in awe of Harrods and suchlike, and just gazed at them from the pavement hopelessly as I walked for miles each day.

And then: when my monthly money did arrive, I spent a big chunk of it having my hair permed! I wanted one of those big hippie

manes. (David, when he arrived, couldn't understand why I'd done it. Maybe for a Jewish person curly hair is nothing special?)
But something is strange here: "If I had a road of orange cloth..." I don't know where that came from – but a few hard years later I was to have a road of orange cloth: Osho's people wore orange then, handloom and khadi, sewn into loose robes to make our meditation more flowing!
And, "witch' is a term Osho reclaimed from perfidy and re-honored with its original meaning: wise woman. And we used it this way when I was in the Mystic Ring in the School of Mysticism in Poona in the 90's.

So, What I've learned since:
1) Perms don't work as they quite soon go all flat, fried and frizzy on you and must be cut off.
2) If we cannot love our own bodies, what can we love? All efforts in this life can be helpfully spent in that direction. The body is beautiful and it loves us and it does its best; it is a miracle, worthy of all our care. We ought to feed it things that make it hum the best it can (juiced organic greens fresh from the ground do the best job of this I know), and coddle it and pet it and soothe it and warm it, and challenge it with long walks and good work we enjoy, and wild dances. Free it, too, with those wild dances, and lovemaking, and emotionally-releasing practices. Delight it with beautiful views, good sounds, and smells that please us. It is our home.
3) Being a witch is a privilege and a blessing. One must earn it; but the tendency is naturally there, and only a little tweaking is needed, and a great deal of meditation, and some tutelage. And then one can have fun, and go deep, and be part of the world of healing and of seeing. It is a good world. And one will have many peers and fellows with whom to discuss things. And one's work will unfold and go on changing.

And: what I've learned since: My own wavy, soft, part-grey hair is absolutely great and doesn't need improving.

Afterthought to Paula

i liked having you here
your red suede bottom
complacent and big.
i liked the finely sprinkled fruit
of your skin.
Your bracelets ring and jangle,
you wear carnelian
like a mountain wears berries.
i like to think you have caves.
i want more of your kind.
Just a sweet girl
who doesn't quite know her own breasts
or the breadth of her bottom.
i will bring yellow flowers to her
and she will lie on my arm and tell me
that she once had a sunny lover,
knew a daring month in France,
understood old age.
Let us be unconscious pirates
to each other's similar thighs,
stories, open necks.

What I've learned since: If one is trying not to eat very much, trying to be slim – one is also unconsciously pruning back the natural female expansion of the aura. In a way, I wanted to be a boy: quick and fluid, I thought; carefree; and above all (I thought) possessed of a superior capacity for pleasure in bed. Now, if I am trying to be a boy – thin, muscular, pared-down – to whom am I going to feel attracted? A "red suede bottom / complacent and big." So, for a few years, as I've said, I lusted gently, intermittently, and uneventfully after soft, rather doughy, simple-seeming girls – mute-ish ones, virginal-looking ones, dull ones even, one might say. Placid. I was, of course, seeking the ordinary, the non-dramatic, the rounded... in myself. All these were things I would not let myself be. I had that terrible fear of being stuck in Riverside; and placidity seemed to invite this brutish fate. (I had a recurrent dream in London that I was *back in America*, and I'd wake up all freaked out, only to sink back in relief to find it was not so.)

When I began meditating much of every day, in Poona in July 1974, quickly everything changed. I stopped dieting, gained weight, and was energetically opened up all down the front of me. I plunged in with all four feet and howled, screamed, wept, laughed... letting out the grizzly bears, pole-cats, ocelots, sowbugs, and everything else that was inside me. For a year I wasn't attracted to anybody – I was celibate, catharting my heart out, cleaning out the gears and carburetors and pistons.

When I woke up again to 'love' it was because Osho put me together with a man – actually a friend of mine who came from San Francisco wearing a coonskin cap and wanting to be my lover. "This will be very good," said Osho. (In those days he sometimes did this, putting two people together. We were thrilled to be so graced! You never knew what the Master saw behind the surface, and we were willing to give it a go.) I still resisted for a few days, but finally succumbed. One thing led to another and by and by I became crazy for men – like, really driven; another form of addiction, like anorexia had been. (I was anorexic in early 1974.) But I was firmly female by then, and firmly oriented towards the opposite sex.

So: if you repress something: hunger, sex, anger, whatever it might be – you will see it and fall in love with it everywhere. Nature doesn't let us kill nature.

Sleep

> David
> elbows on the table
> eats grapes from a paper bag.
> He has darkened his eyelids
> His peeled eyes, wet mouth
> eat me like a dragon.

Factories
railroad tracks
the scabbed backs of houses,
brick skins drying on space
Oil drums sleeping like circled arms
Cluckety-clack of the old train
rackety-dreaming a track to run
a low-ass murmuring dream.

Another train passes close
riffling like an aluminum book
Our eyes, doing chimneys,
suddenly are staring at mirrored
eyes. Two blank faces,
lips parted like pain,
the little white fruit of our eyes
rimmed in black wool.

David sleeps,
legs crooked like elbows,
head back in the corner,
wood and dirty plush.
i am afraid in him,
his mustache reaches darkness;
and he has the sight
of the magician.

Mama, you are right
lavish is what I'm all about
But i am sleeping. Outside,
the country comes
cabbages, rings of trees.
birds abstracting flight.

I remember this – taking a train across London – how peculiar it was for me to see the backs of people's all-joined-to-each-other houses from the train. A sort of privacy exposed. In California there was nothing like that.

green lace outfit (my design) worn to meet David and Carl at the airport in London 1970

What I wore to meet David and Carl at the airport

London, October 1970. Feeling lost!

David had arrived a few days earlier. Now he slept, of course, because he spent half of each night carousing: drinking wine, smoking plants, playing guitar; making love to me. And that is one kind of sleep – nodding off in the train. The other kind, the kind I lay claim to here, is the existential sleep Gurdjieff refers to: the mechanistic state, the not-being-fully-present-and-alive. I was worried by ambition and helplessness, and felt this just-making-time-ness keenly, even as I was preparing for a great traveling adventure with David. I didn't really know about existential sleep… only that I wanted some urgency, challenge and meaning that hippie life seemed to be the opposite of.

What I've learned since: The tributary of writing, and the tributary of meditation (for sleep and waking are heartily addressed by the latter) aren't really separate. Life gave me writing – but for meditation I needed Osho. Then, the two could come together – as they are still doing. So, in writing I was awake, and in meditation I am awake – and the two gradually act on the rest of life as well (the gnarly world of 'love' being a last and late holdout – meditation came to me there only after all else had roundly failed a very great many times!)

What I needed: my Sangha: a group of seekers all working together, meditating together, to raise the vibes and boost us, by the seat of our robes, over the edge, out of the workaday snore and into Presence. And this Sangha functioned only because the Master was there – engineering things, tweaking things, scaring us silly half the time (a great waker-upper) and not suffering fools gladly. Only in that electric urgency relayed by him, could we open our eyes just a little bit – for that is probably what I mean when I say 'awake' here – a little bit, but so much better than not at all. Awake to what is around, what is inside: alert.

I wish this, and more, for you too.

Daydream

A van
Europe and long roads
Mornings in Bulgaria when it's been raining
and we've driven all night
snuggled in against the rain,
windshield wipers thrashing
under armloads of rain –
We'll go out onto the cobblestones,
wetness answering our faces.

You know sometimes we'll feel gray
as a snail's foot. We'll count the coins
that mean belly food, car food,
wondering how long they'll last,
seeing us into how many misty towns.

Your deep scissors get me
slice me mend me.
Under your assault
i lie in the wild weather,
with winds as good as longings
tearing my flesh into travel.

This was indeed a predictive poem, written before we set out

David Gancher, just arrived in London

on our peculiar, lost, yet intent journey onto the Continent. Bulgaria wasn't in it, but otherwise all was accurate – especially the last verse. David tore my soul up, without exactly meaning to, and he was part of my education.
We certainly did feel "grey as a snail's foot" sometimes.
And all the rest was accurate too; it *was* like that.

What I've learned since: Travel is wonderful, travel is essential, travel is divine, travel is joyful, travel is hunger and satiety both. I don't know if this book will be read by the young – I can only hope it might – and to them I say: you don't need a lot of money, nor security, nor something to come back to. You don't need to know where you're going, nor even, really, how you're going to get there – there are so many ways. I read an article by a man who rode buses from the American Midwest all the way to Patagonia, and then hitched a ride on a boat to Antarctica. He spent very little money, he was really uncomfortable some of the time, and he had a glorious adventure. What I'd say to the young is, for god's sake, get out of your home town/state/country and wander the world! It'll wake you up, you'll make friends, get some illnesses, hear stories – and surely, without any doubt, your path will be sewn to your life like the sure sleeve of a garment – *this* way. *This* is what suits me. You'll find out.

What I've learned since: I still adore traveling I don't go with just anybody any more, it's got to feel right; and most often I fly alone, and love that too. I read, write, muse, nap, meditate, stroll up and down the aisle... We humans don't know for how long we'll have this great ease of getting here and there, buzzing off to far-away – do make use of it! (For example, a pandemic might come along to intrude.) You won't regret it.
And – there are probably some people this does not suit, this gypsy romance – but I have a very hard time imagining why.

Anticipating Greece, where I've never been

Greece, a beach;
burn
to madness, death,
burn the shreds
of London cloth
from my temple of hair,
the bars from my breasts.

i eat sun
until my death burns,
lie on the sand
until it burns white,
a sun beneath me,

a hole, mindless roar,
sea eating
a slow hole,
gold-mouthed roar;

die:
a long boat diving
across the sea
melting out flat,
sun on water,

no tiny playthings,
no finger jewels,
no praise.

When David and his gentle brother Carl first arrived, David was planning that we would all go to Greece – hence this poem. And sun sounded good! David bought a VW van from somebody he met in the frigid little hotel where we were staying (Jack and Judi's hospitality not extending to a couple of scruffy young men!)
We ended up in Spain instead.

What I've learned since: The quest for annihilation of the burdensome, querulous self – those things we collect in us that are not ourselves, really – underlies every moment of our lives. We want to shake off that shit! But we cling to it too – hard as hard – so that it coats us like enamel does our teeth.

And yet freedom is so near! This mythical Greece I dreamed of is inside us – a light we can fall into – and it often feels just like darkness at first. But the direction is the thing; *In.*

In fact I don't like roasting in the sun. But I really wanted to be free of my battle with sugar; my perceived sexual incapabilities, self-consciousness – and I fantasized that Greece would be some sort of remedy. Though I think in fact I knew quite well that it would not.

But when I was nineteen I did go there, alone. Back in London then, I'd sold a very innocent story to the un-innocent magazine *Men Only* (!!!) and with the lush proceeds I had bought myself a Eurail pass, with plenty left for youth hostels, food, and postcards. (One volume of diary plus some poems from that time are lost.)

I went to Mykonos, a treeless island baking in hell-hot August; and camped on a headland alone for a week, on a dare to myself, to live naked with only a sheet suspended on poles for shelter. Then I came back to civilization – a beach shack restaurant – and lay all day in the shallow surf there reading Somerset Maugham. That night, in my sleeping bag on the beach, I fell into the intense fever of sunstroke, baking as if I were in a radiant-heat oven – as if the oven were inside me. I swelled up, grew delirious, my head in awful pain, my whole body in agony... I thrashed and moaned. Next morning, barely able to pry my swollen body out of the sleeping bag, I checked myself into a hotel – a huge concession for my gotta-prove-my-mettle ego – and lay for three days in the coolness with strips of skin falling off me onto the white sheet like toilet paper.

None of this helped my by-then-well-developed obsessive-compulsiveness or any of my other unhappinesses. But I was a *bit* more careful about the sun afterwards. This poem actually captures some of what it was like on the way to acquiring that sunstroke!

What I've learned since: We all need some sun – it's very good for us – and lying naked in it is often just the ticket – for a little while.

need to overdo it. The body really will tell us when
̡h. *Will* – the force of mind/self over Nature – has its
t a great part of wisdom is learning when to apply it,
let it go. Ultimately its utter dissolution is ecstasy... at
least for

But the medicine I wanted in this poem was given me later, while I sat on a cushion on cool marble, in India, and was so very much more to the point than the medicine of any blasted sand-beach under the sun.

Bed-and-Breakfast; Windermere

"I was born here in the cellar,
my lips are the color of sheep's lips.
I live near Blake's heart-bath
and every day there are visionary sunsets
and dusks to drown in;
in the morning
the sun comes through the marmalade
onto visionary china.
Breakfast eggs speak to my womb.
I drink the devil in my Twining's tea
and tie my boots up thrice.
I had a lover once,
and the sound of his boots
scuffing over the low stone wall
struck the only purpose in me
I have ever known.
One day I kissed his hand,
and it was beetroot. The cellar
has given my feet to beetroot
and it stains my hands, the clouds,
stains my lips cold. Don't
leak the ink of your sinning
onto my fresh-sliced beds,"

> says the bed-and-breakfast lady,
> taking shillings,
> mouth folded like her arms.

We left London and went, at David's restless behest, to the Lake District – perhaps because William Blake had lived there. For me it was all utterly new, astonishingly cold – and I carried the weight of my inexperience like a stone, especially when I compared myself with urbane David.
I was intrigued by this word "beetroot," where American English just says "beets," so it ended up in this poem – indicating something rooty, rough and dull. And the B&B lady *had* frowned and glared at us.

What I've learned since: Religion, society, and ignorance combine to make many women's lives a terrible frustration of their natural ecstasies. Tantra seeks to unlock these hidden energies, which become so grumpy if denied. In Poona we did so much wild dancing! The landlady's life would have missed that pagan fun.

And, young people in fact don't have the wiring in their brains hooked up properly to be able to clean up after themselves, think of others' comfort as well as their own (or even, really, their own). The landlady was right to be suspicious! As a crew, we were not un-hostile to the status quo. For me, the crisp cold white sheets – just that – were an unsettling revelation. My family had slept in old blankets with layers of newspaper added in winter; there might have been a few sheets in the house, but all were wretched with stains and grime. I was learning about the wide world, and of course it struck me viscerally.

What I've learned since: To *adore* – the word is not too strong – beautiful clean cotton sheets. In India I bought many sets, caused ruffles to be sewn around the pillowcases of some, ruffles on some top sheet-edges, and have shipped them around with me ever since. I sleep on them now for summer (winter demands cotton-flannel). I even splurged, at the beginning of lockdown 2020, on organic as well as normal cotton sheets that I then hired a seamstress to bedeck with lavish ruffles in gypsyish patchworky mixes of floral

patterns and subtle solids. The delight, as the lawny light from hill and sky behind my flat comes in the big window and shows me that abundance, all frilling like huge lettuces above my white velvet bedspread!
Comfort, says Osho, is outer meditation.

Bed and Breakfast, Windermere, #2

I.
High cold
ancestral farm
My hands go pointed dry and cold
on the fur coat i wear.
They will gnarl early
held up like open faces
in the mirror;
beneficent witching.

II.
This country curls in on itself
Sheep-horns pattern the carpets
in the hall.
The mirror marches away with the stairs
as it hangs like a brooch
on the crisp-bosomed wall.

III.
Beds here are serious business.
This one wears its woolies
puts us between thick white slices
of country bread.
Still, nothing encourages loving
Reserve rises from the cold earth
The roses keep their scent to themselves
my ears take the quiet in a cold loud wave.

IV.
In one week the wind turned bitter,
the earth patient.
The winter moon reminds me
that black needles divide us
and sheep don't cross
black roads at night.

I love how I flew, in these poems, totally on instinct. Without my knowing it was going to, without trying at all, this poem captures a moment of eccentric, observational young-womanhood. I remember that moment – standing in that cold, clean, strange hallway, poised at the foot of the stairs, looking about me.
And there is the remarking on the bed again – I had never encountered beds like this – so poufy, so crisp, so perfectly made. And then at the end the reference to the relationship: though David and I made love a lot, I wasn't orgasmic, nor did I feel equal to him. I was just too young and unsure of myself. And I could see David felt there was nothing to get his teeth into in this formal, chilly Windermere – he was also ambitious, for he knew-not-exactly-what, and liked to sit around playing guitar and drinking wine and making up songs about whatever was going on, like any canny bard. All that wine-drinking and guitar-plucking wasn't on in this place. So he'd get all restless and severe and stamp about, and I'd think I had displeased him in some way I couldn't really understand. To change my inner state to be more fitting with his sophistication – which I was just beginning to try to do – of course didn't work.
We took a wintry grey boat ride out onto the lake, and the jaunt felt meaningless, as if such tourist activity was a postponement of what we were actually supposed to be doing – whatever that might be.

What I've learned since: What a joy such a boat ride would be now! No goal – just delight, just simple happiness.

And: My hands have not gnarled early. (Possibly because I avoid sugar and nightshades {potatoes/tomatoes/peppers/aubergine} which contribute to inflammation in joints? Or heredity – my mother's hands were always warm and alive.)

Fur coat: David and Carl, his brother, had found old brittle ones at a flea market in London. This one was grey, a reluctant lend from David. I was allergic to it, as to all fur, living or dead.

What I've learned since: Now, glory be, we can buy nice fluffy synthetic softsoftsoft playful coats/jackets etc; and the world and furry creatures are (we hope) the better for it (though when you wash synthetic garments, micro-fibers end up in the ocean, in fishes' tummies and flesh, and then, as if that weren't bad enough, back into us if we eat the fish). No more disgusting dead-kitty vibes, no more horrible violence to lovely creatures. I have plenty of faux-fur now – collars, cuffs, hats, boot-linings, even legwarmers.

What I've learned since: How to be properly warm! Such a blessing to own gloves, hats, mufflers, boots, coats, sweaters. And of course a great cure for feeling cold is to bundle up and go for a brisk walk. When you return, home is very warm. (The British now also often double-glaze and make their houses un-drafty and weather-proof, which was not the case then. It still amazes me that they made this change.)

As to relating: What I've learned since is that the answer to all divisions and worries is to just go inside myself and affirm my own nature. If it fits with somebody, however briefly, fine; if not, fine too. People are different from each other and we don't have to take differences personally. And this means, we have to be okay with being alone, when the relating isn't happening.

Crossing: Harwich to Hook's End

Rumble
in the boat-heart
Rumble
The sea invents us as we go

Rumble
It doesn't matter how powerful
the sea is,
the power invents us as we go

The boat is bound for Holland
The ocean rumbles as we go
The boat is filled with hunger
with people sleeping on the floor
as if they belonged,
murmuring as if through water
Averting glances,
as if to look into another's eyes
was to look straight at death

Irony is too easy
It is harder to wake in the boat
Step out onto the wet deck
Put your face in somebody's windcold hair
Feel the boat's incredible pleasure
cutting its breast through the water
rumbling, building gypsy foam
as we go

On October 24, 1970, David, Carl, and I finally set off for the Continent. It was all new for me – and here I'm still happy, not yet beaten down by the dissonances that would strike all too soon. I love the natural music of this poem, the way it captures the thrumming beat of the boat through the waves. There is even the transcendent notion that the boat, the sea, were giving rise to us... and I'm wondering now if this was something that I got from David! But in this instance, I think not...

What I've learned since: To revel again and again in an adventure – "gypsy foam." Why not? Osho says, "The heart is an adventurer." Adventures are inside and outside both – though we can choose to focus on one or the other. Sometimes I might go on a lovely ferry ride; sometimes instead I lie down, put my hands on my heart,

... looking face-on instead of "averting glances" – and there. It is all an adventure.

Travel: Amsterdam

They strapped me down under rose-bushes
stuck thorns in the skin of my knees.
Snails circled my breasts,
slow merry-go-rounds
prisoning, glistening,
"Stay in America.
Stay in Riverside,
where the Inertia Band
plays snail music, celebrating
the hour of your birth."
In mud they strapped me down,
in cool mud,
the sun's hot quiet ear
listening to my forehead
listening with sharp heat
through my leafy hair.

"Stay
wrist-strapped
snail-strapped
in cool inverted mud.
Your sun gives you mad visions
of travel, of gazing into the mad sparkle
of an Amsterdam sky.
Your feet may dance the cobblestones,
but every night,
mud-child,
you are strapped down to dream
of the rose-bushes outside your house,
old plaster flaking onto snails,

    the loose roses flaking like plaster
    onto your home skin."

A few years ago, while I was doing some work on this book, I had a nightmare that I was in San Francisco, and my bags were stolen with my passport in; so I assembled, somehow, another lot of bags, with my other passport, and these were stolen too. I was saying indignantly to somebody, "In England nobody would have stolen bags you'd just piled someplace for a few minutes while you took a run around the park!" – which is, of course, not necessarily true – except maybe in the isolated little northern town where I live. In the dream I was a-ruin with paranoid misery – "Now I'm stuck in America! And it's going to be such a hassle to get new passports! Ohhhhhh!!!" And then I woke up.

Some people love their home towns and countries. Some people hate them. Some home towns are lovable. I have tended to find my own birthplace and country brutal, inert, gluey, and sad. (Though a visit in 2017 for my mother's beautiful, well-attended memorial showed me a California amazingly engaging: lush from winter rains, fragrant with so many sorts of sun-warmed vegetation, and belonging now to a generation of my family much more prosperous and upbeat than the one I was born in. Unfortunately, the tall grasses and gorgeous wildflowers watered by those winter rains later ended up creating a terrible, wild-fire summer for everyone... while I was back in wet England. And, later, the longer the current pandemic goes on, the more I am pining for faraway family, grand-nieces and nephews I've barely met or not met yet; and the wonderful vegetation-smells of my childhood. As if the long-ago place I fled has now become the unreachable, the imagined-to-be-nourishing, the longed-for.)

So what is the glue? What is the thing that follows me wherever I travel?

It's that thing the duckling sees when he first comes out of the egg, imprinting itself on his duck-brain, giving him a homing-in place forever.

Are we ducks? Good question. Near enough, perhaps, as makes no difference (as my mother used to say). But – we do have one further gift: the cognition that we *are;* the cognition that we have cognition. Aware that we are aware.

So, alongside all the therapy, where I face this conditioning: "The Inertia Band plays snail music…" and work with it, dialogue with the snail and the rose – there's that further, magic dimension where I'm just present to my awareness of it all. Where I look back, too, into, *"Who* is lying strapped down beneath the rose bush?"
I never expect an old imprint to end – that is asking too much. Instead I welcome each new meeting with it with joy: "Aha! Right now I get to be aware of this, whilst mostly I'm not, I'm just controlled by it!" So, I surrender.
And yet, the gods have brought me to Amsterdam – to India – to England. The world is big and marvelous.
All of me can go to all of it – even, sometimes, once in a bi-decade, Riverside; which comes with me everywhere anyway.
Except in the deepest, the soul, the place-beyond-place. That I trust.

Life on the Boat

>i haven't prayed to you for a long time,
>clouds and trees.
>wind, it's been a long time
>since i prayed to you. moon,
>clouds trees wind
>i haven't prayed to you
>for a long time.
>cold, cold, cold
>i pray to you now, oh clouds.
>
>my love is so pretty
>down in the boat
>with his thin chest,
>his neck a scoop of white,
>his eyes black candles.
>
>ducks on the water
>joined houses, new boats,

> old wind and spider trees,
> the moon a candle of ice.
> ducks cry the night friendly
> flames swim in the room-water
> i am moored at the coal-stove
> down in the boat,
> window of dim water,
> Life on the boat.

The Romance of Melancholy Desert and the Lost Love of My Father is supplanted by the Romance of the Melancholy North and the Impossible Love of David. And in teenage time my Creative Might arose – to make this romance mine. To make it bearable, to make it a celebration.

What I've learned since: The peace of Human Design (that arcane awareness tool I just can't help mentioning again and again, at the risk of seeming in-crowdy and obtuse) having explained all this to me: that this is right, it is okay, it is just how it is. I can live in this music of wind and violins. And if I step back further – observe the edgeless field that is my body – I see that this music does not end with me, nor is it only mine; it swirls catchingly out into the cosmos and entangles itself with galaxies as with long fine hair – and things laugh like lovers, and tumble and play. Why should we be separate from that which made us? I see long fine fingers dipping in distant milky ways and languidly stirring them, like a lady in a canoe trailing her fingers in the water... and my music moves where other musics twine and curl, way out there.

Dingy-Squaat

> The short-bladed knife
> slices pirate bread
> Candles light cheeks
> round above the fur

like eggs in straw.
We live in a boat's duck-belly,
six of us frying onions
slicing bread by candlelight
Oats falling like stars
onto the green wood.
The dull knife saws bread
like flesh has been sawed
for hundreds of years.
Our eyes by candlelight,
and the words from our dark mouths
are as sharp as the wind
that tears leaves like stars
out of the zodiac,
wheeling everyplace far.

That month in Amsterdam, living in that old barge, seems in memory to have lasted a year. The sky was low, it was Autumn, a cold I'd never in my short life known. Everything we touched and saw was ancient and worn. I accepted the group of us – we'd acquired four new souls, two American girls, Terry and Barbara, and one guy, James, plus an older German organ-repairman of great sensitivity and compassion named Kris – without question. All our moods and pasts and karma- loads were in that rough unfurnished boat with us – we lived in one big room, sleeping at the edges, leatherwork and music-making in the middle, cooking on a tiny gas burner at one side – and there was no place for any of it to go save into poetry, and the songs David and Carl wrote – for we did not know about meditation, and the drugs just made everything go round and round.

David was still in love with me then. We did not exactly know what we were doing – most of us were beset by some drive to get ahead, which seemed to have no outlet here. We were having an adventure, but to what end? Still – I felt much rejoicing.

What I've learned since: "Wheeling everyplace far" *is* an end in itself – as long as I use the time to meditate and write and walk. The song of the road is a good song. Ambition I must regard with suspicion; how much of it is made of fear, unworthiness, and so on – compensatory emotions – and how much of it is true energy and creativity?

I'm still wrestling with this one. I suspect that I really wanted to go to some sort of writing school, where there were dancing and performance arts as well. Some people do have to speak aloud eventually, not just to themselves. A meditation school would not have been amiss either. I recently attended a weekend workshop of dancing and writing – and boy, that would have been just the thing then. But the only school I had was travel, relationship, and my own pen. And I do think that a pen and blank book are enough to save a person's life.

In a way, this is a poem of gratefulness… a powerful force, harnessable at will; like asking the right question, it opens up some further place to us.

What I've also learned since: Rocky is now Sw. Harideva (since 1972 or 1973), also known as "Crazy Harideva," to distinguish him from any other Haridevas there might be. He's a mover and a shaker, lives in Goa, and has recently started a FB page where people can inquire of each other about people from the olden days in Poona that they miss and would like to know the whereabouts of. Older age seems to bring out the youth in us.

we sat in the bar

we sat in the bar
drinking beer
before beer
Amsterdam
echoed itself
posters on board walls

thin hourglasses
tenuating

       arted lips
      door mirror,
the mirroring door
one old, lace curtained
the other cheekshiny
like waterglasses

ribboning oil
conversations

people walk to
and backwards
pages

eyes
juggle on cheekbones
like silver fish
in the room-net

and flick-
trade faces

Well, I was stoned! We hung out at De Kosmos, a druggie bar in a huge, ancient building with many bare rooms and the beguiling Eastern scent of Mu tea. Young people lounged about smoking spliffs and drinking Dutch beer and herbal teas. David was a barfly, one of the percentage of any population who finds his life in nervous, idle beverage-consumption and smoke-inhalation, in the company of others of his ilk. Throw in a guitar, and the syndrome goes musical. It was never 'me' – but there I was, and I was learning. Dope made reality do peculiar things, and so, of course, I had to scribble about it.

I was becoming insecure: David always seemed to know his way about, wherever we were. He just slid into a place and owned it. I on the other hand was way out of my depth, and very conscious of what I didn't have: Centering. Money. Transport of my own. Clothes worth the name. Coolness creds. And most of all, *experience*. Man, I was lost! I could really only cling to David and quake with misery and fear, even if it didn't look like that was what I was doing. And I knew through and through that *this would ever do*.

What I've learned since: I like my reality neat – not diluted by substances, save for the very occasional square of raw chocolate; the Tachyon blindfold or pendant, raw organic green juice (if the greens are just out of the garden, the ride's more fly) and other small adjustments. I like the challenge of as-is. I like the sound of things arriving – thunk! – unambiguously. I like fresh air coming in the window at night. And after a spell at the PC, I love to go outside and feel myself arrive in my body, swinging neatly down the road, the good air of the world on my face and hands.

Looking

In alleys
where mushrooms crowd like warts
i am looking
In doorways
chocolate grows in wooden shoes
i am looking
At the flea-market
where stripped foxes are thrown
in wooden carts with rabbit-fur
my wood-grained hands are searching
In toilets with damp shoebox plumbing
i take scant time for the mirror
searching with shelled-egg eyes
for my hair
searching out furs for my family to wear
Onto the bridges in the hail
searching out apples from their cardboard coffins
to slice for applesauce
for my family

> In garbage scows on the canal
> i walk in eagle nerves, looking
> for old pots. Chairs. Hats.
> In alleys
> my heels slip on the shit of old straw
> i look in boxes for stuff. For my family
> i grow eagle-nervous,
> clouds over my shoulders, never alone.

So, we all lived together in that funky old barge, and we had very little money. My inner opportunist came out; ashamed of itself rather. I scavenged. In those days we wore wool and fur and corduroy, all old, all ratty. Fur coats were sold at the huge fleamarket, and we went there, and, I am sorry to say, stole coats. This was a one-and-only for me: I had never pinched a thing nor wanted to, much as I longed for finery or even warmth. It just wasn't what I was about at all. But I loved David, and wanted to impress him, and since he had done it I thought he might think I was daring and cool if I did it too. So, on a bitter-cold day, I took a grey-white coat with swirly fur off a long rack of has-been bearish outerwear, put it on, and walked away with beating heart. I told David later and he was *not* proud of me, but upset. The coat was spoiled for me the moment I pinched it… I ended up giving it to David.

What I've learned since: Trying to prove oneself can get one into trouble – a little or a lot. And there is no need: we live from inside out, not the other way around. Human-Design-wise, trying-to-prove is a thing I'm apt to do, am vulnerable to doing; but it's not really *me*, my nature. It's 'not-self'. (It's the same for so many of us.) This is not an easy lesson though. The urge to love oneself through others' eyes, to get energy from them, is insidious and oft-recurring. It needs great awareness to see what one is doing.

And as to pinching things – much much better to be punctiliously honest – as is my family conditioning and my nature.

Opportunism: great stuff! If the apples were discarded, why not make applesauce out of them? Discards are fair game. In Tokyo once a month people can stack out on the sidewalk anything they want to get rid of. You can furnish your flat on what you find, and

many do. I had a wonderful pair of super-soft grey cotton L. L. Bean track pants I'd found that way which I carried around with me for years. A piece of navy cotton fabric with a design on it in white was carted off to India and my tailor made me an apron from it, which I wore this morning while assembling my breakfast.
Clothes-trading parties are a marvelous joy and female-bonding ritual, to be encouraged. This planet is a place of recycling – nothing's really new, nothing is lost. We burn fallen trees in our own campfire. The trick is to do it gracefully and with a touch of gentility. It can be done.

Amsterdam V

Frying oranges by candlelight
under water
Terry and i, making dinner in the boat

Everybody knows out loud
experiences that still lie
in my corners, between the boards.
Worse yet,
they laugh over their leatherwork
because it's all understood.

The low table is scarred
with leather tools
in smiles of nights
over the chillum, laughing
blowing warm smoke.
Warm breathing, hands warmed
by chillum, and coal-smoke,
and the holding of our strong souls,
strung on the same canal.

David has so many tales

of tapeworms and whores
that I say little,
boots crossed by the table.
All this
(our bowls of dinner, like paints
for our laughter
David hugging Terry
because once she had a baby,
gave it up for adoption, and
brings out plates of chocolate –
after dinner the guitars tuning up
Amsterdam growing colder outside
ice crystals on brick
canals searching the boats
for breath and travel)
this will be a story to give.

David was ten years older than I, slight and wiry with black curly hair, a slight overbite, big dark eyes, very pale skin, a sniffle, a dangling cigarette. He had a louche and languid coolness about him, a way of draping his body around his own scintillating intelligence. I was in schoolgirl awe. To me he was so very beautiful…
He also had leaderly aspirations, and had gathered these people about him with some sort of Utopian vision of ranging about Europe, surviving by our wits and playing music. (He often cited the fact that Gurdjieff, in early years, painted little birds to resemble canaries and sold them. It was somehow spiritual to find a clever way to survive whilst also being Awake.) Thus the leather handbags and belts, which we sold on the street.
This Dutch chapter of our trip ended dramatically: our motorbiking friend Rocky plugged a stereo into a lamp-post outside our boat, and the police came, took the men to jail, for "Schtealing Electrische Energie!"and then deported the lot of us. The police were not very nice to us; one cried, "You liff like bigs!" – whereas *we* knew we lived with dignity and grace. So what if we slept on pallets on the floor?

What I've learned since: Sing your moment while you're in it. And yes, this poem is correct: everything becomes a story to tell.

Carl Gancher, David's brother

Terry reading Nabokov

Cachets of coolness are strictly relative – what's cool one year is gone the next – so that part doesn't matter; but writing about it, exposing the human heart in it, and even just the stinging shoots of ego-bewilderment in it, does.

Tomorrow Morning

Tomorrow morning
early
by the clock across the canal
the gulls will come in
to sit on brown wet things:
pilings, the cracked hulls
of bolted barges...
to cry the sharping slide
of clouds coming in.

We have to wake early
when the mist
is still making itself
The yellow of the boats just waking
The bridge just stretching
its early graceful yoga

We have to leave
Amsterdam,
who wakes a little wild
and darkens at 4 p.m.
Dressed and packaged
so that dreams can go on
by dim candlelight
on canal floors.

The scene will catch itself
dock itself in my hand

i close my hand
where canals run
shouts and barges across my green eyes
close my hand
over the flea market's furs
like a fur egg
or ice wrapped in hide
i shut it away back in my hand

We leave
ladders of discomfort
arthritic in our legs
We leave
to suck the sun
We leave
because we love to leave
again.

This refers of course to our enforced quitting of Holland after the arrest of the guys and their release – and orders to leave the country – three days later. We women had taken wicker baskets of food to the detainees each day – I remember David telling me he had put all his clothes on inside out and walked around the cell backwards, "to stay aware." I was awestruck: How did he think of such amazing things? I would never have thought of that, surmised I; nor did I even really know what he meant, *Stay aware*.
Here, the great drama is over, and it is really time to go. Despite my general angst and confusion, Amsterdam had been moodily yummy for me. And so a poem was born.

What I've learned since: Twice during the 90's in Poona I was able to buy a round-the-world ticket, business class! The Indian price for this was about $2,300; a bargain! And then I really discovered the joys of arriving and leaving. Heady things! I recommend the pursuit to anyone who isn't afraid to discover their own deep stripe of fickleness! "We leave / because we love to leave / again." What a diminution of responsibility! What fun! Householding and moving on has each its virtues for body and soul. If you've not seen enough of this miraculous world, why not go more places? (Ahem – once the pandemic is gone… if ever, oh lord!)

What I've learned since: And yet, this is only part of the story. The other part, absolutely needed, is the inner journey. This can be done sitting still, or moving. Why not have it all?
And there is one more question, of great import: *Who* is doing the traveling? Who in you moves, sees, rests? Who is unchanging in all this change, yet completely alive?
The watcher. The consciousness that sees all that you see, all that you are. This, I am told, is everywhere. What freedom! It depends on nothing – neither staying, nor going.

Night

dread coming
from the toes of the sleep-wish
climbing vertebrae;
crippled crow
ascending cornered stairs

in grey stills
family photographs
you see her over rippled shoulders
filling space,
whistling her stories
through hollow bird bones.

November, Germany
she is urgent by early afternoon,

darkening the road at three-thirty
so that lights come on,
rancid pearls
in the gutter of her collarbones.

On leatherwork-selling trip to Cologne

Terry in Cologne, December 1970

unhealthy black knees
she lowers from the north
with closet wings
feathers wet electric blue
stomach white and wrinkled –

two old pregnancies
dropped
swooping over chimneyed towns
she named them sphincter;
miasma.
they live in pores of germany,
hanging out in urinals,
train stations,
storm drains –
small amorphous brats
begging cigarette crumbs
smelling chocolate wrappers
warming their hands
between each other's thin legs,
sphincter and miasma

as sun feeds our daylight
night feeds us
in our helpless sleep
dropping bastards in our dreams
snakes on our stairs
dropping names,
bird-shit in our sleep.
she visits with dark leaded wings
and we wake suddenly
knowing somebody
was sitting on our chests.

It was November 20, 1970. David, Kris the organ repair-man (who dressed always in leather trousers and wooden clogs), Carl, James (the affable stocky Idahoan), Terry (the Italian-American beauty), Barbara (the Jewish ex-academic) and I... were now in Germany, the coldest, greyest, most doom-vibed place I had ever been. We were staying in a huge old wooden house outside Essen, with a very civilized pair of addicts. I watched the husband cook his drug in a spoon over a candle and inject it; I watched the wife knitting colorfully-striped edgy sweaters on her knitting machine, which she then sold in shops. (Addicts, I was beginning to learn, were stoical people, quiet and aggrieved, who looked always at how to provide for themselves the next buzz; this rescued them from any more usual, drawn-out existential worries.) The house was cold. I took long walks. I was much impressed by the sense of grim desolation roundabout – the closeness of the war not long past, the undigested guilt hanging everywhere – the way it sat just under the surface of the earth like a layer of blood.

What I've learned since: Sometimes, if we are lucky, life takes us strange places. If we can use the opportunity as a mirror to look at things in ourselves, or in the Tribe, or the Collective, these exposures to odd atmospheres can be very valuable. And, when we've had enough, and the gods allow it, we can go elsewhere – sunnier, more joyful places, with more chance of true congress with other human beings. There are such places – but it does no harm, for a while, to experience and allow the darkness and the dim.

Germany Nov. 30

I. March of the thin clouds.
In the forest of Thin War Wood,
cannon thunder crashes
across the ears of the sky.
I run where grouse-feather leaves fall,
Go under in short rain.

II. Fantasy traces me,
a relentless gun.

What if one of these leftover Nazis
shot the girl in navy blue
running in his woods?
Hit,
reel down into smashed mud,
ribs burst,
straining my throat
to the armored house,
"I am precious, I am
precious"
trees balance delicate
in the sky

III. In the wood of green trunks,
peanut butter mud,
Fat Hans is taking his unconscious
for a walk.
It trots with pinched barks
little asshole eyes
beside loose trousers.
The gun over his shoulder
is to sew up the world with
yellow skin to grey sky.
Holes make thunder
leaves fall,
Airplanes in a short day.
Fat Hans
teeth of barbed wire, cement tongue
is an overcoat for pain.

IV. The attic has aluminum windows
from an airplane which fell
through screech-empty dusk
kaptain krunch box breaking;
cheerio muscles and kellogg stars
lost in leaves.
German children breakfast
on bones and milk.

V. The love of purges.
Earth rolling languid in barbed wire,
grinning foxholes,

thunder grinding stones to snow,
trees stripping
"break me, break me,
let me suck bullets"

Fat Hans moves gravelled sausages
from his bowels.

War must be beloved.

VI. Through the window
of the Armored Eye.
Twigs stir the sky.
Safety for supper,
doing fine.
To laze through grey warmovies,
lie before sleep
listening to wind.

I found Germany a grim awakening. The seriousness of it all oppressed me: war and its aftermath seem, above all, grey. It was all the Uber-UN-California. I had seen few movies in my life, so I wasn't projecting. I had read only two books on WWII: *The Great Escape* and a book of poetry written by children in concentration camps (this last a life-altering horror), but even these could not convey the wraparound *atmosphere* I found there. The deep chill. No, it was something *felt*, like a bruise under skin, a layer of memory just below the present. It was everywhere – in every field, town, and woods.
I've been to Germany many times since, both East and West; and have had little cause to alter my impressions. On every visit, I've somehow ended up crying.

What I've learned since: "War must be beloved." Yes... Osho says the world must have a war at regular intervals, as a catharsis,

since people live such emotionally-repressed lives. So: Dynamic meditation *works* – you can vomit out your rage, release your frustrations, harm nobody in the process, be free of it, and feel *so much better.* And if anyone still feels soldierly, and wants to march about and fight: well, why not let those who love that sort of thing go off and do it as a sport, just with each other; and not bother the rest of us? Wars suck in the innocent and the unwilling. They are often brokered by elderly noncombatants. Why not let *those* fellows duke it out? And leave the rest of us alone.
Osho says, "Do whatever you like. Just don't interfere in anyone else's life."
That about says it... and on the domestic front too.

December – Cologne

i lean to you in the dim room,
open my mouth over your neck
my breath cold as mercury,
my fingernails
iced roses in your shoulder.
The cat noses your pants like a fox.
The sun is in the mirror
split in three.
My nipple is a hazelnut in your mouth.
You breathe, clouding the glass
the cat's nose is in your navel
You shiver. The sun disappears.

My eyes grow ripe and fall
like marbles from a knifed bobcat.
The cat breathes a little opium note.
You are kissing my mouth
and all the sharp teeth and fur,
the cat eats my hazelnut nipples
scratches my white arm

like a broken mirror,
You have a mouth of black roses

We are turning over and over
on a floor of cat-bones
sucking each others' eyes
like red windows
setting into smoke.

Well, that was an adventure – making love with David after smoking opium (the one and only time I did that drug); and then, Coleridge-like, turning to poetry for further expression of the experience. David and I were briefly in Cologne for some reason, staying again in some big cold house. We were in some nearly-bare, frigid bedroom, having fervent, spacey, intense sex on the floor (!). David used to stare into my eyes at such times, passionate and commanding, and yet searching too – and I always felt miserably that I failed him, as I didn't know what it was he was telling me, and indeed I seemed to have no adequate place to receive it in.

What I've learned since: Once was enough for that drug, and: no substance unlocked my orgasm (unless you count red wine, eighteen months hence, in France; but maybe it was France that did it, and the most patient, non-phallus-oriented lover I ever had. And even red wine only worked that one time. The lover, though, persisted for a while...) And, while this opioid event was memorable in an aesthetic way, it was the usual big question mark in terms of real meeting... though it's arguable how possible real meeting is between these creatures called 'male' and 'female'; although on a heart level I think meeting is possible between anyone and anyone. This wasn't that.

What I've learned since: One must try out all sorts of things; and then find one's own place, one's own people, to go where one feels safe in one's own true passion (and I don't mean necessarily sexual). I call it "The art of blundering."

ember, to David

The creature that lives between us
is a cat with a changing body
Swinging from a trapeze
tied beneath our closed eyelids,
it drops feathers for breaths –
i lie at night with my head on your belly
listening to the merry-go-round horses
being unscrewed inside.
i want to suck at your polished shoulder
until I sleep.

The creature that lives between us
is a river
with banks of fur.

This was that same place in Cologne. I remember there was an oval mirror on a bureau with feather boas and other theatrical bits and pieces draped about it.

What I've learned since: Lovemaking, if it is merely instinctual, is not good enough. There is too much conditioning in the way – and Nature's manifested inequality between the sexes (man fast, woman slow) means that instinct equals, all too often, frustration. Even apparently successful lovemaking can leave depths upon depths undiscovered. And if the woman is unfulfilled, how, really, can the man be satisfied? The two are in this thing together.
It is his job, his duty, his discovery, his journey, his only hope, his challenge, his crusade, his holy grail – to slow down to her timing, and to learn her, to listen to her, to find where she lives inside... so that both can be uplifted and given illumination. This will require skill, compassion, friendliness, patience, and great self-awareness – all of which are very, very good for him generally. (I was just enjoying a novel called *Separation*, by Dinah Jefferies, in which the heroine's lover says, "Sex is all about the woman. Most men don't know that.") So while David was a passionate lover and did his best, he did not discover me; and I did not really help him to – for I had no

thought of a right to selfishness then, in bed.

From my diary: "David said that I fuck like a guy – not my movements, but the way I use the energy... To come, I must let that state happen that is like just before I write a poem – that receiving. The whole point of a man's fucking, he says, is to make the woman come, which makes him come. I have emotional orgasms, he said, because I don't really seem frustrated, but of course that's not enough. he understands so well!" (One day I would like to edit and publish those diaries – daunting task – 2400 pages!)

What I've learned since: The woman's timing is all. If she can sink into eternity, all the better. Women, speak your truth in the moment, even if it's unpopular: yes to this, no to that; wait, please; a little more of this, not so much of that. Now, wait please while I stand up and dance madly, arms above my head! Whoooo! ...Now we meet again.

We are not just bodies here; we are all the rest of us, too. Shall we explore this? It is a wild unfoldment. Shall we enter this world entire, and see, feel, know here what we are?

barcelona

>   dark
>   pension hall
>   you approach
>   white and nervous
>   in dark drug alert
>
>   she killed you
>   the mother
>   stabbed that snake-slim tree
>   white flesh home
>   i have stroked
>   in infinite undoing
>   now you see her

in doorknobs
in dark hall
and in women,
their wombs
worn on their faces.
for the first time
you admit you are afraid.

i come toward you
candle held aloft
swathed in a black
wool cape, inside
naked –
today for the first time
i have surrendered.
in an hour
the belly swelled out
full and huge with death –

a sluggish bat
turns, urinates
in layered guana
bloating to the cavern walls.
my only centre,
his heavy dreaming meat
within.
you tell me you are crazy.
with candlelight
over black belly
i tell you silent

i am mary
mother of jesus
insanely doomed
to die with birth of god.

in all this
only the candle is alight

    a hot storm
    burns black rain
    on barcelona;
    ancient smells
    incense the vapor
    all is stark
    doomed drama,
    myth pinnacled to abyss

    david, it was spain
    and it was eternity
    jesus in crashing drops
    in tile courtyard
    in urine smell
    of barcelona
    rising,
    rain beating, falling
    clean
    and ancient
    on sleeping barcelona
    black grave in love
    with the dead

We left Germany in December in the rattly old VW, spent an uncomfortable night trying to sleep in it, at the side of a road, and next evening arrived in Barcelona in a crashing, hailing, light-flashing storm. We found a rustic *pension*. Barcelona was a moody, dark, stained place then, Catholic and mysterious, full of old buildings, ancient ways. I felt it all through me as some strange familiarity, as if I had lived there long ago, before memory. We roamed around, looking for food, and took in the atmosphere. I loved it!

Back at the pension, David ingested whatever drug he had about him – I don't remember what it was this time – and began to drink his usual red wine. But something must have gone amiss, for he came to me all freaked out.

The swelling belly: I had eaten tapas with bread – the wheat made my belly bloat – very unpleasant.

What else I've learned since: Going back to Spain, and seeing chain stores replacing indigenous shops and neighborhoods with cookie-cutter edifices selling shiny whatever – a teeth-gnashing disappointment! Spain was Spain then – its smells were all its own. I mourn her, though (and maybe because) she had her darkness. This poem is steeped in Catholicism – of which I cannot of course approve – and yet the melancholy of it all was wonderful. That too has largely vanished.

Rigging

three hundred years ago
this island was covered
with vines of rain,
like a brain
shy with persuasions
of constant hiding.

then the sun lay down here
for three hundred years,
and his yellow belly
caused the vines to smoke
away, up in ash,
and houses were carved
from white rock and red rock,
and ships drifted into the harbor
with noiseless prows.

today i stand
on an eyelid balcony
watching the birds flying
and flying
in the water,
and the masts and rigging
like ghosts of vines

> in the sun.
> one of my hands
> with cracked adobe lines
> remembers vines,
> stray and tangled.
> the other
> bears the straight lines
> of sun, masts, rigging.

We took an overnight ferry to Ibiza, sitting up all night in chairs. David asked around, and quite soon found a *finca*, or farmhouse, to rent, up in the hills. The old man who'd owned it had died just the week before... and yes, there was a ghost! I think he didn't like his house being overrun with hippies, for he knocked on the foot of the wooden bed a bunch of times *very hard* at midnight on New Year's Eve! When I was there alone waiting for David to finish celebrating and come on up.

I had heard that the Baleares Islands had once been covered in

View of Ibiza, December 1970

forest. Goats had been introduced and they ate the trees down to the ground. I was much impressed by the loss.

In the last stanza I speak of left side, right side. I had only begun to live then, and had not explored the two sides in any systematic manner – for we all have both: the sere, visionary spear-bearer of the Male; the lush timeless blossoming of the Female. I knew only confusion about these things. I projected the Male onto David and felt badly inadequate in the Female.

What I've learned since: There are different styles of Male and Female in people – and even the ones we own can change daily. Meditation has honed my male energy into a still, clear objectivity; for a long time he was too strong, overbalancing me – but brain surgery persuaded me to give up on his over-exercise, and he calmed down. My female energy is light and light on its feet – it never was the jungly, spring-fed, earthbound sort. Human Design has helped me make peace with that. I'm even relieved –. It was lush enough in its time, for this incarnation. No more need be expected of it. Its gifts are different.

What I've learned since: If you're a woman, there's a small technique to help you see your own Inner Man and Inner Woman clearly – at least, their current state. You'll need a watercolor set, a piece of good paper, a notebook and pen, and half an hour of free time.

Paint a picture of your left and right ovaries, just allowing whatever wants to appear on the page to appear. (Important to use actual watercolor rather than just crayons or pencils – the water unlocks the subconscious.) Gaze at the painting... then step physically forward, out of 'you' and into your left ovary; then close your eyes and 'become' your left ovary. Ask it what its name is. Trust whatever it says, no matter what your mind thinks. Write ten lines from this position, starting with "I am..."

Then bow, say "Thank you," step out of the left ovary, back into 'you'. Rest a moment. Then do the same with the right ovary: step out of 'you', into the right ovary; close your eyes, ask it its name. Now let the right ovary write ten lines beginning with "I am..." Bow, step out of it, thank it, step back into 'you'.

Illuminating!

You can try the same thing with your breasts. (And if you're a man you could try it with your testicles – though I've no experience with this!)

a bleak night in Dec. 1970

you rock the wooden doors closed
like ribs locking.
your guitar hot as a candle,
you climb the stairs
where i am digging at my pain.
the air is bitter.
i remove all traces of envy
from my flesh.

red turkey fruit
grows from the green hide
of the cactus.
i saw an adobe-walled yard
where the cactus grew spiderwebs,
layer on layer, dusty
you were not there. i was walking.
It was good to be alone.

the stars shine like birds
like glittering water
like travellers,
smiling in seablack cold.
your black hair glitters like a sky.

i am up here making dusty blood,
too quiet,
your guitar plays the candle
i will be generous
but it is hard.
blood. red dirt. Island.

A teenager can have a rich emotional and poetic life – but that does not mean she is mature. The English novelist Elizabeth Jane Howard says in her memoir, *Slipstream*, "Pete was a gifted and interesting man; he was never wittingly unkind to me, but he didn't understand that my youth presented him with responsibilities as well as advantages." The man I was with was like that. He'd been in the Peace Corps in Turkey, wrote for *Rolling Stone* magazine. He was rocking with the 60's. Who was I?

It's odd that I use the words "making dusty blood." It sounds like a period, but wasn't; I didn't have any from age seventeen to twenty-two. The Pill had messed things up, such that when in Germany I'd gone to a gynecologist she had diagnosed, *Unterentwicklung der Gebärmutter,* or something like that: Underdeveloped uterus. So I must have meant some other sort of blood.

What I've learned since: The goddess in me needs, has always needed, an immense amount of time. She needs to see the color of a man's integrity, the true bent of his intentions. (In those days every man had a story to explain why his romantic inconstancy was a great idea.) And she needs to be seen, courted; understood, even.

When I was young I gave myself away to scoundrels, fools, and idiots – mostly idiots. I wanted love and attention. I was not ready for sex; because no man bowed down to the Goddess rightly, courted her justly, researched her ways. And because I did not know how to abstain from performing and competition, and *just be.*

Young girls should be taught their value and their power. Each should be taught how to access their own Inner Authority, as Human Design puts it; so that they know in themselves whether they really like a man or not, and if this is the right time for him to be in their lives. I suffered from a wholly unnecessary effort to please – and I suffered from being unable, when I did make my boundaries clear, to enforce them. I had been taught that kicking and screaming were bad things, evil and witchy and unacceptable. I had been taught to acquiesce to grownups simply because they were grownups. And so I was forced into intimacies I wasn't ready for, which then embroiled me in emotional morasses I am still untangling, if gently now, to this day.

What I've learned since: Women, even young ones, are the Goddess. They deserve the utmost respect for their sensitivity and their power. If everyone – men and women alike – lived in the service of this law, the world would clap its hands in revelation and so many, many things would fall into place – for all of us. And what is so beautiful in a man is often the feminine that is assisting his masculine to be civil and helpful: the sweetness of his chivalry, the gravity of his protection of women and children, the depth of his feeling for a male friend, the observant beauty of his art. The feminine principle has been feared, maligned, stomped on. It's time it was re-instated in the position of Massive and Helpful Mystery in our lives – even as the Underwriter of Existence.

In this poem I was trying not to be envious of David. I was trying not to be jealous that he had now added an additional gifted teenage girl, Doris, a bottle-black-haired German drugs mogul, to his harem. I did not have Dynamic meditation yet. I did not know how to trust my body; to see what it really liked and really did not like. What was healthy for me and what was not.

What I've learned since: Learning to trust this body is the most worthy endeavor for the rest of my life.

Ibiza Winter Lament

i'm always waiting for the bougainvillea to bloom.
i'm always waiting for them to come home.
i'm always waiting to tell the poisons goodbye –
the speed, the sugar, the sleep.

Was it raining again? When i tried to get to you?
The fire is eating my face.
– You're sweet like the sun is; bone-sweet.

From where i sit the fire is sharp, sliding to its death.
Why do i detest myself

David, December 1970, Can Juani

for sitting in front of the fire?
Laziness, and merry-go-rounds.
Why should i not detest myself?
It's only fear making excuses to love
for shadowing the true.

Let it be precious, this low fire
me watching all the cheeks in the house
(for they've come home)
turning like pink clocks,
in a sooty adobe finca
on an island, in the rain.
Let us fry up some nonsense
to eat on cracked plates.
The butane light is not merry,
doing its share of sobbing.

Was it raining last time i wrote here, too?
Dull smash of wind, low trickles
on the ears of the house?

i know that i do these things over and over.
Inside, i'm solid bone, like the walls of this house.
My efforts taste adobe.

When i write, there's always a chapter on the fire.
i stare at it, feed it, with terrible gratitude,
Gather at it like a sucking moon.
There was a little worm on a twig-husk
thin as a thread of saffron. He tried so long
to escape the fire, in tiny
shaking terror.

Ibiza is cold and damp in the winter. The one fireplace provided the only heat – and smoked like a grampus, so that ceiling, walls, and us and our hair were black with soot. I didn't know what to do with myself – once I cleaned up our bedroom and made it tidy, and David got very angry with me for being bourgeois: "You're ny mother! I *left* my mother, I didn't come here to be

What I've learned since: I have a particular mandate, in Human Design terms, to love myself. This is a lifelong exploration. And it's nobody's business but my own. I like this job – which really just means, to *be* myself. Then I have so much permission, for what I wanted to do anyway. This is great. The Tribe, the Collective, don't really want people to love themselves. It might take them out of the group effort, the group mold. And it's true – it might. But some people just *are* like that. Would you make a cat try to be a turkey? Wouldn't work.

Fire-Wish

the dark room,
my mother's body,
one-breasted
against me,
a damp sleeping curve;
wind in the pecan tree.

no
it is David,
sleeping.
He has made love to me
and i am swollen
like a cut fish.
i allow trembling.
Wind rises out of the trees.

shall i burn his guitar?
In a well-made fire,
shall i watch the strings
melt and snap,

one by one?
i have a good reason,
built on voodoo
and hollow bones –

i am missing
my triangular fire,
and the music
that i should play so well.
curled in the dark
birth-damp,
i want the sleeper
to wake and hold me
hold me,
and make safety in my ear.

When I was twelve, my mother was diagnosed, or mis-diagnosed, with breast cancer. There was confusion with the test results at Kaiser Permanente. (We had a medical plan there because of Glen's job.) Mama had a brutal radical mastectomy. As she was coming to afterwards, the doctors announced in pleased tones that no cancer had been detected. This was the beginning of the end of her marriage with my father; she insisted later that he had refused her the $30 she would have needed to get a second opinion. $30 was a great deal of money for us; I'm sure he didn't even have it, but... The fact is that in our family there are different versions of the story. One brother insists that she *did* have a second opinion and that there really *was* cancer; that our mother's story-telling skills extended to her own history. In a way I would like to believe this, to spare myself the burden of her rage and indignation against my father, and the doctors, that I have carried all these years. But in another way of course I don't want her to have had cancer!

At any rate, her recovery was slow and painful, yet she still had to care for us. Her left arm remained swollen, as the lymph glands in the armpit had been removed. She often got infections in her cracked fingers – cracked from desert dryness and overwork. I still feel a sort of incredulous sorrow when I remember that time...

the children gathered round the bed where she lay with her arm elevated via a scarf tied on the bedstead; our gatless fear and empathy, our helplessness at her helplessness. That helplessness of hers soon turned to rage, and then we had to weather that as well. I can barely stand to try to imagine what she suffered. Our father remained stoic and unspeaking. *What dark ages did we live in?* The poem is also about my sexual inadequacy and frustration. And my shame.

These two themes sit weirdly together, yet this was how the moment was.

What I've learned since: A doctor is not a final authority. You might very well want a second opinion, plus as many alternative supportivenesses as you can find. We have to be proactive with our own health – finding what suits us, educating ourselves when something goes wrong. You might want to consume a lot of organic home-made fresh green juice, my favorite and most reliable health booster.

It might be a good idea not to wear underarm deodorant. My mother thought she smelt awful and no matter how poor we were she managed always to have Mum deodorant, which must have contained parabens, which preservative has been found in breast tumors. Whether or not the lump she found just near her underarm was cancerous, the chemical insult given to that delicate area could not have helped.

Second: First of all, these emotions can have an outlet beyond poetry; cathartic meditation does the trick. And cathartic meditation, in turn, is best done in a group, within a Sangha, a meditation community – at least in the beginning. So I was missing my Sangha.

Third: What my sexuality needed first: a compassionate, experienced wise woman to give me counsel and lay to rest my fears and shame. Women are so very different from men, and those differences need support and understanding – and plain old *knowledge* of what they are. (A dear friend of mine, Leena, a Cranio-Sacral practitioner, once said, "Most of the wisdom on the planet can be found in post-menopausal women.")

Fourth: The relationship needed to go to a relationship session! It was unbalanced in so many ways, and in my vulnerability I had no voice really, and no champion. We needed to bring out what was inside us at a deeper level than just the ego-strutting wannabe-cool attitudes that seemed to be what was available to us. There was much possibility there – if we could have gone deeper – to appreciate and feel compassion towards each other's humanness. We could have had *love* – friendliness – mutual respect and awe and joy; even if we could not be partners in the conventional sense of the word. Men seemed to insist on everything being easy in a relating (the woman was not supposed to complain or fuss) in order to spare themselves the excruciation of self-examination and most of all, *feeling*; men need support for that (as I did for my sexuality); they are vulnerable there. Denial doesn't help.

And lastly, if having children is going to throw you into such poverty that you can't take care of your own body, don't have them. Be grateful for effective birth control – find out what sort you can live with, what works for you. The happiest parents I've seen had enough money and only a few kids. Why be poor, sick and desperate if you don't have to?

And: If you're female, but only if you're female: be selfish in bed.

Formentera Departs

Island hill-stubs
birds cling to the water
waiting on the dock,
dark crowds of Spanish
and the lighter flurries
of freaks
twinning and laughing

rabbit coats and goodbye

Cristina's ponytail,
pink paper roses
rabbit coat, she waves with
Doris –
merry gravity
hands in her belt,
i cannot stand to be with her,
beauty punishes

Ten hands
wave
like birds dispatching
from a tree,
wave and hold
the air a solid instant,

the water pulls the boat
away,
Doris' face eating into mine
a small shrinking purr

Oooohhhh… Doris, David's young paramour. We'd been visiting her in her white thick-walled house on the little nearby island of Formentera. She had lush red cushions on a couch in her living room, and I was so amazed that she had been able to get all that together, whilst being no older than I.

I was now the dejected wife. I remember this ferry journey across the narrow strait from Formentera to Ibiza – the pain of jealousy, of envy, of comparison; my own lostness in my scruffy, dry-skinned sorrow.

What I've learned since: Take care of myself. Do this abundantly. Put this before all else. Lavish on myself beautiful clothes, and boots, and hairdos, and jewels. Revel in the things I love: books, writing, soft fabrics, particular foods. And above all: Go inside myself, so that I know what I'm about – visit my various inner provinces, and then the Empty Center, the groundswell of Being.

And: A poem lasts longer than a love affair.

Formentera II

it was the port, like a black elbow

i won't care,
i won't care,

then a Marin County boy
kissed my open dizzy hands
you know, Kat,

Confident, magnetic Doris, David's paramour

you know what you saw in the sheets

a hideous uncareful fear.

always looking for me, me, me
buttering bread
the butter still on the bread
i looked for it to answer

they're rollicking
about Doris' U.S. Army socks
over there.

the open mouth
they're whiffing poppers
over there
(wingy seaweed
milk and braziers)
gritting my teeth
over a stainless steel balloon

of course
it leaves everybody cold.

Invited into bed with David and Doris – looking, then, in Doris for the love David had withdrawn. Bizarre. Peculiar. For I wanted *David*.
The Marin County boy was Tom, one of our number for a time. Even in the trying-each-other-out of youth, there was no chemistry between us. (He later tried to stiff me for the payment for the return ticket to New York I sold him. I finally found him in Sausalito, two years later, in his jewelry studio; he *very* reluctantly paid me $90.)
By and by the weight of my unhappiness combined with the effects of unrelished drugs, and I could not tell if the buttered bread was speaking, or if I was. The others in our coterie were alert to people 'going off the rails' – it happened, in drug-land – and, no doubt from fear, rejected these un-centered beings. I was becoming one of them.

What I've learned since: If my body does not want a thing, do my best not to consume it.

And: If I look for my center in other people, I will not find it, and they will reject me.
Go inside. Find me first. Then relating can follow. (This was a hard, hard learning and took many years.)

And, if jealousy arises, let it sting. Nothing else you can do. And have a little look: am I jealous because I am missing something in my own life? What might it be? Can I give it, somehow, to myself?

Can Juani – February

We look at each other
with rivers now,
the days
we walk down the road
into sure sun
almond trees
thick with white flowers
feeding us
(we are an eagle,
arms thick with feathers,
who dreams of wings)

In our eyes
the master water,
on the road
stones parting to show the sky.

The nights
we camp in the kitchen
bread and onions
feeding us,

    the ragged sleeves
    of the fire
    our solid voices
    our flickering cheekbones.

    The nights
    we wear each other's bodies
    like gifts
    and in the business of sleep
    sweat, and turn over
    and let the dreams fall in
    like the night
    through the little
    high window.

Even in a sorry time, with the wrenching decampment of my lover's affections to another – even with the psychic displacement drugs bring – there were these times of bliss and luminosity. I remember the night this refers to – our crowd were staying at the house of an acquaintance, on another part of the island. I remember the flowering trees, just outside. We took some Dormondinos (ridiculously large and strong Spanish knock-out pills) – I remember I saw stars and fell down – and I must have woken in the night or early morning, somewhat recovered, and written... or perhaps later in the day. (We did so *drift*.) Or perhaps we stayed two nights and I wrote it on a previous night, before we took the damned things.

I have learnt, through experimenting (and this only happened after I saw a really nice vid on YouTube where a young man from India went around filming all sorts of people singing and dancing and speaking gratefulness – and that day, this principle, of claiming and speaking gratefulness, just hit me right) that, if I wake in the middle of the night, I have a distinct choice between worrying, and doing the opposite. And this opposite is what I call "doing my gratefuls." I just lie there saying to myself, "I'm grateful for that black dress with sparkles on it I got at the charity shop today. I'm grateful that I took in to the shop a bag of stuff I don't

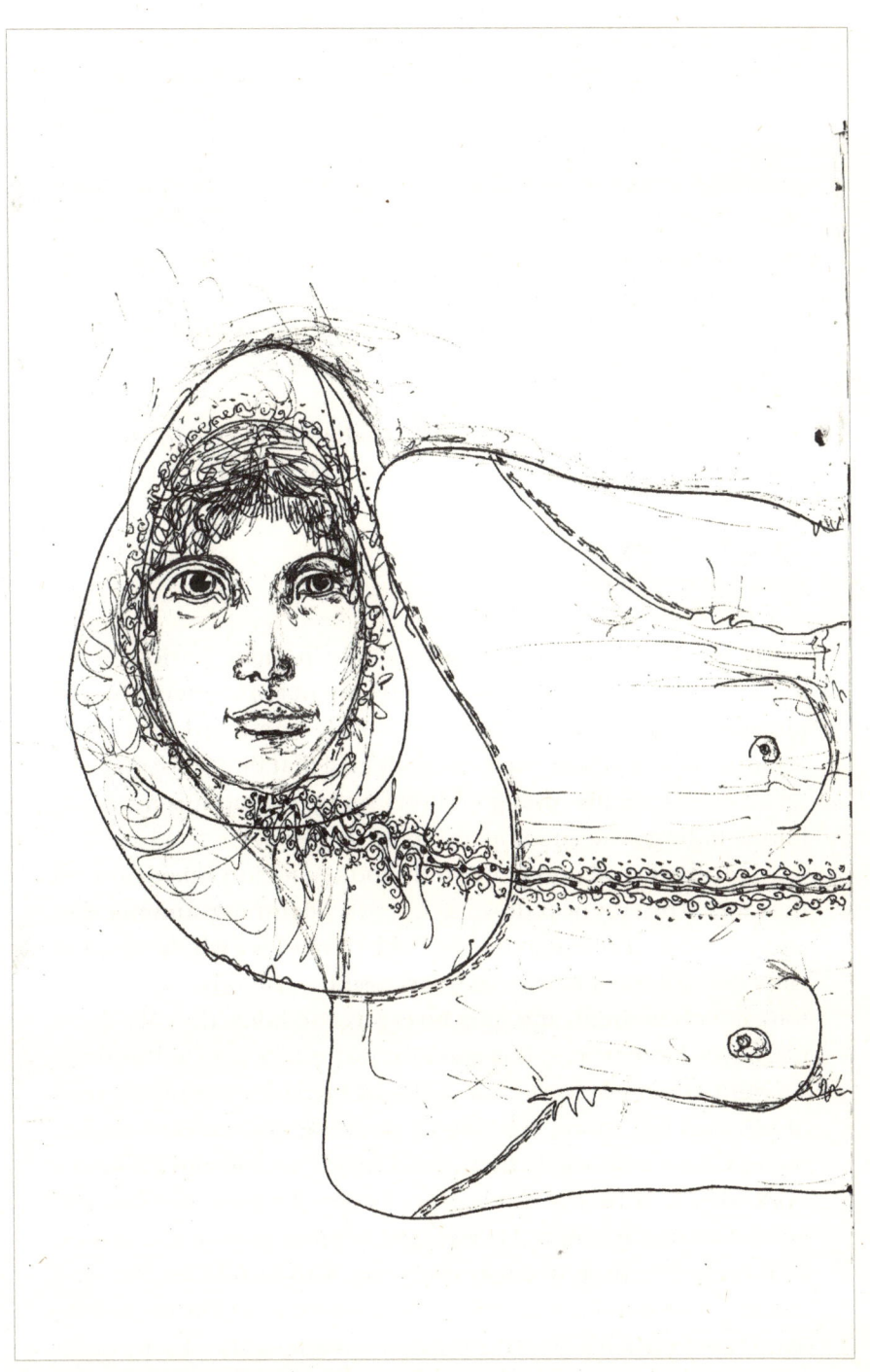

Drawing, Ibiza, January 1971

want anymore. I'm grateful I'm reading *Passage to India* by E. M. Forster, because it's just brilliant and makes me happy to read. I'm grateful the recycling trucks came today and took away all those bottles and all that paper. I'm grateful for this house! I'm grateful I went for such a good long walk. I'm grateful for my clean sheets. I'm grateful so-and-so said something nice about my book. I'm grateful there are some nice leftovers in the fridge from today, so I don't need to cook tomorrow. I'm grateful I got a lot of ironing done." And so on. This is so soothing, and lifts my heart so gently and surely, that I soon fall asleep again, happy inside my cozy being.

Only one drawback: now, in the daytime if I start to think of something I'm grateful for, I right away feel sleepy!

From My Diary
Ibiza, February 1971

...Got black velvet pants now, with a hole in them. David and me and Doris all fuck together, and when I was in Formentera I fucked Okesha the Algerian, and David was in the same bed with James while he fucked Morris. I am infinitely glad that things are opening up all over. I am just young and very hung-up, and it is necessary for me to be gentle and not ever to lie to myself.

Today David and Doris and I took Acid and hiked around the cliffs. The sun beat down as hot as a beginning summer day, and the water shone that dazzled blue. There is a whole world of cliffs that I never knew were so accessible. The other day David took me up to them, and it feels very free to know they are there whenever I want them. It is good for me to take acid at this time. Though David got pissed off and said I wasn't even taking care of business any more, cooking or cleaning, just either freaking out or taking acid – well, fuck him. I'm all I've got, and I'd better work with it. If he doesn't want to be worshipped, the bastard, he sure makes it tough. He's so goddamned groovy. He says he feels himself getting stronger every day. And he told me the ways in which I've been a drag. We lay down on the pebbly sea-beach, and I had to talk because the tension was killing me. To my slight surprise, I learn what a drag I've been. "You still think of yourself as Katy and Serafina, queens of Riverside, incorporated. Well, it's just not so. You don't even carry your own weight. You're a *drag.*"

So. One thing I've come to is that I know now that whatever I do, it's what wants to be done. If I have to leave David because of all the unbearable shit I put on him, so be it. It's very possible I'm just too young... Doris is not afraid of him. I know that anything I put on other people is just misplaced.

...I feel regretful that in my disconnection, I leave out... so many beautiful things – the Ibiza people, the happenings, the lives of my people. Well, there ain't too much lower I can get, so when I come out of this, I'll have to be pretty high. I'll be interested to see. Someday I want to learn firsthand of the two-thirds of the brain that we don't use...

The log burns on the fire. James, Doris, David eat in silence. Omar the pale Afghan hound slurps spaghetti from the floor. I am wearing beads around my head like a headband. I go to sleep thank god. I will know the best things to do. They come.

Sunday

Katy: "Do you suppose La Tierra is like that every night?"

David: "No. Tomorrow night, for instance, it should be much groovier.

And that's what you're concerned about."

Me: "You read a lot of things onto me, David. I'm really embarrassingly innocent of ulterior motives."

"Horseshit. You're rife with them."

David and Doris are playing chess, and she wins. Katy mends her long orange dress. James plays guitar in his room. David wears the white pants I gave him for his birthday. I'm very zonked on Dormondinos.

David: "I'm going to bed." Stretching his striped-sweater body. "You coming to that one?"

Me: "Yeah... I gotta mend for a few minutes."

I look up and the room sways. David is holding a candle and it burns his hair all to shit, a flame taking the front part of his hair. He brushes it with his hand and it goes away. The black residue is on his white pants.

As of this morning, I am not David's old lady anymore. I am free. God I feel better.

Like shit.

Monday

La Tierra, the very fashionable bar in Ibiza, where people sit fashionably around on low leather chairs, cracking sunflower seeds and drinking and smoking and talking. Doris is here, freshly showered and beautiful in her white skin and black hair. Rocky is back from his adventures in Germany, Amsterdam, and Moscow, nineteen now, to a warmer Ibiza. He made a lot of money making pornographic films. David is leaning over the table in his striped sweater, and I am still afraid of myself via him. What incredible things I must be made of! James is here in his Levi shirt with the string of beads I made him around his wrist. The song "meet you in the fallin' rain" is on.

Last night David popped two Dormondinos in my mouth, and I got more stoned than I've ever been. I talked at incredibly slow space speed, and saw flashing lights, and we all had a real talk, lying in bed together. At first David called me a "hippie twat," which he later apologized for. I'm so glad I'm not his old lady anymore! Now I can often see him as a real person, and not put all those heavies on him. What a relief!

I have been totally empty. The beginning again.

La Tierra is where Everybody hangs out. We are part of everybody now. Melody complimented David on his dancing today, said it was sexy and inspired her and turned her on.

Last night we went up to Casa Weirdo, as David calls the glorious finca up on the hill. Lots of people were there, and a Cancer chick and I told each other ghost stories. David was arrogant. The road up there is rocky and bushy and we get afraid of ghosts.

This morning David and Katy and Doris woke up in James' bed, where we had somehow ended up. Dormondino still plodding through our veins. We all began to murmur and move and smile and breathe, and all my openness is challenged to watch David and Doris moving together, she recieving [sic] with her open legs and soft body, her mouth open breathing pink, sweet, eyes almost closed, moaning, while David in exquisite triumph and balance, his long beaded neck arched, pushes and pushes and all my fear is the excitement it wants to be, and I move with them, we all look at each other from our night's talk, we really love each other. And he fucks me, and I know just to take it, take it, feel it like the warm woman I want to be. *[Note added afterwards in blue ink*: bullshit I felt like *shit* pure *crap shit* – K.A.]

James and I talked about that – the infinite power of receptive absorption, rather than my accustomed shallow aggression. I am learning the most difficult – complete surrender. When I am jealous, it means I want, I am, I see, but am afraid to believe I am all of that.

Chicks are something incredible. I love them. I want them. I am so ready to make love to a chick now. Today I ran into Christine, the gypsy-looking chick from the caravan, and she was lovely and excited and open and luscious, and I want to see her…

Wednesday
[I Ching hexagram drawn in]
"Stagnation – the superior man goes back into his own real self, and disregards everybody else."

Thursday
What beautiful things I see, what beautiful things I am. The whole day for me is a workshop, ironing out whatever in my thinking is deathdealing – I accept, open, and think through any hassles. I hope to have it so that I don't have to go through the long thinking riffs every time, but for now it is absolutely necessary. I can neither regret nor hope, for both are too unreal, and have been hanging me up. David: "You have to do your approval for yourself."

Now I write to Mama, who sent me a $10 bill today. I send her poems. I wrote a beautiful one the other night, when I stayed in town alone. Talked to Gypsy-from-the-caravan and Black Butch in La Tierra. Black Butch said, "We ought to get together sometime." He is right on.

Tonight, a huge party at Can Tunicos for Terry and for Day, the two Pisces chicks. Presents, wine, food – I made lemon pudding and bought cookies, we had numerous variations on rice and vegetables. Of course. I was outta sight, book. I sang all I wanted to, and talked to people, and recieved *[sic]*. Terry wants to talk to me, she's all excited about Doris-David-Katy, she went up to David and began ranting, "You're crazy! you're insane, and you're trying to make Katy crazy!" I laugh.

...Mas Tarde. I am sitting in a bar in Santa Eulalia with David and James. We are all growing with each other, bit by bit. We have scenes that we visit, on this pine-tree island, things we all talk about together. A Leo, an Aquarius, an Aries – we take energy about with us like flowered robes. James is my friend in much the same way Taffy was – the way we talk together, the way he expounds theories. I sit beside him when we drive into town for hamburgers or a James Bond Spanish-dubbed movie, and we talk in abstractions that we both understand perfectly, leaving no part untouched. James is medium-short, with a stocky body and a curiously round ass, big thighs. His face is narrow but long, with the sort of mouth that looks like it is wrapped around his face. He has pretty brown hair, and is always cool. So is David, even when he celebrates and charges around. James says sometimes that he will make love to me fantastically. Especially when he's stoned on Dormondino. Dormondino is the Ibiza anti-thrill. It makes you soft and warm and dreamy-drowsy, and your sex opens and unfolds like an old daisy going to brown seed, and you can be merged and mellow all night... The word Dormondino is as common in the Ibiza air as a strand of flying pigeons.

...Here is a thing. Drugs. Lots of drugs. Acid, Dormondino, speed, poppers, hashish. Wine and cigarettes. Lots of pastry. I was sure I was going crazy. Wild-out schizophrenic paranoia. I lurched around all day feeling like I had fingernails in my throat, eating pastries and going to the post office and clutching my black wool cloak around me in the rain. Cleaned the house this morning, packed, anxious as hell. Bid goodbye to the *señora*. A thing I have noticed is people will not meet my eyes *except when I feel present*. That I have almost no will over, it flashes in and out. I wanted to feel all my ghosts and devils, let them roll. But it's freaking everybody else out.

Tonight a girl told me to take some vitamin B, so I bought a bottle and took a lot. I began immediately, surprisingly, to feel all sane and better and happy and just when I needed it, too.

David put me in a poem, about me lost and drifting with my mirrors. Well, Kate, that is some burden to make beautiful in this life. But it could be worse. Mundanity, for instance.

They have all gone more or less to bed. Doris sniffs. James grumbles in his throat. I am sorry to have been such a drag to them all.
Don't be seduced again by that mirror, sweet chucklehead. Your white soft belly, criss-crossed by the leather lacing on your velvet pants. The delirious worlds in your head... Do you remember what the gypsy in London said? My "boyfriend would be stolen by another girl," also my friend. I'd say it has definitely happened...

February 13, Formentera

the boat slides
into port
past tremulous lights
on cold water.

i can
waver to my knees
beside you,
in smoke
and torn lace

saying,
baby
let me
guide you down
and unbuttoned,

    let me
    heat your throat
    so welcome,
    i can
    sail you again,
    give you
    wide rocking murmurs
    on the warm
    waves of the bed.

That scene again… the small ferry-boat pulling into the harbor, the low white thick-walled buildings, the sun… and this time I'm just exposing my need, my neurosis, my pain, my desperation.

What I've learned since: Sexual maturity is a storm lasting forty years. Before it: peace. After: peace again. During: only those lulls caused by satiation; so temporary. Nature is a cruel master.
And yet. That powerful stuff is so valuable to us if we use it rightly. Let the madness of passion burn us completely – in dance, in Tantra, in wild lovemaking, in senseless howling at the moon. Only by living our love-madness totally do we get the benefit of what comes next.
Women's brains do fixate on one person and become addicted, enslaved. It just *is* like that – we need not take it personally. As Osho told me, "Just be a witness to the biology."
And, only by throwing it all in the ring do we ever get to come out of the ring at all.

Ibiza Vision

    Behind fig-tree waters
    the music of sitars
    searched out my grief

    and unmasked it:
    You have been silent

for so long
locked in lost houses,
licking flames
for comfort,

trying to out-die
the dead.
The shy old men
on their hobbled canes
have more life
than you,
look at their
sea-wet eyes.

Time has better plans for me
than those i give,
and makes wide dances
for its stars.

The fig-trees
play my music,
with grey skin
and nobbled fingers,
as old
as my old can see.

The water flies
on wings and blue
wings,
and the clean rocks roll
in the water's mouth,
and the rocks are thick
as flowers on the fields,
and the stars dance wide.

"**Time has** better plans for me / than those i give…" Yes, this was a vision, and a true one. That's the way it was, and is. It is a thing I remind myself about, every day.

e learned since: If I don't over-plan my life, but rather ..., and allow, and listen, particularly for very interesting invitations; life might just have something up her sleeve that is beyond my dreams. It has happened like that… Like the man says: "You can't always get what you want / …But you just might find / you get what you need."

Ibiza Triangle Lament #?

David and James
shake the rug out
by the clothesline;

a hat and four arms
flapping

the rain

Wind in the house
i fold
a red shawl with two
holes,
like missing breasts

i fold
a burned apron
David's pants

Do i steal?
Rip silk
in thin jags,
push red ribbon through

to hang in the VW
to go away,

the bottles are lined up under the table

Doris and David sleep

and animal James
sleeps at quiet attention; the door
the black mirror
of the frying pan
on the wall

Milk heels,
my eyes,
shuttered hexagrams.

The wind ploughs the wind.

I have heard Osho say that if a relationship has more suffering in it than joy, it's time to leave; more joy than suffering – stay.
In those days it was deeply fashionable to be unfaithful to your partner in the name of freedom. Nothing less, in fact, would do. I have no quarrel with unfaithfulness per se; biology loves it, the gods and goddesses love it – it does so stir things up and make them lively! But things must be faced in their entirety, as they really are in us; and faced with love and compassion and heart. There were too many 'shoulds' going on here: I should be independent, centered, enlightened enough to let David have Doris. (Though without *my* actually going to bed with someone else! Which I did, once, just to try to even things out and impress David – a friendly if heartachey meeting in a bunk in a ferry-boat – and David freaked out!)
I was not any of those spiritually great things. I was in the mad grip of certain hormones women are heir to, that imprint them with the lover's smell and make them turn towards him like a flower to the sun. I was in the mad grip of neuroses, too, exacerbated by chemicals: LSD, hashish, Dormondinos, etc; sugar (which is a drug, not a food, whatever the culture pretends), caffeine, the long aftermath of antibiotics (which strip the inner protection of the very core of your body and leave you shaky, fearful, and all-at-sea). And I was in the mad grip of the fact that I had not

had a hands-on participating father to underwrite my life with stability and a sense of my own value! Instead there had been that abstracted, distracted, abdicating, sweet-and-sorry presence I could not effectively communicate with…
None of these things was a *fault* of mine! Each of them was an opportunity to grow and learn – did we but know it.

What I've learned since: If I have no power over things in the outer, I can at the very least (and it is a great, great deal) reclaim my place in the universe through meditation, Self-Healing, giving myself trance journey sessions, and getting helpful sessions from relevant practitioners. All these things help *tremendously*. And then things on the outer tend to shift. That's what I've learnt.

Around this time, David wrote this poem:

Las Sirenas

I have a strength
to endure
many sleeps:
delusions of the guitar
theoretical harmonies
the broken loves
of my friends

are hungry,
they will try to eat
these sad island
stones.

My sleep comes hard
strain after dreams
my voice grows clay
   it rains,
My hands close up
  sad
they never knew you.

*I have a strength
to endure
many sleeps,
Mad David
his head hung down the well
summons his drowned magic
from the caves
so he sings
louder for the echoes
louder for the morning
louder for the water.
in the dead well.*

The Dog Curled Ghostlike

The dog curled ghostlike
in the corner of the house
of your heart
guards a metaltooth door.

Not to show his power,
he represents himself
but is not himself.
He hides under the floor
in a dark chamber of no design.

From the house's hill
the sea shines down a rounded
slope. It's Spain,
and many dreams of Spain
burn useless fires around
your arms.

This is not important.
Love translates everything

into a verging moment.

The dog of your power
piles power behind it
like bull-pawed earth.

This is all okay.
These powers
fly their massive shoulders
over the earth.
They fly –

I don't know if I wrote this to myself, or to David. But "This is not important. / Love translates everything / into a verging moment."

What I've learned since: The 3rd chakra: power, mind – and the 4th: heart, endlessly spacious, unconditional love and acceptance – have an interesting relationship. It is safe to go into the often-scary 3rd (just below the ribs) via the tender, non-judgmental fourth. There are all sorts of powers on this earth; yet love is a quality that can unlock them. Undo them. They change character under its glow. This happens because the heart regards them without choosing: "This is all okay. / These powers fly their massive shoulders / Over the earth. / They fly."

All sorts of energies are needed in this world. Our job is to observe them; let them be total, yet not ourselves be wooed. Strangely, this gives rise to love; and love in turn draws these energies up into itself.

But one must never, never judge. My own experience: this is possible in deep meditation, when observation is sharp against the stillness.

From my diary
Wednesday February 17, 1971

I don't want to think about those old days now. It's the new days I love, the warm wind and the sad-housed grandmothers, the midnight sausages of Spain.

Book, you are beautiful and beautiful. The little boy who lives next door to Doris made the boat on the back cover, and I put almond blossoms on it... I (also) made envelopes, and I was happy. It is a strange Kate nowadays, unlike any before. One minute she is alone, running, looking at the sun go down over Formentera. "The flagship sun," she thinks, "Leo Maximus." Then she is crying softly behind a face she cannot see, while around her the friends laugh. The French astrologer tells her the map of where the stars were when she came into the world this time. She is wretched within her skin, and yet she feels she can fly... Every minute now is heavy. You may be sure I am glad of the rebirth, but also I keep coming up scared.

The wind rattles the wooden curtains outside. David and Doris are in bed. This makes it necessary for Kate to come to reality with herself. If she compares herself with them, she dies. It is so tempting. But how can I live gracefully, feeling those eyes on me? David and I talked about it tonight, after I got back from my long Formentera groove. It is definitely astrological – "The Aquarius' place is to understand the Leo. The Leo's place is to get off on the Aquarius." "I read this blurb in a magazine once," I said, "It said that with a Leo and Aquarius, they would have one hell of a time, but both had the character to make it." "Yeah, but for what?" said David, in his Aquarius t-shirt, his twenty-eighth birthday today. Then – "Come in here, I want to talk to you. Bring a candle." Just what I'd been wanting to say, burning up watching him, like nobody else does to me, I want that black hole in the center of his eyes. I followed him into the bedroom. He put the candle on the nightstand and began to take off his boots, sitting on the edge of the bed. "Oh," I said, for this is one thing that I let happen.

"How could you go off and leave me to fuck all these girls that I don't dig?" he asked, for he had been fucking Morris and Doris. "Well, one of them, anyway," he added. He is so proud, so cool, that I may just leave him.

This time we had each other though, and I was fierce with grief as much as passion, and passion was connecting our electricity, we fucked like mad creatures, equal and wild with each other. It is what we have.

I can only say this openly, for I am laid open like a wound.

re selfish," said David, "you only care about me where
ur changes. I'm tired of your changes." He showed me
em he wrote to me when I was gone to Formentera.
It's to Doris, too," he added, and the familiar thing came down, that Doris is a fiery Tibetan monk, and I am on the edge of being a lostling, falling off the planet altogether. That would not be so bad, floating and sailing in the proud dark.

I will go to bed and dream again, and tomorrow I will take a lot of acid. I am sleepy from the long day waiting for the boat in Formentera, and traveling on the laughing, bucketing boat to Ibiza, and walking partway home in the black wind, while stars shone thick in the sky. I left Okesha's house at sunrise, while the moon was still bright, and walked much of the way to the port, where the sun made the adobe pink, and the transparent turquoise of the water leaped into white jutting waves.

And it was strange to come home, as I knew it would be. Doris and James and David fixing dinner, full of stories, David hugging me with endive in his mouth, thin and in a felt hat, very together, immediately I am shattered again. Again. again.

Who had been mended with such gentle langour [sic] in Formentera. The I Ching: Taming Power of the Great, with changing lines to The Gentle, Wind.

If David loves me, why is he making me crazy?

February 18
He is not making me crazy. I can indulge in you, book – "God revels in abundance"... I find myself in attitudes of prayer a hundred times a day, and positions of fear as often. I came to a thought tonight that maybe I am just crazy. It was a good feeling, a let-it-all-hang-out feeling, and i know that the term "crazy" is an indulgence. So be it – indulge the abundance, my nature is essentially sweet, and this is the kind of crazy I would be.

So perhaps I am crazy. Today I took the acid, a purposeful searing scald of all my brain – and whatever remains intact is thankfully fluid. Did you know, sweet book, that on Formentera (my sunset place) the French astrologer did my chart. And I am Leo with Virgo rising and moon in Taurus. Incredibly strong, incredibly full of tension – do I feel it! The staying Virgo hand, the

Leo pride, and then something else – if I *trust* my energy, then that is taken care of. It remains to trust the callings that come to me, and to resist no temptation. I need to write in you, book, because of the incredible restlessness of my mind – it traffics my skull like a caged cougar, looking into the eye of the moment, cupping itself around point after point of – stuff. So is my anxiety, such could be my peace. So is my fear, such could be my flight.

The astrologer spoke of callings. He said that in March and April I would have an attraction to solitude, and I would know depth. I love to think about these things, to eternally just open, open. He said I was very intelligent, and this could manifest itself in anxiety. And does it! …Mars in Scorpio, like Doris and David.

…So. I sit at night eating from a salad James made, while David fixes his tape recorder and James works on leather… I say now that if I have some calling, however strange, go with it. I am wearing a bunch of old raggy things, a brown scarf, a black shirt, black crepe skirt, Angela's tights, the long coat Angela gave me. I don't like my hair like this, but I haven't much choice now.

I look at the table, the jar of flowers, the bowl of oatmeal in front of David, half-eaten, the typewriter. All I want to do is go to bed and contemplate the infinite.

Sunday
Another day of freak-out in sunny Ibiza for the ridiculous Katy. Surrounded by grooviness of all sorts, *[page ends]*

I've been holding off dropping the big goodie. I haven't written in you for a long time, and I feel good about it, because what wants to happen, will happen. You've been wondering, I'll bet, when I'd wake up and see how I was fantasizing all over everything. It's a long process, like forever. But I was sinking, you know. And you know that sinking is even good, for it's taking you back to where you need to go. I have had to surrender a lot, and there's a long way to go. It's funny – one night, stoned on hashish up at Casa Weirdo, I came to an inescapable conclusion, one that I welcome whenever I am open enough – something wants me, and is giving me no quarter. What wants to happen, will happen. I light a cigarette and look out the door and see that the wind is blowing, and remark, "It looks stormy out!" holding my cigarette aloft, fantasizing in a split-second that David will think, "She is putting on airs with that cigarette," realizing that it's all in my head, remembering my I Ching reading this morning of Shock, Thunder, with changing lines to Fullness.

I am equating Casa Weirdo with my sweet awakening, for it was there that I thought and thought, or rather my thinking took wings, and I discovered about everything being one. Take it from there...

March 6
Amazing, my pen still writes. Writes as though possessed, Delighted! I have made myself crazy, I guess, about as crazy, anyway, as I can get.

The air is brittle and cold. Outside, Spanish lurch in threes, drunk, and I don't want to know of them. In La Tierra, it is the show – and Kate on acid in the middle, to put it bluntly, and people looking her in her drowsy eyes. A French chick, whom Kate used to think she was, danced with a tongue like a lizard's chin, her breasts in a thin white shirt, dancing from round hips with serpentine swithering motions. Kate lay back in a gathering confusion, thoroughly obsessed with Everybody's judgement of her – selfish, freaked out, vain.

It is back at the apartment. God, I'm glad to be writing in you – I have been prepared to lose everything, and why? To test myself, as these new testings have done.

I look at Doris, and cannot love her, for she is too nasty, too perfect. The fire seeps and smokes. There is a bracelet of blue beads on my wrist.

"I guess you know we're through," said David, leaning against the door of the toilet. "You always make out in front of me in public, as though to make a point of it. Go ahead, be eighteen! Go on and make out! That's what you want to do." Our mouths and cheeks are mulling and writhing, with all these little patterns. Katy is thinking only. (I am so confused. Is this what it's like? I want that coat-collar to lay my head on.) That's what made me crazy – it was the coat-collar of the black suede coat David got at the sale at Ivan Spens gallery. It looked like Glen, god help me. That was a dangerous thing you did the other night, David. Pretending to be Glen for me. It was funny – I almost didn't like it. In the dark with you, David, I am so good, so unafraid. It's just when the light comes on – Those eyes. Those other people's eyes.

Sure, David, I know what it must look like to you.

And I don't know what I am to anybody else.

Tried to stop caring.

How can I live so close to David, who is so sane, and go so crazy?

That is why. He is sane for David. Who knows what is sane for Katy? How have I gotten onto those terms? Sane and not-sane? That belie the turns of the corner onto the Montesol, the sideways looks into the mirror, the long nights cradled in sweet dreaming watery cradles?

One of those horrid clingy festery things, is that what I'm becoming? Aha! that's what I'm Not Supposed To Do, is cling. So I am doing it.

The thing I guess that bothers me, did I have to go so crazy? Well, says something, you did, so I guess you did. Perhaps, David, you would say it is not so. But I have rooted out some things once and for all.

Like my thing about food. How amazing I am! Who does not know what she is. It disturbs me that in all this I have been a drag on my fellow man, but shit, let him take it.

What is confusing is these Ideas about myself. I guess I decided to discard All of them, and here I am. Idea: Leo. Idea: Virgo influence. Idea: all those psychiatric terms for things like father complexes and mother complexes. Idea: you have to lose everything to have anything. Idea: David's old lady. Idea: any idea, I don't know, I decided to test them all. Because some were constricting me. My usual goddamn excesses. And I got this Idea about David, and it's haunting me, over and over. Like shit, can't I make it behind this same old thing?

It's wet today. I have an urge to run back to Jacques, knowing full well what I'm doing, saying, "Jacques, take me and hold me and take care of me."

This morning David and James went to the San Juan police and they said we have to leave Monday. The sun rises in this diary in Ibiza – who knows where it will set?

Later.
The reason to go crazy, is to give up. To have somebody help you back. And this they can never do, except with words. But what a shame to go back to the States for that! I wish I had never heard all these terms.

I said, "Do we really have to leave the island Monday?"

James said, "There's this chick who keeps coming up here and breaking my bubbles. She's done it three times now."

Everybody laughed. I laughed. They were talking about me.

The ashes flap in the fireplace like little fishgills.

...All stories for me end with the finding of inner strength. Hmmmph.

It is so clear. I can look at everything so clear. I must go to the bathroom.

It is later. It is suddenly clear that everybody else is just a person like me.

I read David's mind. Twice. David was furiously scribbling a poem. Suddenly I laughed. "I just got a sentence in my head" I said, "'dancing in hideous glee'". I laughed with bright eyelashes.

"I was just writing that," David said. "Almost exactly." Later I was drawing and suddenly said – "you weren't writing about the pharaohs, by any chance, were you?"

"Just the pyramids," he said, and a few seconds later Doris and I looked at each other and laughed, it was just too good, yes, a nudge with the shoulder in the shoulderblades like that...

...So here we are. We have to leave the island Monday. This morning: rain outside, the first in months. Our neighbor Walter stomping in the garden saying over and over again: bummer bummer bummer and in the other room, Beatles playing "two cats in the yard, remember how life used to be so hard," but very soft and mellow, and in the middle us, Doris and me, making some good love, sometimes I could really love Doris, hold her close and do some of my Leo pawpainting into her back, kiss her – "we don't kiss enough," she said. "I like it, to kiss you." For we have had bussiness *[sic]* talks and dagger-talks, she and I. Just now it is daggers from her black and blue eyes, for she certainly DOES NOT approve of all this.

What a blessing, to be able to think without pain. So purely. What a blessing, to know that tonight is not, as it seems, the last night on earth. Or if it was, I suppose it would not make a difference.

...Doris looks up from her drawing and cluck-clucks back and forth like a nurse. Goes back to her drawing, after one flash at Kate, who is paranoid and has earned it, by now.

Death Sky

Perfect as Mediterranean
knife blue,

i'll slice the pain
through open
wrists, all the way
until the black lid slips.

It is no good,
living with one eye.
my eye wants to open, open,
take the cold clay road
underlining the hill,

The gull
who dived an inhaled cry,
the rock in water
and sun,
the milk and marble sky.

It is no good,
living in an adobe mouth,
feeling the sun like a whip,
hating my sweaty bed,

> the bread on the table,
> the slow chewing.
>
> i want to run
> on the earth's bare body
> without envy;
> with two eyes,
> through green junipers
> the hills humming like bees
> in a blue milk sky.

This was not really a death-wish – the last stanza imagines, "I want to run on the earth's bare body / without envy," – so I really wanted to live, but just to be free of the terrible ache I was feeling at being slowly shut out by David (who was, quite rightly, recognizing my limitations). Then there was Doris, whose entrepreneurship David admired as well as her unshakeable cool. Then those strange *ménage à trois* in bed, warping my sense of myself further as I tried to grapple with sexuality with a female, when I didn't know what it was with a male. All this, plus the drugs, were shredding my still-unformed persona and making me seriously question whether I was located within myself, or somewhere outside, as I've said – in others, in the walls. This was horrible! I used to buy vitamin B syrup and swig it, to be coalesced, then, temporarily, eerily, back into a 'me' in this one body. Then I'd fall apart again.

What I've learned since: *This* sort of longing for annihilation is really just a broken heart; mixed with the natural longing of the human to go beyond her apparent boundaries. It was also a cry of longing to inhabit my own body in dignity and peace, rather than letting others inhabit it – sexually or psychically. I was crying out to belong to myself.

This is still, every day, a challenge to some degree: to recognize my own gentle, often shy body's clear knowing about what suits it and what doesn't. For me, the body is the fount of wisdom, or at least prudence; it signals me with little 'ulps', and falling tummies, and heart-wincings, when it doesn't like something. I don't need someone else's ideas about how I ought to be (even a lover's;

especially a lover's) but only this little silent signaling in my chest, my belly.

I was so envious of David – he seemed so sure. Yet his sureness did things that hurt me – so it was not mine. How to not waste energy on envy, but find my own sureness? I wish someone had taught me this early, early!

It's about closing my eyes, listening, observing, and *respecting what I find.*

As a teen I was terrified of leaving the broad life unlived – and so I threw myself into things, pleasant or horrible. There is some worth in this – the worth of stretching something till it nearly breaks, to find out what it is – but what it is might end up being something quiet, which keeps its precious stretchiness in abeyance, until the right moment. There's value in stretching – and yet, the value is in the ultimate coming-back to what works for this body, right now.

Teenage friends and relations have occasionally written to me of wanting to commit suicide. Things seem to them futile. I wish for each of them a start to the meditative life; I know no other that really works for supporting the human being in all joys and sorrows; and for helping it find its center. And, awareness is never a bad thing. Any occupation or art or craft or calling can be a meditation – and so daily life can be.

Diary Excerpt
Ibiza, early March 1971

…So I'm going to keep on the vitamins. And last night I meditated a little and felt better. But that's not all this is – I've been sicker than hell most of my life, I'm beginning to believe. The vitamin B is cheap. It's what they shoot into paranoiacs, in massive doses. I'll get some E and C, too.

A friend of Carl's promised to give me Anais Nin's address in Los Angeles. He's talked to her, and she's very interested in young writers.

Everything I do, say, write, or think, I compare with David. Automatically.

Fantasy: lying on the beach in the Canaries, lying on the

beach and lying on the beach and lying on the beach. Reading sometimes, soaking in the sunlight like a cat. I may do it. I am tired of being crazy. Maybe I can O.D. on it, instead of fighting. I don't want to fight anymore. The Canaries sounds like just about the best place in the world for it. And whatever is real with David and me, will not deteriorate over time and distance. He wants a caravan, and especially he wants Doris to join us, which she might do in a month or so. I could go to India with them when that happens... David wants to go to Zurich to earn money in coffeehouses. I'm tired of fighting.

The wood burns into little feathers. David thinks I am a lesbian... a real lesbian supposedly is looking for her own cunt in another woman.

Lying at night with one hand on David's cock, one on Doris' cunt. Between them, a child's joy, a child's delicious erotic joy. She is kissing my neck, and then he makes me from behind, talking within me like nobody has ever talked before.

Last night the wind howled all night. I stayed up after David and Doris went to bed (they do love me) and wrote a poem, which I haven't decided is good or not. Maybe writing has helped make me crazy – it encourages the idea of two people within me. Sort of. But otherwise, that tremendous energy – where would it go? A lot went into running, that now is loose.

I'm burning boxes that we get from the market. I smash them up and burn them and they are gone too quickly. I am crazy, crazy, I think of when David said, on that ghastly acid trip the second day we were here, that he was making himself crazy. And I *encouraged* him! He's never reproached me for it, but I too believed he was a sort of other-worldling. He has since righted himself in grand style, subtle and constant. Playing his guitar at Can Juani in front of the fire, the candles waving from the wind that comes in the door we keep open to let the smoke out, James there too, head down over his harmonica, how strange it is that I don't think I can bear to be with them. How strange, too, that leaving Can Juani and Ibiza has not sunk in yet. I see the house like it always was, dim and stoop-doored, our bed, our clothes hung on the rack, the little stand with the tapestry, an ashtray, a wine bottle holding a candle, a hole burned in the tapestry. The tangled bed in the morning, which I sang and made up again. My trunk of ragged clothes by the door, dripping impractical crepe and torn velvet. David's clothes thrown every which way on the floor. Even now I write with only half a mind, waiting for David and Doris to return.

If I went to the Canaries, it would be with the people from Casa Weirdo, over the hill from Can Juani. Nobody is (so far) as groovy to be around as David, but I am becoming a pair of pained, watching eyes.

So Finally

So finally
i lean
to you
    It has taken weeks
and our bodies meet
like old friends
in the hollow
talkative dark.
They are late
but catching up.

Outside
our distances wait
like bored sailors
    in the empty port.
Black drug velvets
your cloudmoon skin
Take me down
Roll me over
Play glossy blues
on my body.

The seagulls
perform mathematics

    in the metal dawn
        out of time.
    The sun comes up
    frightened
    over a tense sea,
    the harbor is closed
    like a mouth
    in the wind.

    No crossing that water.
    It's upset and evil
    No island
        no sleep.

    So finally
    i lean to you
    in music and glances
        Your statue smile
    is a secret
    at least 10,000 years old.
    A Tibetan monk
    peeks through his incarnations
    beneath your strict eyelashes.

    We listen to music
    a dance out of time
    and in our cursed alchemy
        of fire and air
    we are amused.
    We are hungry.

This must have been some brief reconciliation. "…in our cursed alchemy / of fire and air…" Perhaps this was after I'd returned from Barcelona, where I'd gone to see a doctor. And had had there a few days alone in which to locate my own self again.
    We made much of astrology then – though for me this enthusiasm has now vanished into the larger body of Human Design – and David was an Aquarius, aloof and cool, and I was a Leo, supposedly

fiery and warm and 'me-ful'. We two mused on this a lot, and I longed for his unattainableness as I'd longed for my Aquarian father's. I felt disadvantaged from almost the beginning. How can one argue with Cool?

What I've learned since: Life is not about cleaving unto other people most successfully. It is about finding out what I'm here for, and meeting that 'me', and respecting her; making her tenderest acquaintance. It is about respecting every morsel of her sensibility – her Yes and her No – so that in union, she is a full player, with the right of veto in any given moment. Her reality counts as much as his does; and in a sense she has more to lose.

Love is about the woman saying what her experience is, and standing in the truth of her sensations and her pausings and stoppings and flowings; not at a mind-level, but from being actually plugged in and observing what she feels. (It is awareness that allows us this distinction.)

Brief reunions don't count for much if they are part of a rollercoaster of mis-matching and bruising and judging.

Diary Excerpt
Wednesday, March 10, 1971
Barcelona, Pension Central

30. *Li, The Clinging, Fire*
The Creative has incorporated the central line of the receptive, and thus Li develops. Fire has no definite form but clings to the burning object and thus is made bright... K'an means the soul shut within the body, Li means nature in its radiance... [and thence for two pages of I Ching text I copied out, ending with:] *...And take captive the followers. No blame.*

It is not the purpose of chastisement to impose punishment blindly but to create discipline. Evil must be cured at its roots. To eradicate evil in political life, it is best to kill the ringleaders and spare the followers. In educating oneself it is best to root out bad habits and tolerate those that are harmless. For asceticism that is too strict, like sentences of undue severity, fails in its purpose.

na. Dim pension, a Western on TV. Before me, the
y: two letters from Ron Schreiber of *Hanging Loose*,
letters, telling which issues my poems would be in... I
wrote him a letter, newly brief and succinct, it felt good. One letter
he wrote from a hospital on yellow paper: hepatitus *[sic]*.

An open box containing Witche's *[sic]* Bread from Serafina, that she must have mailed in November or so. I fetched it, slightly brutalized (smashed in the ribs no doubt the morning it crossed the Spanish border), from the train station today.

I. Who has no personality. Doris's apartment, Kate in a shambles in bed... Paranoia, where you can't look at anybody. I was really into it, lying naked and clinging to David's every smile and knowing it. We walked in the wind and he said I should go back to the States. He was fed up. Later he went with Doris and saw Cassius Clay on TV in a bar, and came back and said he decided to accept me and help me, instead of reject me.

On the boat, there was Jim, who held me in La Tierra my acid freakout night... with the help of drugs, I was becoming separate selves. Looking in the mirror and watching my face flicker, pale, shrink. David also opined that I was going technically crazy. I stood in the hallway in my black cloak facing him, lips quivering, unutterably young.

Let the hell roll... Hugged them all *[who were staying on the island]* goodbye. On the boat, tall Virgoleo Jim and I went down to his cabin and took off our clothes, locked the door, climbed up into the top bunk. Pulled the curtain and made love. I did not strain. When I surfaced, I was glad; when I hid, I was okay. His chick Lucille, a Taurus who is psychic I am sure, long blonde hair and immersed eyes, slept with James in the bus down in the hold. James was in a purple sweater and Romilar.

Within five minutes I had told David, and he was ultimately pleased. I was a little astonished that he experienced insecurity. But he was glad to sit out of the sex king scene for a while, he took a Bustaid and stayed up all night reading, and taking notes on, *In Search of the Miraculous*. On Gurdjieff.

So tonight at the Pension I stay with Jim, and eating the aphrodisiac Witches' bread, am warm. Did a yoga meditation sleepthing, totally informally, in a dark room here this afternoon.

Everyone else has gone out on business and godknowswhatelse. Lucille and Jim are here to deal shit.

I love I Ching.

From my diary
en route from Ibiza to parts unknown
Thursday, March 11, 1971

A windy beach south of Barcelona, the morning. My curls blow at the sides of my face. The last couple of days have been so heavy that I hesitate to try to describe anything of them – nevertheless, I want to converse with you. David is asleep back in the car. Heavy for these people: David, me, James, Vicki, Lucille, Jim, and a man we met last night, named Marty – I want to be with him again. On the stairs at four in the morning he asked me to stay with him, I said no, he said okay, I followed in my black cloak down the stairs. He paints much like Jim Chambers, and he raps like nobody I ever heard before. Nobody. He has offered us his house in Tangier for as long as we want.

I see, am beginning to see, how things are heavy for other people. When I speak now, it is from a spacious, centered feeling all inside, and I hear within the same place.

If I were Tom Wolfe, who wrote *Electric Koolaid Acid Test*, I could put in the nuances, glances, rollercoasters, raps that bounce off anything and everything in the world.

And we sang last night. David loved it, and I am so glad he got to rap like that, finally, I'd love for him to be able to do it more. Take some pressure off. Marty lives in a third-floor apartment in Castelldefells with his wife Bix, an Aquarius, who is blonde, beautiful, has a strangely-shaped upper lip.

I feel in these last days like part of a library of eyes, a circus of eyes, a ten-course meal of eyes. Watching Doris' face shrink, purring, on the dock as the boat pulls away. Jim's eyes again and again, green and deep and welcome. He is so easy, but his earth sign is not quite at a pace with me. Deep and easy, tall and spare and even loving.

Pension Central: Lucille goes away for a bit, I am with Jim in the candlelit room, good. Always a little frightening, but good. We never have to talk much. He and Lucille went out later to Plaza Real for dinner and perhaps to sell some shit, and I stayed in their bed and drank wine and read Koolaidacidtest. David and James came back from Castelldefells, and David was Freaked. They had had an incredibly heavy scene, on acid, at Vicki's mother's house... It was also David's mother's birthday, and he felt exactly like her. I was beginning to realize we are separate people. He needed me. He accused me of not caring, and tried to stare all his black voodoo into me, and out of some well I came love, and he knew everything I felt ("Look, Baby, I can feel it all tonight. You said 'get out of this room, David, I don't want you here' with all your little vibes just now. You don't deserve me") and then he went down to the rambleshackle VW bus and slept, I presume with Vicki, with the midnight Barcelona thinned-out traffic all around. I slept in a room with a lot of other chicks, and lit a candle, and said a long dream-chant-poem for David, and concentrated my love-vibes on him, which left me exhausted. Two scenes – me leaning against the doorjamb in the long dimgreen hall of the pension, with the old mad wallpaper, some doors ajar, the shadows, a vase of plastic flowers, colorless in the dim, somewhere at the end. Wrapped only in the black wool cape that Doris gave me, my hand on my unloosed stomach, in that last moment that he left, as we traded love for a single spidery flash, I felt the love growing up out of my stomach, as though I were pregnant with it. Me in the candle-lit room alone, looking in the long mirror on the wardrobe, my cloak over one shoulder like an ancient black-clad Grecian woman-witch-goddess, my eyes immersed in the liquid of the room. I spoke aloud; I made unashamed spells to him, and strained my new-found spaciousness.

Eyes, meliquidous eyes. David's – have I noticed before? – are huge and as though there were delicate, peeled eggs behind the brown pupils. The reason... that I am frightened around him is because I resist the full force of my attraction, refuse to believe so much could be inside me. It is. Lucille's eyes, steady and searching, always on somebody from behind her quiet hair, her glasses. I loved sleeping beside her down in the boat, it was like sleeping with a moon. Her eyes are a little like Serafina's. Taurus.

I hugged her once, and she said "outta sight"! a wonderful little circus jar (sic) from the psychic Lucille. I gave her some witche's *[sic]* bread that Serafina sent to me, and she ate a few crumbs delicately with her long skinny fingers, and asked for the recipe. Serafina has kindly included it, mimeographed off, with a blurb at the beginning about the witchiness and aprodisiac *[sic]* qualities of it all. *[Note: Witch's Bread was a solid dark fruit-studded spicy loaf.]*

James' eyes, on Lucille, on Romilar cough medicine, on... *[page ends]*

Mid-March
We are going south now for a couple of weeks, supposedly to make leather bags. David wants me to leave him in Zurich. I have an address in Denmark... Vicki looks at me almost with pleading. Lays her head on David's shoulder. "I am a sweet girl," thinks Katy, "and you, David, are an asshole."

March 16
Traveling, running, traveling, in brown ink rain. I stare out the window and the thoughts run clear and painless like rain. When I speak it is from a throne inside. We have hitched the old Boogie bus to the beige one in Gerona, Spain, where Carl left it, and now David rides in it, steering, a bit harrowing. We're in a cafe somewhere in southern France now...

Today David said "We'll see," and I know we're all getting easier, thank god. We're still south of Lyon. James writes letters beside me. It has rained for three days. I loved one night we spent by the sea... I loved centering the fantasies in me, instead of strewing them messily on everyone else. James says he can talk to me now, he doesn't feel that I would suddenly weird out on him. I feel scoured. David has fallen all unglued, too – we bob along in the rain, low and a little unsteady. A couple of weeks ago David said, "You'll see, when the sun goes into Pisces, I'll fall apart." And it's been true. He is out in the bus now, reading a trashy murder mystery, his nose getting red in the cold. My David, whom I don't know. So what. (I read that and laugh – it's senseless.) Sufficient unto the day is the evil thereof. Last night we crouched in the warm cushiony bus, candles going in James' elaborate candelabra, copped from dead Butch *[Note: Not the same as Junkie Butch; Dead Butch had whammed his motorbike into a wall]*, the Butane going. I made hamburgers and we had coke and wine and yogurt and chocolate things, smoked a couple of joints, my customary anxiety kept low-key. Night before, we were headed south, slept by the beach with the rain blowing in the tall childhood weeds. I made wonderful sausage with tomatoes, onions, peppers, fried eggs. Can Juani fare. Next morning we decided to head north instead... My money is hereby gone. It has been a grace to just ride like this, free to roam in my head...

Bits from Diary
Zurich, March 1971

...to a sauna, where healthy Swiss women showered and sauna'd and went in the icy cold pool, and my head was tight with thought, thought, thought, which somehow I managed to abandon later. The I Ching spoke against strict asceticism, something changing to Inner Truth.

Clothes, all the clothes in the boutiques, I want them. Tonight when we went out for fondue I wore a beige shinystuff Aretha Franklin dress, very short and tight, the classic shorttight dress. Black cape over it, lizardskin belt and beads and bracelet. I'm funny-looking, I give in, flatfooted, bigassed and stomached, shortbodied. Fuck it.

David is always improvising songs that I suspect are about me.

Last night we made love. We slept up in Copi's room on the mattress with Copi's clothes scattered all around, and it was sweet like always, and very sweet. Afterwards I lay awake, half-awake, and David's hand was over my shoulder on my nipple, and I was melting, so I pressed fingers on my pussy, just moved them and pressed them, eyes closed, relaxing before it and before it, and then one moment the whole room of darkness gathered under me, warm and warm, gathered up like a warm flood bath, and pushed me up, up, to it, over it. I lay with my thighs quivering uncontrollably, and suddenly I was satisfied, changed, satisfied, and I slept.

Current fantasy: a big band, all of us and Copi and a kid with a piano. We have a band and practice regular and play gigs, and I

Get to Sing. Yay! Yay! That, I think, would save my life. To Sing! In a band! Have to work with other people!

  David woke up. "David?" "Uh huh." "I made myself come, I never did that before." "Oh yeah? When?" "A little while ago." "Hey, that's outtasight! That's great!" he said, turning to me his white thin shoulders in the dark. And I am embarrassed some, damn it, and lie awake longer and longer, and our bodies mingle so much friends, no matter how the friction goes waking. I need other lovers, projects, passions.

Trogen – March

The second floor
of a huge old
Swiss country house,
in a gorge
filled with the rushing clatter
of melted snow –

i stood by the barn
and heard ice cracking
like old voices
from the eaves.

The dead girl is dying
one hand flung out
across the electric heater –
this is the time.
of no more pretending.
No smiles to the pretty ones
playing guitar,
no heat withdrawn,
no playing in the snow.
No more girdled
stomachs, smiles, tears.

    i lay in the big chair
    in front of the heater
    and cried
    Rocked in a comforter
    cried all the names I knew.
    Mama! No! i have never
    been happy!
    When this was done
    i became a dark egg
    floating in darkness, and warm.

    The lit-up room
    Snow on the ground
    So this is why they play
    flute, guitar,
    long crying,
    melting, no more
    pretending,
    just light falling
    murdered on the snow.

We were all kicked out of Ibiza for "Promiscuidad," because Rocky (who'd also come to Ibiza, though separately) had made a porno movie on the beach with his voluptuous little German consort. So we drove the van to Switzerland, as we'd been offered a chalet-sit in the mountains – a musician David had been playing with knew the house's owner. There was a well-known band in the village, Die Minstrels, and so that was it – the next weeks or months were going to be all about guys playing guitars night and day.

I think David finally realized he was an idiot to expect equality with me, and, uncomfortable in blaming himself, had to blame me – though I saw him wrestling with a certain compassion. (His brother Carl told me in 2007 that indeed I was thought to be so talented that I was expected also to be emotionally mature.) David didn't value the me that he now saw, but that me needed to reveal itself and have its time. You can't ask an eighteen-year-old to be twenty-eight. She needs to be eighteen.

Everybody among us was melancholy, really – they'd fled structures and rigors, school or work, and thought that looseness and the unplanned life would give all the pleasure the 60's promised. Instead, ripe and ready energies found themselves restless and uneasy, with no work to do. So they played music – which is wonderful – but then they would have liked more people to play it to; and we were up there in the crashingly thawing snow-covered Alps in March.

By common unspoken consent (except mine) nobody was to do housework or any other sort of chore beyond the reluctant buying and assembling of simple food. Housework and chores were middle class: the enemy. But for me, housework and chores could usher in the promised land – cleanliness and order.

What I've learned since: The teenage troughs of pain such as I describe here might be explainable by chemistry – but I still feel the value of what I got by sinking to that nadir. Those troughs, perhaps, are a necessary part of our orientation into adult bodies and lives – an extreme we must go to to locate the median. When I say, "Mama, I've never been happy," it just isn't true; but it seemed like that right then, and allowing the totality of that darkness gave me the necessary impetus to leave a situation that was unhealthy for me.

Yes – it is wonderful to fall to the bottom of a thing. As I write this, my body takes a big, deep sigh... It is wonderful to dig down as deep as I can go, and examine the sorrow objectively as well as feel it utterly, and then fall even deeper... and not count on the outer world to make it up to me; but face things, down and in; and not run away.

Osho gave me the strength and courage to do this, just by being there and being steadily a source of light. By telling us again and again that death is necessary every moment; dying to the past. Making that idea palatable, and wonderful too. So that we can face our inners with a bit more equilibrium each time.

What I've learned since: It's very simple. If I don't feel recognized or valued for my being and my contribution, *as myself*, I'm in the wrong company. I'm supposed to wait for an invitation to go elsewhere – but I didn't know that. David had, basically, invited me not to be his girlfriend anymore – but he did reluctantly invite me to Switzerland (when I refused his suggestion to go back to the States). That was *not* a good invitation for me! Therefore I should not have been there in the first place, and whatever happened was wonky and awry.

When I finally left him, there were many months of dogged, troubled drifting and a few gnarly adventures ahead of me until I found a home – one to which I was invited. I'm just grateful it happened by and by.

What I've learned since: This too will pass. Seasons change, intolerant boyfriends are left behind, new people come on the scene – vocations arise and are embraced. I can have my own life, as me.

Bystander to Musicians

Inside a black house
four men sleep
and i do not need them.
On the morning
they awake from their dream
looking for my arms

i will be down the black stairs
weeping
but not for them
And the sunlight
dirty and half a-mist
will fondle my hurrying back
through a small window
it has burned in the wall

Ghost made of sunlight
Men made of ghost
Time of no resolution

More teen angst

Old woman house
you planted these rosebushes
two rows in the hall
athwart with wrinkled grey-lipped buds
They stir like sly fingers
when i try to pass

The door of course
is huge with some disease
A giant vegetable or human limb
rotting against the only exit
Bulge, termite oedema
an Earth rolled tight
against the hole

Black house
what penalties you exact
The roses chatter silently
wanting watering

The chalet was an hour or so from Zurich, in the Appenzell area, in a hilly little town. Urs and his three musician friends lived down the hill, and the guys all played away the afternoons and nights.
I felt purposeless, adrift, and as if there was some other urgent thing I was really supposed to be doing! Instead of learning my own body, I had sex with David, which didn't help at all. I felt during it my passion and clinging and longing, but the lovemaking seemed always to raise more questions than it answered, and I was too shy and mortified to voice those questions. (David would not have understood them anyway, I suspect, being in a male body. I thought – and I think he also thought – that women were supposed to orgasm from penetration alone. I've read that some do; most don't.) I consoled myself with chocolate, great slabs of it, Switzerland was paved in the stuff. And my thighs grew alarmingly. My smart shag haircut, acquired off-the-cuff from some hippie hairdresser we'd met in Ibiza, had grown out into a limp, shoulder-length frumpiness. David criticized me impatiently.
Within me, roses chattered silently, wanting watering.

What I've learned since: If I find myself someplace uncongenial, it is extremely useful to notice precisely how I got there. Did someone invite me clearly? Or am I just there by default? Or out of fear? When I was invited, how did my belly and my heart respond? My body in general?

In this case I was along more or less by default. I did not feel valued. If I had been asked whether or not I wanted to come – and this I don't recall – I must have responded from fear, from addictive 'love'. This is how a lot of things are done in this world – by sloppy default. Human Design strives to bring crispness and respect back to human relating. I applaud this.

The Fog Rabbits

The fog rabbits
mist hares
come out from barns
and shut-woods hutches

when twilight fills
the windows
with numb turquoise vapors
and mist fills

the windows
like a sea

And we sing
furthering with mouths
of rare metals
the annihilation;

The mist rabbits
fog hares
come bump-gliding

>   e fur feet
>   ken ships, like ears,
>   their lost bells
>   ted hollow tongues

The world was so foggy to me then… I did not get its workings, was somehow repelled by them, as if they were innately closed. I had heartbreak, and eczema, and sugar-cravings. I had only a few patched, raggy things to wear, of which David disapproved. He and Carl were from a prosperous family, which he considered woefully straight, but its vision crept in: no rags, no 'failure', allowed.
This poem is fog-song… for I found fog wonderful, even in my fogginess.

What I've learned since: There is inner fog and there is outer fog. Outer fog isn't really foggy; it's just a mass of crisp moisture-droplets suspended in the air. One has to be careful in it, but one can be careful crisply!
Inner fog is also a mass of particles, suspended in inner air, or the air of the aura – same thing – with an amassed weight to them. This is more problematical. It can also be caused by wrong food and substances, ingested or breathed. One has to figure out which it is; and for substances, avoid them. For emotional fog – for it's mostly that – we have Dynamic meditation! Fantastic! My inner fog cleared dramatically within the first months of my greatly-applied meditation life.

Red Snow

> Red snow
> sunset
> trees pouring their icy shadows
> down the hill
>
> i'm going to live

The Bomb in dreams
dropping slow
almost backwards
like the pearl in Helene
Curtis shampoo

Beebelly
my feelings all over you
like hard gold bees
and the way
you left on your belt
and boots to fuck
brittle jaws dissolving –
Red Queen
hurting before the fact –
anything unsolved
surfaces again like skulls from The Blob

When I was a child, the Bomb was a great and fearful threat hanging over everybody. My father therefore saw an opportunity to dig a Hole, and so one was dug in the back yard – using a hose to moisten the dry earth; then shovels, a winch and a bucket. Robbie was the most enthusiastic brother in these labors.
The shelter was, of course, never finished, and stayed a Hole until my mother covered it up in disgust, using boards and dirt; *after* she had shoved down it numerous dead appliances my father had gathered for the cannibalizing of parts, for his Invention.
In school, during regular bomb drills we crouched under our desks while shielding our heads with our arms. (Even we children could see this was absurd.)
After listening to Glen and brothers talking about the Bomb at night I'd go worried to bed and have a terrible dream, of airplanes flying over all flat and manta-ray like and a bomb falling out of one of them, tumbling ever-so-slowly, slowly down… falling in dream-time, as I watched helplessly, terrified. Such an ominous slowness.
Also as a child I saw television only a few, memorable times, at other people's houses. *The Blob* and *King Kong* were the only movies I remember seeing on TV. *The Blob* was scary! It featured an

illustration to a dream

Sketch of a dream

extraterrestrial lump of slime that grew and grew, eating everything in its path, and then regurgitated the bones.

And there were commercials too. The fact that TV was at other people's houses meant that the products on the commercials, as well as the people in the shows, belonged, in my mind, to the big world of "stuff other people do and have and we don't and can't." So all of this came into the bad fate of my romance with David. "Hurting before the fact" of separation, which duly did occur. (At my instigation, for I knew the situation had become direly unhealthy for me. I was pulled off-center entirely by his presence and there seemed no cure for this painful state. To save my sanity, I'd have to leave him.)

What I've learned since: Yes, anything unsolved does surface again. Yes, you have to keep going over it from every angle until it vanishes upwards in light. But you needn't worry it – just watch it, through and through. And cry if it cries, beat pillows if there's anger; restore the balance in whatever ways the body wants.

Hard gold bees: Much later, in 1986 in California, I took Ecstasy, twice. My then-boyfriend Subuddha didn't take it, but he was with me. Under the influence of the drug I saw precisely what I was doing to Subuddha (even as I felt myself to be a victim of his uncommunicative indifference): I was enshrouding him in a web of strong fibers of my own energy, that I had cast out around him like a net – lassoing him, imprisoning him, keeping him near. I was as determined as a kitten climbing up your clothes – I *held on* via these astral cords. I was working unknowingly to control him – and I thought it was love. (And I must say he was graceful in his refusal of my snare.)

So I know about those hard bees I sent to patrol on David. Strangely, I had an experience in meditation last week: I was at the time undergoing distance healings from a bio-resonance machine, and was divested, by its agency, of an old Haunting, which looked like a cartoon Trojan Bee in my belly, filled with nasty, heavy little bees who did the real damage. All this was taken out of my lower body and sent far far away...

"Anything unsolved": Hormones are, I think, unsolvable; they can only be witnessed, danced, and can thus lend some of their energy

to awareness. But I am not *only* a female, programmed to latch on helplessly; I am a human being, with a responsibility to myself, and decidedly, a mandate *not to bother someone else* with my stuff. If David didn't want me, why stay?

Today's I Ching

    dawn
    he got up afterwards,
    and read in the front room,

    I stayed in bed
    watching the sky widen
    stepped out into my body
    and leaned
    on the light falling on the snow

    bells rang and rang

    morning congratulates our bed,
    a fringed canopy, a crown,
    a living tousle
    "you have three bodies
    but you must give yourself a soul."

    midmorning
    throws the coins,
    "keeping still."
    I get tense. I forget
    everything except ideas,
    done too softly, too often.

    afternoon. walks out
    down the swiss hillside,
    steep and housed and fenced,

some forest,
the berry-vines, snow-smashed,
just lifting.

I drink and drink
the air
off the three bodies of the land.
"to think of what is not
immediately at hand
only makes the heart sore."

sore for my thousand
drifting bodies
and fishhook soul.
the little paths are muddy,
but the grass
lifts its color week by week.

evening makes
a gray skin sheen
on the windows
in the room's dark embrace.
breasts find my hands.
The steep hillside mounts me,
I look at the window,
sight becomes incredible,
I'm not sure I trust it,
how did it get in here?

so a miracle is the flash
of cloth drawn back.
I want to draw a series:
a girl lying down –
legs, forearms, the dawn head,

and little spikes emerging,
widening,
become a crown,

her body changes
flash by flash
to a lion's,
and the crown
eclipses to a mane.

the body shrinks off
like a rocket stage,
and the mane swells,
until it's a sun,
flying way off up
to the corner of the page.

What I've learned since: Well, I've delved deeply into the I Ching, that human-genome-numbered, archetype-stuffed ancient tome, because it's part of Human Design. I enjoy it greatly. Keeping Still: ah, how much I've explored that: sitting with Osho, utter quiet in the hall except for the deepest-ocean, space-between-the-stars sound of his voice, watching the internal energies whilst the body sits immobile. Lying down in my own Self-Healing, still as still... watching inner doors relax and open beneath me, so that I fall into some deeper level.

Three bodies: David must have gotten that somewhere – I'm sure it didn't mean much to me then – and I forgot all about it – but later, when I'd become a meditator, and was exploring chakras as a beginning Reader (nobody taught me this nor did I know that anyone else did it; the endeavor just arose in me in response to Osho's discourses on the chakras) I discovered those three layers in people. The three bodies, if you will: the surface, the unconscious, the superconscious. (There are other systems of layers which have more numbers to them – and that is valid too. Why deprive ourselves of a richness of systems, when all else on Earth is rich?)

As to giving "yourself a soul": I think Gurdjieff said that. Osho remarked that this was a Device, to spur people on; that we *do* have souls at birth, but must discover them; be reborn to them.

"I am sore for my thousand drifting bodies / And fishhook soul..." Yes. And so I was eventually brought to Osho, by my little sister, who had by then become a beautiful woman named Sarita. And Osho could knit all these bodies together, into one.

From a letter to my sister,
Zurich, April 6, 1971

My Serafina!
...When you stir cream into a coffee, have you ever noticed that the thin foam makes galaxies, exactly like the ones that whirl so far and high in space? As though there were great spoons at work, mixing stars, creaming stars like butter, sprinkling stars like sugar into the bitter black. Drink it in...

  ...Look on your left hand. Heading up and to the right, from near your life-line, *[note: actually it's near the heart-line]* are there small, thin, thready lines? Those lines, like little zippers to be undone, or threads to untie for a package to spring open onto the great black coffee of the sky – those are the uneven sutures to the unknown.

  Now I climb back into the Odeon and wish I had money

for another coffee, for we rushed into town this morning sans breakfast, and I'm hungry.

I love to watch the girls here – there are so many fine ones, with red lips and shiny hair and admirable asses, and I feel a sort of wonder at their sparkly eyes. Am I in the spell of the feminine mystique? And is it a cop-out? I say this to you, my sweet sister, I feel more round and soft and relaxed than for years, more accepting of everything, including that florid bushy place, and these round breasts, and the belly that smiles triumphant. People from every country are known for something – the Swiss for Clean Uprightness, the Italians for sleaziness, the Spanish for their negative auras of grime. Americans are known for their psychoses. Funny little word, mindful of clicks and clocks and television talks, the creeping insidiousness of a way of life, punched out in superballbarbiedollvitaminlessschoolcounselor days. You don't know how sad it is till you learn something else, you have your method of survival. For us (besides just being and loving and smelling the orange trees) being the Most Beautiful. For me, being skinny, talented, a mite untouchable, and Planning to Get the Hell Out. Now here I am, and how can I get touchable, stop caring about being skinny, and live NOW? I got to. I am. Yummy. Oh, love, how groovy of you to call me a genious *[sic]*. I like it better the way you spell it, it doesn't look so clinical. If I am genious, you are a hot sweet thunderstorm.

Now... by the river with my black Moroccan cape spread out and the bags we made laid out to sell. All sorts of strange people walk by. We have made wonderful bags from soft suede. I made four of them, each very different. I want very much to sell them – ...

...Damn it, nobody's buying the bags.

Now, Feena, you will think that I have neglected your wonderful letter... not so, it made me feel better than any I have so far received from you. Your letter peeked right into this soul. Perhaps you will never have to do what I did... I had to lose my pride, for there was no longer anything to be proud of, and pride ate itself like a hungry coat-hanger.

Deary Fina, we all sit at the Odeon and it's Friday, or something, yesterday I sold 3 bags for $25.

...New York, New York... and you there, my unpoisoned pear. It occurs to me that my attitude towards drugs was not so much natural prudence as a plastic virginity. Sure, lots of people get fucked up behind them – but David shows me that a person can do them, work inside them instead of using them to crack yourself up. David was always onto himself, and drugs have only helped him to dig things. It is strange to live with somebody who is so excited, so together, so gorgeous – and be yourself all-fucked-up-feeling. If I need to go through the fucked-up – and apparently I do (I remember ways that I've felt like death ever since I was born, and now I can understand *every one*) – it is good to be in that household, where anything goes. But I do suffer for lack of anybody to really talk to. Ah Sera, I love our Trogen house.

Later
...Now I'm scratching my chest because of eating brownies. I sure still get scared of getting fat. *Scared* scared *scared.*

Me and David had a fight. Physical I mean. He took acid today. We talk'd in the bedroom. That asshole, he's sure he's a god. That asshole. I hate you, I said. You're insufferable. He thumped his skinny chest with his finger, me me me, he said, I'm a god, and I'm not ashamed to say it. Hear? Laughed happily and generously. I hate you, I said. I really do. I don't believe him, when I get away he'll just be a ragged hole left in my heart with the word god pulsing in it in little red juicy beats, alternatingly like a neon light with the word fuck. Godfuck Godfuck Godfuck God...

Hey Serafina luv, come over here 'bout July, and you and me'll travel together... I wanna split.

The Swiss Clock

    from agony
    (sun falls on the face of the clock
    from grass gone green overnight
    (the Swiss clock on the tower

from long hauls
in the back of the VW
riding on torn Kapok
sitting on a tire
my friends sing
in the front seat
whatever comes to their heads

hatred of my body
puts me in a kind of wonder,
but no more can I deny
it –

(sun lifts the clock face
and turns the hands

(my naked body
is a grey statue
sawn in half,
laughed at, and set to roam.
if I weren't saddled
with my mother's stomach...
if my legs were longer...
my thighs not so soft –
In Zurich, so many girls are beauties,

(the clock is green and gold
like a peach-beetle
buzzing around on a string
tied to one black leg
the sun glinting
on the metal in its wings

∽

when I was beautiful,
I envied myself
my tight thighs

my molded breasts
my deft eyes.
my legs approaching me
in the window
caught my breath
ran away with it,
ran like thieves.

I've always been robbed.

(on top of the clock
in the center of the town
there is a sun, a moon,
a gold star.

(I dream of cows

and make histories
and lie on a hillside
this morning, happy,
and my face goes around
in the sun.

What I've learned since: I've already said!

Accents in Oxford

Hearing the jammy chattering
of high school girls
from perhaps Alabama
(they roam Oxford –)
i vow to curb my hammy twang
which slithers out from under my tongue
like a water moccasin
from some past life

in Appalachia, as Daniel Boone's
coal-stained grand-niece,
or perhaps from
the soft black tar
of south Los Angeles –
July, and cruisin', and my
lower lip hung out
like a sunning snake
in the ancestry and the fashion
of the time
Strut so good
in my velvet
i don't care,
and ain't nobody listening anyway,
is there.

We're taking a jump in time here.
I left David and the rest of the crew on a roadside in France, where we'd judged I'd have the best chance of getting a ride north. It was goodbye; painful but necessary. Cold Turkey for my addiction to David. The VW bus drove away... and I looked about me for a bit, at the empty road, the big sky, the flat land.
I felt much better right away.
Which is not to say that I felt *good;* but things were simply... simpler. There was just me to worry about, not what he thought of me, as well. I don't think I had a plan exactly – I was just away, on my own. When a car came along, I stuck out my thumb.
In Amsterdam I met a young American, Gregory, at the American Express office. We hitched to Denmark together, to the flat little island of Fejø, where there was supposed to be work picking fruit, which never materialized, and so instead we milled about, feeling weird. I didn't feel loverly with Gregory. He was a complicated boy. There was a friend-rape. I wrote a story. I left.
Went down to Zurich, then a night hitch-hike through Germany where I suddenly felt spooked and demanded the truck driver let me out in a rainy, black wilderness. "You are *dahft!* You are *dahft!*" he protested and I slid out the door the long way down to the road. I huddled all night in my soggy sleeping-bag, listening to dogs bark

at a farmhouse not far away. Another time a truck driver let me out when I asked, and then spoke wistfully: "No luff?"

I had a strange sojourn in Copenhagen, where I was vaccinated for various diseases because I thought I might go to India, as my sister was planning to do. Feverish and unwell, I then asked strange girls on the street if they knew a place I could stay. They took me home, and I sweated it out till I felt better. Then, on the street, I bumped into a man I'd met at Jack Grodsky's place in London, in those early days – an American physicist, short, mild, and very hairy. He let me stay at his house in the suburbs, and exacted the predictable payment, which I felt I had no right to refuse him, despite my utter disinclination for the task. Urgh. This was what 'freedom' seemed

With Phil Dauber at rock festival, Denmark

to mean... He then took me to a rock festival in the country.
I went down to Zurich again, had compulsive liaisons with a couple of different men I had no business going to bed with, saw Nureyev leap high across a stage, then finally wended my way to England, and Oxford.
There was no rhyme or reason to any of this.

Later: In 1972, Gregory, the tall young man I'd gone to Denmark with, turned up in San Francisco where I was then living. I visited him at the seedy old downtown apartment he'd rented on my recommendation, and which he didn't like. He was studying some photos when I went in – of just-pubescent girls, maybe even pre-pubescent – I don't exactly remember now. But I think there were children... and he told me frankly that he was sexually attracted to them – that that was his real thing. I retorted indignantly that I thought that was weird – what was sexually attractive about young, young girls? But it is a sign of the times that I did not consider it a criminal thing; it was a preference, and everybody got to have his taste. I was probably jealous, in fact – though I did not want Gregory at all. I don't remember whether either of us thought of the little girls' feelings. Poor children! I wonder what happened later... I never heard from Gregory again, and Googling turned up so many men with that name that searching was hopeless.

What I've learned since: It's not the accent, but the voice itself, that gives the listener clear access to the soul of the speaker – if she but listens. The timbre, depth of connection with the inner, or not; pitch, and indescribable nuances say so much.
We love to differentiate by accent, as we love to differentiate by skin shade or a dozen other variables; that's because our minds and bodies are still in thrall to our monkey past, where hierarchies and territorialities are the order of the day. We can laugh at someone's differentness, and they at ours; and each of us feels like Somebody. Monkeys like Somebodyness too. (I remember reading a great naturalist who studied chimps in the Serengeti. He noted that they only had to gather food for a few hours a day as there was plenty, so they had all the rest of their time free "to be vile to one another.")

If we sit on a bedrock of love-for-ourselves, we can enjoy these differentnesses without being serious about them, without punishing people for them. It's nice that somebody has pretty caramel skin – or long black hair – or a great facility with cooking *pasta alla rucola*.

We can laugh at ourselves – our own outer layers, our own accents. It's part of the fun. I'm thinking of Poona again: the meditation community in India where I lived for most of the years between 1973 and 2003. Four acres, numerous old mansions rehabbed for a very busy community; lush gardens, immensely tall flame-trees. One shining man, speaking to us day by day, about our own souls and minds and vast potentials. And telling lots of jokes! Thousands of people, from a hundred countries, all living and working and romancing together. We saw each other's depths and inners, because we were engaging with our own; their outers were of only passing interest, like the clothes one wore that day. English was the lingua franca, but with such a hash of accents that eventually we all developed strange ones!

Goody for us – why shouldn't an accent be as fluid as the associations one has? That is nature, adapting itself endlessly. (I have heard cut-glass accents, after a long sojourn in the States, taking on hard-ish 'r's and sounding quite peculiar; I have seen these same new accents in print with dropped 'u's from the word 'colour', for example.)

Bring it on.

P.S. I am really Daniel Boone's grand-niece, with a sizeable heft of 'greats' thrown in there – which brings in another excuse for prejudice: who our ancestors were. My own reading: it's of value to excavate one's ancestral line in meditation, whilst assuming that that is not the only line one has had; one has been a number of colors, nationalities, mixtures; and none of this has described the Empty Yet Unique Center of ourselves.

What I've also learned: My own Human Design says that this kind of aimless, hopeful wandering is really not a good idea for me. I need to have a good place to go before I leave a place behind, or could end up wandering in the wilderness for much too long. I've often thought that the trip across America with my sister worked as well as it did because of *her* karma, not mine. She's a born Pioneer. I can only say that in the various wanderings, I must have had a compassionate guardian angel hovering to take up some of the shortfall in my good sense.

**looking down from a 2nd-story window
at turkeys in an apple orchard**

>Afternoon... sleep,
>uneasy dreams again,
>across the sleep-face
>like a handful of drops
>thrown on July dust
>from a grey uncertain sky –
>Turkeys, soft idiot grey
>squat huddles in damp grass
>One rests apart
>wing over its chick
>like a heap of soft ash,
>a magazine burned
>to feathered quiet
>over a sundry gathering
>of kitchen bones.
>
>Green chalk apples.
>How i hate to speak
>of the highway,
>beyond the back field
>glaring and droaring forever
>like the mind; a vise band
>across the forehead
>of the sleep, the land.

It was July 20, 1971. I had gone, rather uneasily, to some dull

Midland city with Ken-the-mad-teethed-Scientologist, a scrawny little fellow, a sort of friend, who lurked about Oxford. (He fancied me terribly but I never gave in.) We stayed in a house with some people I don't remember. It was my first experience of the Midlands. It felt to me like parts of the States – uninspired, flat, bewildering, monotone. And that highway – like the freeways of California I'd fled, people going somewhere going nowhere, cloaked in unyielding metal.

I seem to have a strong, rather fixed sort of mind. In those years it got to troubling me a lot with its repetitive intensity, telling me bothersome and untrue things, trying to make out like it was the boss. It was a form of obsessive-compulsive disorder really, but I knew nothing about that and only felt imprisoned and ashamed. I did not know about *watching* the mind, having some distance from it; nor did I know how to follow any disturbed state back in to defuse it, then further to where health is found. These things I had yet to learn... and nobody I met then knew how to teach me. Certainly those Scientologists only aroused my grave suspicion!

What I've learned since: Be careful what you say Yes to – you never know where you'll end up. Note who it is that invites you: is he good fuel for your unique journey? In this case: No, and no.

What I've learned since: Ahhhh... how to rest in my Being, my belly, my core, my inner emptiness. How to turn energies over to the body, in dance. How to sit and watch, breathe and explore, ignore the pesky importunings of the mind. How to enjoy what fun the mind can give me without believing all its tales. (It does so like to 'get you' when it can. It knows just how to do this, what your weak points are, when you will believe it. That's how it survives.)

All this, of course, came through Osho. He spoke to us on this subject every day. He gave us techniques to try out for ourselves. He da man. Thank heavens I came along, and he came along, all at the right time. Thank the subtle forces that be.

In a Pub in Oxford

Ain't much to write about
sitting upstairs in Victoria Pub
wearing velvet for the first time in months
and an ivory pin
to hold it together,
And it's no surprise
to feel sexy again
after so long,
my birthright of course,
it's been said by certain friends
That i'm too hung up on myself.
Well, i'm eighteen years old,
what do you expect?
You see, this ain't much of a poem.
so far, no images
except the ivory pin,
and that i bought
for half a pound.
i look around
for somebody to maybe find me,
but really I find myself
right here, not much to find right now,
but I'm anchored
in not knowing who wears velvet; looks around
this dark old place with beams of wood –
seeing what there is to see –
book upon my knee.

What I've learned since: Even when there was not much to write about, I am glad now that I wrote it. This poem is a succinct picture of a time and place – and why not? A bit of blathering, painting a picture... why not? I love description in a book – something that anchors you, tactile and visual. And is not every detail sacred really? On this unlikely planet, in this astonishing universe?

Maybe it will only seem interesting or important to some great-grand niece or -nephew of mine, sometime… or maybe not even then. So be it.

And: "…anchored / in not knowing who wears velvet, looks around…" Well, yes. Suitable moment for Koan meditation, Who Is In? But here, I already knew that I didn't know who was this person I found myself to be, in all her amorphous mystery. Good beginning!

Interview with the Social Worker

Look,
stupid social worker,
chosen for idiot benevolence,

don't mess with me.
i don't have to lie
about how many men
i've loved for a night,
my truncated schooling,
my greased travels,

my discoveries on this planet.
i dress them in words.

i speak well,
better than you do,
foolish social-worker,

You are required
to inquire like a false relation
after my loneliness, my clap,
my shame, sour-tinted like old milk
in the garbage-can you
hope i am.

> You can offer me
> a plane ticket, a plan
> for painlessness.
>
> i give you
> my ready sweet artless
> words, they are even true,
> to elude you. Then i leave.

Well, this was a sorry tale; in retrospect, it fills me with horror! Neither my body nor my mind are as tolerant of either diseases or medicines as once they tried to be. Tracing back, I must have gotten the gonorrhea during a pleasureless meeting in a tent at that rock festival in Denmark. I then took it, hidden away and unguessed, to Zurich, where I gave it to a tall redheaded American I felt no connection with either. (In those days I knew only how to strive, and blame myself, and pull at people, and disappoint both of us. I did not know how to wait.) I had no symptoms and so was surprised and chagrined when the redheaded youth told me he'd gotten it from me.

I lived then on that $60 a month from my father, and stayed in the houses of kindly folks I met along the way. So I had had only enough money for half the antibiotics the doctor prescribed. My International Money Order was one day late, and for that one day I had no medicine. As soon as the stipend arrived I immediately went to the *Apotheke*, bought more and finished the course. Then I went to England, and eventually Oxford.

I was symptom-free; and don't remember now how it was I realized the disease was still there. Medical care in England were free to tourists as well as residents, so I went along. It was discovered that the disease had flourished underground and would now need to be fought with some horribly strong antibiotic called Kanamycin. I had a bad reaction to this stuff: my face swelled to twice its size, I had a crusty rash all over, and I felt just dreadful. *And* I had, before I realized I was still infected, had pitifully worthless sex with a poor plummy Mick-Jagger-looking wretch who had been reluctant because he was engaged... and I didn't know his last name or where he lived (it had been dark.) I only knew his name was Teddy (*so, so* sorry, Teddy!) So I could not find him to tell him.

In those days people went about ruining or decorating each others' lives with stupid sex everywhere – and lord, what a mess! I had a bad sugar habit then, knew nothing of probiotics, so was laying the foundations for a mighty river of Candida (to mix metaphors) to plague me intermittently. (Swearing off sugar a year hence helped greatly. So, strangely enough, did a little nightly treatment suggested by Kohrogi-san, a wonderful Japanese healer, in about 2016: Sit with feet in a basin of hot water for eight minutes. Then go to bed. This helps to warm up one's insides and vanquish the cold situation that fosters Candida. I did this for a while, then switched to just putting my feet on a hot water bottle in bed. It really helped.)

The social worker must have been part of a comprehensive and benign system to help people – even foreigners. Like the young snob I was (the young do *know* so much, don't they?) I paid her no attention at all. My adventures were the thing, not my health!

What I've learned since: How to wait for men (possibly even forever). How not to jump on any poor idiot and get/give STDs. (In the Commune, after 1983 all of us were tested regularly for HIV, so that was great. And during the latter part of the Ranch in Oregon condoms were mandatory, and STD frequency fell dramatically. Consciousness was definitely raised.)

- That balancing the needs of an adventurous nature and the needs of the body is a very fine and worthy project for a person. I am not sorry I went all the places I did. I am sorry about all the unrewarding and risky sex, which didn't address the goddess in me at all. But I didn't know any better.
- To avoid antibiotics if at all possible, but if I really must take them, take the course as properly as possible and follow it with a lot of probiotics. (When I say "…as possible…" – it sounds a little hairy, and it is. Twice I've taken antibiotics and felt so horribly deathlike and ill that I stopped them before the end of the course. One of those times was for Giardia Lamblia (an intestinal bug of dramatic manifestation), in India. Luckily it seems the

cure occurred anyway. The other was for an infection in the jawbone. After five days I just could not bear another dose of that stuff and how it made me feel. *Could not.* The extraction of the offending molar led to the infection's demise. That was lucky and I'm grateful.

There are times when the doctor prescribes antibiotics and it just isn't necessary. So I've learned to have some sense about that. For example, a sinus infection can be profitably addressed via colloidal silver snorts, twice-daily tea tree oil steam inhalations, and getting a good strong dehumidifier in the house. But the clap? Oh god… you've got to throw everything at it, I guess; the evil and the benign.

- To continue to avoid bureaucrats if at all possible, but if I need them, or even if they just think I do, to be gracious and kind and grateful, even if I don't take their advice.
- To look very kindly on socialized medicine: It makes for a much happier population, attracts doctors less motivated by greed, and has a rough-and-ready nobility about it. Governments would do well to spend money there rather than on so many idiotic things, as we all know. The Brits love their National Health Service even when they criticize it. And I am so grateful to the competent and kindly health visitors who attended my dying brother Garth/Rudra in Vancouver in 2010.

And I'm shocked at the ungratefulness in this poem!

Fat Poem #15

Why did you do it this time?

Well, it was the two women.
With faded hair.

They can't see me like this,

a guilty film over my eyes
like nearly-eaten melon
over the rind.

The strong one
thinks i should earn a living.
i use Aries' strong bones
to beat my body
cranch cruckle kick.

The other
is a mother
with a clean house, sad skin,
no taste for sweets.

Hee hee,
i slide redberry jam
onto a biscuit
quick,
crunch munchle sweet
crumb pain

in the dark pantry
again.

Into the river of my own particular eating disorder, there had been several tributaries. Not wanting to grow up and become my mother; therefore no belly, hips, please. (This felt quite desperate.) BC pill trauma: I'd better diet fast and furious not to bloat toad-like overnight. Sugar allergy, wheat allergy, dairy allergy – all these allergies promoting addiction. Love-hunger: though our mother was adoring, indulgent, and fond, nobody else in the family was! Nor was the culture, in any place I'd yet been. Sex: it did not perform as advertised, and what could take its place? The nearest thing – or, let's say, the superior thing – was a bagful of greasy, warm, *sweeeet* pastries from a baker. The bakery was my porno-master.
English pastries were greatly inferior to the ones from the mom-

Victoria Hodder and me, Oxford 1971

and-pop bakery in Ferndale, with its giddy-making perfume of vanilla and heated wheat-molecules and cinnamon issuing of an early morning out onto the street. Much inferior to the delicious cakes I had baked from the Woman's Day cookbooks, with lavish icings and seductive weight, richness, freshness. But these poor confections were all I had now. So, after vowing I'd never do it again, I'd do it again a few days later: take my hoarded shillings to the dingy shop, choose a pile of rather antiquated-looking cakes – dry they seemed, and studded with unnecessarily lurid candied fruits, and often icingless when they should have been iced – easily the awfullest cakes I would ever see until Indian ones. Then I'd carry my forbidden-feeling bag with its live-seeming contents to some place safe and hidden, and ritually scarf them down. I'd feel great for five minutes after eating the first one; but could never stop there. So I'd eat as many as I could afford, as many as there were. And look around for more. There was always that awful little adjustment to the fact that there *were* no more.

Then I would feel horrible. Just awful. Self-loathing, depressed, stuffed, confused, somehow poisoned. Secretive, miserable, aghast. And so then I'd go running, in whatever raggy clothes I had, counting the laps around the field opposite Mrs. Hodder's house in Oxford where I was staying.

Also staying at Mrs. Hodder's was Corinne Wood, the escaped mother of the Woods clan in Riverside (it was in their garage I'd first experienced a make-out party, complete with boy-orthodontia and potato-chip shards, when I was thirteen). I'd bumped into her on the street and she'd rescued me, taken me to Mrs. Hodder's, where I had a small clean room in which to do my nefarious sweet-stuffing. But I sometimes did it in the pantry instead, with cookies and jam that didn't belong to me, making Mrs. Hodder cross. (I was not above stealing sugar in those days, in the form of other people's sedate supplies of tea-snacks or puddings.) Corinne used to lecture me on Practicality and Responsibility, but I was deaf to her advice. (She thought I needed a proper job, for which I would need an education, and so on. Like herself – she worked in some medical-auxiliary profession.) I did not confide about the sweets – it would have been like confessing masturbation.

What I've learned since:
- The body is so resilient. Stop abusing it, and it will reward you right away by *feeling much better*.
- If you are sensitive to a food, intolerant of it: simply stop eating it. Put it on a 'taboo' list, where it becomes the devil, and will cease to harm you thenceforth. Cold turkey is the only way. Kohrogi-san says that honey, agave, and the like are thieves; sugar is a murderer.

Many people are sensitive to wheat, dairy, and sugar, and if they removed these things from their diet they would lose the weight the body carries as water (for some reason toxicity encourages bloating with water).

It's my opinion that sugar is not a food at all – just a scary chemical. If you stop thinking of it as a food it's easier to shun. The desire for sugar can be met with a luscious piece of ripe fruit, which is what the body, if not the mind, wanted in the first place. Fruit refreshes, delivers hydration in a peculiarly assimilable way. And it's not addictive… just delicious.

I recovered from my eating disorders (binging later morphed to anorexia. I never had bulimia, thank god) in Poona. Recovering from anorexia is very scary, but with Osho's benign help I got over it, plumped up, then slimmed down again when I launched with a sort of fixed vigor into… sex addiction instead! Addiction per se took much longer, and much alertness in meditation was required: how not to avoid emptiness?

What Did I Eat On My Birthday

Well, i got up late
Thought i'd stick to my schedule, but
after breakfast which was very nice
(i had run four times around the big
green field across the road,

not picking the red poppies)
i went shopping to the North Parade
which i didn't really feel like doing.
It was raining,
and i shouldn't have to do anything i don't want to
on my birthday,
though i observed that nothing
is exterior to a birthday,
and it had been holy even panting
around the field in my tennis shoes;

Anyway it was an excellent breakfast
a peach sliced in half neatly,
stone discarded, the priny cavity
like the roof of a monkey's mouth –
on a brown plate; a slice of white cheese,
and a very small and to-me-novel bowl of bran buds
and milk (grains, if eaten with leisure, release
flavor on flavor in the mouth, and this is perhaps why
people can dig brown rice diets, i thought) –
and i had tea, of course;

The fact that it is my birthday went through me casually
like the wind leafing through my clothes,
as i walked to buy mushrooms. It struck me halfway there
that the shop sold fresh brownies
so after buying carrots mushrooms onions, i indicated brownies
to the shop-girl, feeling exactly like a man in his overcoat,
don't they know how slurp wicked this is,

Oh lord i ate them out of the white bag.

On my birthday,

Two thoughts
A) The sight of a girl eating is sexual
B) Anybody eating an apple looks like a virgin.

> For lunch (i am fond of my schedule)
> i had two scrambled eggs, two Ry-Krisp, and a bit of old salad.
> Tea of course; tea and toilet-dashes
> run alongside me.
>
> What a foolish birthday, i snicker. i expected reverence.
>
> Now let's see, dinner is a project,
> pork pie and baked apples, Mrs Hodder the landlady and
> Ken the mad-teethed scientologist will be here.
>
> Today's stomach preoccupation about usual.
> My nineteenth birthday.
> > i'm damned curious about the twentieth.

So. That was August 12, 1971, at Victoria Hodder's boarding-house in Oxford.

And, what I've learned since: Tea (or any caffeine) makes me blather a lot. I now drink tea or eat chocolate only if I'm traveling (caffeine also makes me feel protected) or have not had enough sleep. Then I enjoy the high; but I consume only a little bit, or I get the jitters after a while.
Milk makes me feel low and snuffly.
Bran buds have sugar and wheat in them. Don't eat.
White (or any) cheese makes me heavy and snuffly and makes my left breast feel dense in the milk-duct. (A nurse confirmed that this is because the breast begins to think it is supposed to start feeding calves.)
Ry-Krisp has yeast in it, which Candida seems to like.
Pork is, to my mind now, a hideous food. And the pigs are treated abominably.
Eggs are fine once a week, but eating them oftener brings heaviness and headache.
It's important that peaches are organic. Apples too. Conventional growing uses lots of evil spray.
Mushrooms aren't really veggies. They're beasties. And I'm suspicious they support Candida.

It's important to eat enough.

Men will whistle at young girls (and not just whistle) even if the girls look podgy and sad.

It is a bad (but tempting) idea to cook for other people on my birthday. I tend to go overboard, cook for three days, and get exhausted.

It's nice, but a bit sad too, to get birthday greetings from lots of half-remembered old acquaintances, on Facebook.

I can also celebrate my birthday alone: movie, hot bath, good book, buy self prezzie. Take self out to eat. Walk in woods.

Food isn't sex.

Nobody need be ashamed of eating. Sex isn't shameful either, just peculiar and bizarre. Everything that's seen as shameful, will cement itself to you with truly vigorous and undissolvable glue. Behind shame is anger: "I want to have my natural desires!" Desires made shameful cause all sorts of messes in the human.

What I did on my twentieth birthday (since the end of the poem is thinking about this): Much water had gone down the Ganges. I was in a tiny village called Saint-Privat, in the Hérault area of southern France, with my lover Paul (whom I was yet to meet when this poem was written). (Just to name-drop here: our host in Saint-Privat was Ted Simon, who went on to write the famous and incomparable motorcycle adventure story, *Jupiter's Travels*). I had gone teetotal about sugar (bless my cotton socks, as the Irish say) and looked MUCH better. I'd had my first orgasm from oral sex in a hayloft near Nevers, with dear patient Paul. I'd sold a story to a magazine and poetry to other magazines. I'd been raped twice – once in Edinburgh (this was technically consensual but was really a gross exploitation by the older man, the now-eminent director Max Stafford-Clark, an hour after his wedding) and once in Rome, in dastardly fashion, by an unknown cold-eyed young Italian. I was tan from spending weeks in Greece and Italy. I wore a pretty, flowery dress I'd made myself. I refused to eat even a crumb of the fancy white cake neighbors had bought for me at a bakery, which caused local consternation.

And, here in West Yorkshire (where not long ago I worked for the half-brother-in-law of the aristocrat who employed me in London in 1971, and at whose house I met Paul), I've been packing for a trip to London to meet Paul's little-daughters-all-grown-up. Paul himself drowned in New Zealand in 2002, on New Year's Day, in a heavy sea where many people died.

Madame DuPray's

Basement shop
in a grey brick block
smelled of catshit

There were pools of catpiss in the shoes
but it didn't matter,
the mates were impossible to find

She beckoned me close
with a crooked hand
eyes like dissected fingertips
skin laid back
to show the eyeball bone

"Listen to me, Dearie, I'm eighty-six,
Don't walk about without shoes!
It may be right for India or Africa,
but Scotland was never meant for it!
I used to go barefoot
in the fishmarket in Aberdeen,
and that's what's wrong with me now!"

Moaned of her backache, knitted at a sock
with crippled twists

while i pawed through moist grey piles
of catshit and rags.

Sketch, Edinburgh, September 1971

In September I'd hitchhiked up to Edinburgh to go to the Fringe Theatre Festival – entirely because someone suggested I might do that, as I was at a loose end. It was a strange journey, one lost soul entering into a place of souls in various degrees of lostness and foundness – perhaps the actors, in their art, were somewhat found. I met an actor with curly hair...

But first, a big house full of supposedly-celibate female Jesus Freaks, whose fruitcake I stole out of their private tins in the night to eat alone in the dark – and a male Jesus Freak who stuttered terribly as he asked me if I wore a b-b-b-*b-b-bra*?

But as to this poem... How can it be that it's a delight to settle down into an old scene as insalubrious as this? And yet it is – the atmosphere of Edinburgh then, the greyness, the tall narrow buildings packed tightly together, the utter foreignness of it all. This was before cheap clothes made in China covered the world, and a garment always *cost* you something – at least in Europe it did, if not in the rummage sales of America. I'm a born clothes-freak; I remember the blue leather sandals with little cut-outs in them I had when I was two, the light-blue dress with ruffles I wore to the Catholic church with a family friend when I was four. The first entire paragraph I uttered in this life was a description, to my mother, of what a lady I'd seen walking down the street was wearing (grey twinset, matching skirt, and pearls). So in my travels I was hoping without much hope, to find a few items of clothing with which to pad out my patched, meager supply. I carried my old Swiss Army knapsack and couldn't fit anything else in it, but still. One had to look.

I'd seen a second-hand place down some steps at the corner of a square, and had gone down there to find a lumpy, rag-bedecked old woman presiding over a dank and smelly emporium, where grey and brown wool and old, cold cotton were heaped on tables – and where, indeed, a cat had been to do his business. Incongruously, this shop was called Madame DuPray's.

When the old lady chided me for my bare feet, it reminded me of a similar admonishment I'd received in a supermarket in a 7th-Day-Adventist stronghold near Riverside, where I'd been shopping barefoot and an Indian man (himself a great novelty) had cautioned me never to go barefoot: "This is not India! You will hurt your kidneys! And even in hot climate it is bad!"

What I've learned since: If I don't wear slippers or wool socks indoors I have to pee *very* frequently. There are acupuncture points on the soles of the feet called the "kidney poles," where the kidney meridian debouches, and they are very sensitive to temperature. The kidneys like to be warm, and keeping the feet warm helps greatly. And, speaking of India: I apparently got hookworm there – I think from going barefoot in Goa in 1975 – because in 2000 some very thorough tests showed fragments of hookworm eggs in my gut. So that's another thing to watch out for.

And I'd not recommend Africa for barefoot joys either, though I've never been: eye-worms that burrow in your feet and come out through your eyeballs! And so on.

However, I've heard that it is also very helpful to walk barefoot over gravel, to strengthen them.

What I've learned since: Second-hand shops (or charity shops, as they are known in UK) nearly always smell bad, if not cat-pooey. It's off-putting. But I still like them very much – it's just that whatever I buy there (and I'm convinced it's not only cheaper, but virtuous to buy many items one wants used instead of new – and whatever chemicals the new clothes were treated with, or dyes were used – have all off-gassed long before. Not an insignificant consideration!) I wash immediately – clothes, dishes, books. I learned how to clean books while working in Osho's library. (Damp cloth wipe on covers, spine, top and bottom, and endsheets, fan through pages with hands quickly, put out to dry, stood up and wide open.) It perks them up greatly.

Happily, second-hand stores are almost never as disgusting anymore as the one in the poem. Even I bought nothing there.

And: My Human Design says, "If you feel that life has no meaning – don't *do* anything!" I went on that trip precisely because of that meaningless feeling. And there happened on it a meaningless relationship, an acquaintance-rape, sore feet from wearing a pair of awful rust-colored canvas lace-up boots with thick, hollow high heels (the only footwear I took with me). A truckdriver who showed me porno pictures, so that I leapt out of the cab in a lay-by.

From the Jesus Freaks' window, Edinburgh, September 1971

Poem Seven Years After Crashing at the Jesus Freaks' House in Edinburgh and Stealing Their Cakes in the Night

Jesus' unknown spinsters
Young and wide
And desolate in grey Edinburgh
Keep their cakes in tins
And their biscuits
And shortbreads
In tartan tins.

In the night
Creeps pagan
Katy,
Young and wide
And desolate
In grey Edinburgh.

And thieves
And rumbles
Fumbling through the tins,
The guilt-thlop of suction
As cake meets air,
Sultanas, crumbs,
Marzipan thick and wide
And rich as night
Can never be
For Jesus' wives.

Hands meet bricks
Of butter. Body,
Dark as lovers,
Black and scented,
Cake and brandy,
Steals the thief
The girls' love-feast,
Steals their innocent

Self-portrait at the Jesus Freaks' house

Sweet-greed blind.
Guilty munches the
Crumbler,
Eye on door,
Guilt on pubis,
Door on street
To slanting city
Dark and wide –

Meeting walls of tin
And jam-tart,
Possession outraging
Her mouthing thirst again –
"I have a right!
God, give me! Give me,
God!"

Jesus' spinsters
Meet their noses
Snoring. Jesus' pagan
Steals their bodies,
Sleeping, pimpled,
Young & wide –
Half-awake,
They mumble possession.
Awake in fear,
She grabs and hides.

Just for the heck of it, I'm including this poem, written in 1978 when I'd already been living in India for four years. It seems to fit better in this book than in *The Poona Poems*.

Backdrop

i don't want to do it myself anymore

with the shower-water
or even with my own human finger

i want your tongue
willing   patient   steady
Yours
to applaud me
with slow licking
(and beating on my unbarred doors)
fluttering in my hearth-place

Earning a tiny bit of money doing sleazy modelling in London

making & becoming fire
i want the steady sound of night
in the window like a forest
and you making me lost to sound
(or love or time –)
mirroring my woman-musk
with your studious blind mouth-flesh
loving the scent which I love

Weren't hot nights in New York
in the soiled 30's
spent like this
each of us
thrilling to our role

in such studious
such effectual application
weren't we well employed
didn't i have a red dress hanging
on   a nail
Didn't i fail to get tired
but, when tired
Didn't i forget you

Teach me to forget you
steady with the rudder,
hold the sail

After Oxford, and misadventures in Ireland, Edinburgh, and Holland (with an Irish actor, Tony Rohr, who drank Guinness or whiskey steadily throughout each day) I went to London, and answered an ad in *Time Out* for an au pair in Islington. (My sister and her boyfriend passed through England during this time that was a lost drifting for me. She and I practiced Primal Screaming together at somebody's muddy cottage in the frigid countryside, then the pair of them continued on their travels.) As the bus went up the road I happened to glance out and see a man crouched by an old car, repairing it. He was bald on top and had a luxuriant mustache,

Me, Renard, and my sister, London, autumn 1971

wore round glasses and old jeans. For some reason I noticed him… Soon afterwards I sat in a sunny kitchen with a garden peeking in the French doors, with vivacious Valerie Fox, a young French-American woman with curly hair and a crisp accent, for whom the word 'insouciant' could have been coined. And there having tea with us was the mustachioed man from the street, who was a good friend of Valerie's.

That was Paul Winstanley, whom I've already mentioned above. He became my lover that night. I spent more time in his basement flat a block away than in my own, the one that came with my new job

Tony Rohr, my sort-of boyfriend

looking after one Thomas Fox – for which I was wildly unsuited.

Paul introduced me to oral sex – I mean, the kind where I get some, not just the other kind, which of course I knew well by then. Paul had premature ejaculation problems, a big full mouth, and the wit to employ the one to make up for the other. I was nineteen, and this was a boon for me – to be free for a while of the demanding penis which sought to flatten all before it; the penis I could never live up to. The penis which ignored the rest of me.

It took six months with Paul for my orgasm to free itself, even so – and it took a roofless hayloft with stars above, and France, and red wine – in Nevers, as I noted already – but it finally happened, and I celebrated by inking big red-and-yellow sunburst designs into my diary. Indeed a hallelujah.

The New York reference, by the way, was about a past life or perhaps just an alter ego, I thought I had caught a glimpse of – as a young woman of color, who owned a good red dress and liked to wear it on the street.

(Weirdly enough: At some point during the nine months I lived in that little basement flat in Islington – spending most nights with Paul – Doris turned up in London. {It was a small world then, in the counter-culture realms!} She was now dealing in cocaine. She looked a bit more haggard, less fresh than before. Paul and I tried a dose of her wares – the only time I did that drug. I hated the comedown – like tiny sprinkles of cold broken glass falling through the veins.

(I had of course told Paul the whole story – he was my best friend as well as my lover. And, as we all lurked in the inner doorway of some freezing old house – I can't remember whose – I saw Paul checking Doris out with diffident hope in his eyes: another threesome?

(And I saw her take a split second to grok all that and turn it down. Paul was not up to her standards.

(But nobody said a thing.

(My main emotion was shame and pity for Paul, along with a bit of annoyance at what a tail-wagging opportunistic dog he was after all!

(I never saw Doris again.)

What I've learned since: Even the delights of oral sex (during which I did not feel exactly connected to the man, but rather lost in my own generally effortful attempts to connect to elusive pleasure) did not comprise Tantra at all. Pleasure was the goal; a sort of striving for success, not awareness. Orgasm was a goal – so that I could shunt some of my shame into pride.

(That being said: I recently found, in *Woman and Home* magazine, this little entry on the Health page: "It wasn't until 2005 that the full size and scale of the clitoris was accurately represented! Women's sexual function and pleasure has never been prioritized by mainstream medicine. But the 'rediscovery' of the clitoris has heralded a new understanding of the importance of clitoral awareness – for women's pleasure and their health." I would add: read *Vagina*, by Naomi Wolf. It'll blow your mind. And: fie on poor old Sigmund Freud, who ruined so much for so many for so long, by insisting that clitoral orgasms are inferior to vaginal ones… when in fact, it is all connected, and vaginal orgasms always involve the clitoris. What in the heck did old Sigmund cite as his empirical authority, for gosh sakes?)

Awareness looks at all of it – the beings, the acts, the moments, the sensations, the true feelings underneath, the underneaths of those true feelings – with such attention and absorption that a whole form of love is born; inclusive of all that is there. Thank you, Tantra.

Sentences in the Desert
To Glen

I.
Out into the desert
into tall night
the family comes walking
sad Okies, books' images filming
over their skins,
Invisible amoebas of words
with slipping colors –

Not here, the family
no brothers no father
no desert boots
no hands
innocent and dreaming
no faces hid by dark:
We are shades in the moving
crystal, beetle dark.
The Coleman lantern swings
from tall father,
murking the dark with light,
frightening the border
where dark jumps into light.

Beetles run
made huge by isolation
startled by instinct;
crabs
in the deep sea we plow before us
in the sea black night
over cold dunes
which suck and slide under feet,
running before us when we run,
filling our boots with sand.
So cold
and crystal is the night.
We are lost in desert
with our Okie lantern
hunting the big black beetles
and rats with tails long-tufted
hopping   plumed over loose dunes;
in tiny holes and doorways
nocturnal spiders weightless
on legs like arched haired fingers;
plump mice, dime-tiny
delicate as seedpods
on grasswaved leanings into wind.
Catch the tiny desert mouse

or kangaroo rat trembling
into thy big pale hand
thy sculpted gentle
curled bone hand.

II.
He is the cool skin desert.
He allows us all.
We love him.
We are tamed.

III.
We are lost.   We climb the wash
to the ridge,
push yucca over.
He makes a bonfire in the night.
We wait for the VW
to be unlost,
for the others to find us,
the safe big brothers.
We run to look again
over the black ridge-edge
for the long roof somewhere –
Blue van, home.
Bonfire brave and crackling
warming our father
making invisible the coyotes
who howl far over ridges –
And I wondering
why it was dead,   the eight-legged tarantula
hand-huge and brittle
velvet-upholstered
like tomcats' balls.
It was on a rock in daylight
dead like a leaf out of season.
Others appeared then too, all dead.
We lie down
on cold sand

pillowed on the talisman
awaiting coyotes, rescue, or dark.
Then soon the shout –
Huck found us!
The VW had flown backwards
up over the ridge,
shown us the rooftop
we had seen and not known it.
Home was frosted metal and warm
rackety breathing
morsel in vast cold dark.

IV.
Later, one purple twilight
my first guru
with black-ringed eyes…
was only a man,
a friend; he walked with me
to a wide rise
and looked with purple-cast eyes
over purple sage
to the violet mountains.
Sky hung down around us,
a wispy settling shade.
In the dim spare whisperings
we could feel the peoples
who had been spare,
and the austerity of sage.
We were violet.
He cared for me. The family
was old doom; this Jim
magic talisman. New
old eyes, soft violet twilight.

He tried to lift me
from beneath the feet
that dreams have,
up over desert's

wide disarray, free
heart-pained floating
over the dotted sage.
He tried to fly me
too high
into the pull of that upper gravity,
and I was eleven,
and the mountains cut me,
and the weight of this mountain called earth
held me down.
I sat in worship
in the temple; sleep and sage
mixing molecules in purple dark.
He told me I could skip it all.
I want to weep.

V.
On the campfire
demons laugh in quickflame joy
and I am safe
in the illusion of my father,
his sage's shade
reaching, his arms' gentle sphere
harmless, innocuous, sublime.
My sleeping father is a blade.
My chuckling saddened father
with his wealth of peanuts
in cashew cans, macadamias
and man's marshmallows, cider fresh
and fermenting,
is the pool I sleep in.
His wealth of paper phials
and annotated spiders
and his last dollars to pharmaceutical
supply houses for the medicine bottles
enclosing centipede, scorpion, muse.
His love escapes me.
He is mysterious as woman is to man.

With Paul, it was easy to write. He sat tapping at his typewriter, I sat scribbling – and there was a settled happiness in his little tidy flat below-stairs. And in that space, to my own surprise I began to write about my childhood, my life in Riverside, and the rutted, eroded Badlands around it, and the Mojave desert we used to visit.

Yes, this was my Glen's world – an innocent surveying and exploring of that desert and the marvels of Nature. He was an expert at insect-reconnoitering, but inept in the hard and rushing plane of business and commerce or the visceral minefields of emotional negotiation. Completely clueless in all that. I'm tearful again as I read this over… it really does capture the wonder of our desert trips, in which we'd get lost and found again.

The word "Okie" isn't accurate: the family weren't dust-bowl refugees, but pioneers who came West in the 1700's, 1800's, 1900's – Wester and Wester, till there was no further left to go. Glen was born in New Mexico in 1914 – his family migrated to Santa Ana, California, shortly before the Great Depression.

But the kerosene lantern and our poverty reminded me of John Steinbeck's tales. Though we were not uneducated or the slightest bit redneck – we were pale-necked and studious to a fault.

The verses about my first guru: that was of course Jim Richard, the kindly tall scientist family friend who used to go on nice respectful walks with me around the neighborhood, to talk about Time and Consciousness. I cannot find him on FB (he went east to Virginia Beach to be at the Edgar Cayce Institute, by and by). He who was so good to me – I would love to see him again, or to write to him, a thank you. He was only good; completely generous and non-exploitative. And a mystic.

What I've learned since: The world is full of rich deserts – there for the finding.

Sadness about fathers is a normal state of affairs, not to be denied or eschewed, but rather surfed in, each time it arises; yet not clung to. It is okay if it goes on and on. That sadness keeps us deep and humble; but it need not keep us prisoner. Be doggedly, obstinately yourself too. Be happy. That is your greatest rebellion. It will not harm your parents. We are all in this together. It will make them whole.

From Letter from Mama
Casa Naranjal, Riverside
December 1971

Darling Katy,
I'm home from work early – dusk – and here's your celebration of a letter with the exquisite glowing seal. I've got to piss, and put away the groceries – and take off my good clothes and then – then – …I sit in the big chair and feast, read. There's so much. I want to answer right away, but I've got to cook red meat for your long lanky brother – who will be so tall – and so sweet, when he is grown…

The pkg. gets mailed tomorrow. In a pocket you will find a small amulet of this our earth, in a little leather pouch Jim Chambers put together in 3 or 4 minutes.

A collage of a letter this will be. *David* "typed in his usual dense sharp scathing way" – I didn't know David, but from this and the quotes, I do know him. His misapprehension of Serafina is stupendous – it overwhelms all his other perceptions, however bright they may be. And it is very strange. I'm glad I was permitted to miss him.

Serafina Yes I worry – always under my sleep I worry. Renaud is not merely a reed, he is a rotten reed. Better she should make her way alone. And I have not heard for a good month. A lovely drawing and letter from Franny mentioned a special delivery from Sera and R – asking for money – the Garsts sent some. Phil *[Phil Smith, the Unitarian minister]* says $100 per month should be ample for Sera: "I'll bet he's living on her bets Phil. So do I."

My guts: It's a pleasure giving them some wear and tear so I can send Serafina and you a driblet of money (or in Sera's case $30 per mo.) but I do not want to lift a finger for Renaud. I resent the very god damned hell out of being put in a position to have to do so.

The innards are fine now. I went to Phil and Auxier both *[Mama's longtime friend Dr. Auxier, who also delivered me and some siblings]* – he gave me gestalt and she a pelvic and some pills to relax the stomach. The pap was negative – the hormone levels OK. So I'm good for yet a bit more loving. I have dark suspicion that all that aspirin I took when I had flu in November could have started up some internal bleeding which took a long time to get over. So the other day when I was down with the current epidemic (like a combination of pneumonia and the worst hangover you ever had) I didn't take any aspirin at all. And now I feel quite well. It was felling people right and left so with all the agony I had the security of knowing just what it was, and that I'd survive.

Jim Chambers: When I came home the other day, there was a note from him with address and phone. Though tired, I called, and he came over. I gave him tea and bread and cheese; he took me and Ian to his house, which is full of groovy things, and luscious purses. He gave me one I just love. It goes with my new dark brown Brazilian boots and dark brown suede hat with floppy brim. The boots are fabulous – like Sharon Smith's... The first time I've ever lavished money on myself at Christmas.

But to get back to Jim. He is in deep unhappiness right now. A relationship has ended. He showed me her picture and it gave me the creeps somehow – she looked like you. But with none of your softness – sweetness – soul... He feels no one loves him or cares about him – he says people no longer turn to look at him – he does not really exist. He is thinking of self destruction. And if he has really been living on whites for the past year as he says – perhaps he is on his way. I told him I cared, which I do. And got him to promise to go see Phil.

Other Lonely People: Within a 24-hr period, two others reached out to me. Poor old dumb George still comes around from time to time. He says the same things, and so do I. It seems to comfort him, I know not why.

And then, on an impulse, I called Bob, to wish him Happy Hanukkah and shining Solstice, and he told me he had tried to call me the night before and got that *Sorry number not in service* recording, and was going to come by. We hadn't been together since July. He asked me eagerly to come over. I did and my little wooden boy is getting realer all the time. So his fairy with the red hair loved him and massaged him and petted him – and slept with him. When I left he said he wanted me to come back. I get lonesome he said simply. At first I felt funny about it, for as you are aware, the great love of my life he is not – and someone else is – soul of my soul. But then, it was just nice and companionable... and sort of fun.

The jolly holiday season out at Boys Town is one grand snafu... Fr. Peter is being a shit. My good Jerry was sleeping with his next-door counselor girlfriend and for some reason some of my monsters went up the hill and complained to Pete – not to me, as they should have if they feel like complaining. And Pete won't tell me who the little finks are. "Why didn't they come to me?" I demanded.

"Because you're a woman," gloats Pete.

"Oh shit!" said I. "And my staff?"

"If I were working for a woman, I wouldn't tell her either," he says triumphantly.

"Woman as n****r," I cry indiscreetly.

"Drop it. Right now!" he demands. "I don't want to get angry. It's too close to Xmas."

"Well god bless us every one. And bah and humbug," say I. And leave.

So now I and Pete will go on feuding for a while, neither of us wanting to. He can be so dense.

Jerry and I had a heart to heart. The dear lad is so innocent. He simply couldn't understand why you can't fuck on the job if the kids are in bed. But today he and Judy went in and told Pete they are Getting Married and now suddenly everything is OK with Pete. He's a marriage freak. Jesus, I'll probably have to get married, I know I will if I ever want him purring over me.

We have our gross old lady too. She's been at the switchboard or somewhere in Boys Town since the year '02. Friday staff were discussing the day's lunch – tuna fish – and she said, "Can't stand tuna fish. Smells like a woman's butt. Not the back end. The front end."

Brother Lawrence, with his prim little turned-in mouth and his sneaky pubescent face said, "I wouldn't know, I'm sure."

Oh yes, we had a fire. One of my E.D. (emotionally disturbed) 15-year-olds stuck a stick of incense into a very dry Christmas tree and lit it. The fire alarms pealed right merrily, the kids' room was a sheet of flame, the fire door opened – I ordered them all out. The GD fire extinguisher didn't work. No buckets. I sent the staff next door for an extinguisher, poured water from a kettle on the blazing tree, and took it out in the yard. The kids were really fine. They're feeling the lack of matches though. They won't get anymore until they pay for the floor – or rather, the culprit does. Six units came roaring up from fair Beaumont City as I was airing the place out – all eager for the treat. When I got home my horoscope said, "Danger to loved ones from fire." Well.

One of my freaking out angry ones threatened to hit me – just brushed me though. He didn't really want to. So Bro. Russell rushes out for reinforcements, and I was doing just fine in there with the door shut with my angry one...

...Have you read *Dibs in Search of Self* by Virginia Axline? A lovely book – one case of a play therapist. Now there's something I'd like to do... Behavior modification is for the rats.

I read *Black Elk Speaks* too, as I believe you suggested – another beautiful, but almost too hurting, book.

...Oh yes, my Christmas tree. The first one I *ever* had to *my* taste. A two-foot fir, in water in the old green ginger jar on the hatch *[table made from old ship's hatch, found on beach and much-varnished by Jim]*, hung with clear fake cut glass – some stalactites, some pear shaped. Candles on each side and a low one under the tree. A red pot of scarlet flowered winter cactus, my little elephant... It's charming and mine all mine.

I like everything you write me about Paul. Even the sad things...

12/21/71

All day I sat in my big chair, arranging papers, writing reports. They're done now. In the morning I recopy, rush them out to BTD *[Boys Town of the Desert]*. I only took 1/2 hour off to trundle over to Woolworth's and buy long legal pads to write them on. Isn't buying paper neat when you really gotta have it – can't make do with wrapping paper and old bags?

Last night I had various ungood dreams I forget – but one gleam of pure joy remains. Tom *[Mama's great love]* asked me to go fishing with him. And seeing a stream and a smooth rock canyon wall (I do this in dreams sometimes – things are more than one level all at once) I accepted with delight & relief...

Katya, the Garcia Lorca got damaged in Boston, but I'm sending it anyway. It's all there and I think you can put it all right with your bookbinding skills. I don't know whether or not I wrote you about the vicious speedfreak's dog which chewed up the journal of my journey – I think I did. She laid tooth on the Garcia Lorca, but not fatally. All the *un*valuable stuff in the room she disdained to touch.

...I love reading about your clothes, and I'm so glad you have them, recalling when you had next to none. (I like my new clothes too, but i may have no place to wear them. Just as I can't really wear my new eyes anywhere. I got some luscious dark brown eye paint, and I draw a line along the lash line all around, tipping it up at the outer corners. Groovy. I'd wear them to the Uni Uni *[Unitarian Universalist]* New Year's party, only I gotta work, dammit...

1:10
...Ian and I are off to the post office...
More soon, love, love, love,
Mama

Patriotic Lovesong – to Joe

Grope a continent

Squeeze Idaho's tits

Bite Oregon's ripe-apple cheeks
stroke with sun-buttered lascivious shudder
California's belly-warm sand

Put it in Texas, good and greasy
fold a hot prick taco
prick with hot sauce
hands fumble breathless
in Washington State forestry
you got one knee

in the ant-pile of New Orleans
black-pepper ants boogeying on your sweating skin
while summer asphalt yields warm tar under your elbow
and your right hand is up in New York Ciddy being stabbed
and robbed and having bills posted on its fingernails
and the sweat-grime lust of your palms
feels like summer to the inhabitants
and they rob and murder and fornicate even more
while your prick down in Texas speaks soft Mexicano,
arouses low-uddered herds of longhorn cattle,
is lassoed eversogently by firm circling sun
and your balls are buoyed warm and salty
in the Gulf of Mexico
Oh   Idaho's sweet tits   Nebraska's corn-gold bottom,
the wiry black armpit of Detroit's factory stench
America the wench! Rub your hard belly on soft Arkansas
nuzzle and lick in Cool Neck Wyoming,
roll your tired head in her horse-flanked sleep!
Trust your ribs to the Rockies
wildflower honey drizzles on a thousand mountains,
warmed to runny delirium by you, by you!
Slips like the Mississippi south to irrigate
palliate   to slicken   to suck
your good branding-iron, oh my cowpoke
my cowboy   my tonic   my lovemilked ram,
sheepstealer   horsethief   wetback and immigrant alien
and inbreeder and stealthy savourer of the lips of the
flashflood wash!

Dig deep your well, and drink, and deep-fry in petroleum,
and fry your drumstick deep, and butter your sturdy brown
biscuits
and honey your butter from our wildflower bees, cows,
cowslips –

oh Joe, fuck America, fuck me!

I have to laugh when I see this. I remember writing it in Paul's dim, sparely-furnished flat while he clacked at his bitter, sarcastic fiction, full of alliteration and obscure words. I was in one of those odd bursts of nostalgia ex-pats are prone to. (The nostalgia is safe since a wide ocean lies between you and the birthland!) It was published right away, in *Transatlantic Review* and *Hanging Loose,* where the editors were definitely male! There was no Joe; he was just Yankee Every(young)man.

What I've learned since: I can still get the odd rush from thinking of Mark Twain's birthplace, Hannibal, MO, in the soft, muggy light reflected from the Mississippi; I can feel a twinge of blues-style longing and mournfulness when I think of those Santa Ana winds, the train tracks, rattling palm trees, in Riverside, California. But it's not the same as wanting to *be* there.

Inyo County Subastral Blues

It's dark
lying in here alone
but I welcome you
my sweet one.
I always welcome you
my sweet star-face
moon-face
my sweet beebleberry
my algae-mouth, my love.

Come over the mountains to me
star-face
wiping your hands on the trees
where the cold red star-juice
gathers like rain
and falls
and I pass later
and my cheekbones are grateful

for the blood of your spoils
moon-killer, thief.

You are always welcome in my house
where pale neon flutters in the window
spelling Katy's Cafe.
Red neon juice stutters in my veins
and you're always welcome
through the door, hunter love
to lie with me on the sofa
and unbutton my breasts
trace your fingers
in the dust
blow gently in the crevices
so dust rises about us in a cloud
like some astral dust-storm
humming, palest grey

And from your shoulder
my mountain rider
starshooter
I see the far berry of the earth
twiddling in the air
over the candy-bars by the cash register
milky way bars, mars bars
in boxes on the dusty glass.

This whole thing was simply channeled, as-is. What does it mean? I don't know. It does incorporate a nostalgia for a certain day, in about 1963, when the family went out to a tiny settlement called Kelso in the Mojave desert.

Previously, ore trains had stopped there, from mines, but now all that was left was a cafe and an old train station, and a house or two among the leafy sycamores. The ground was just a fine white sand. (I don't know why my father loved the desert so much. Perhaps he considered it radical, and other beauty spots bourgeois? Or perhaps the austerity suited his scientific soul? But he loved the abundance the desert hides – the amazing variety of jumping,

Rather plumply doing yoga, Islington, late 1971

creeping, crawling, side-winding, buzzing life you could find there. And the sun.)

The air was so dry that day that our lips split and bled, and we'd rubbed margarine on them from the lunch box. It didn't work very well, and felt greasy too. Taffy was with us, so my joy was magnified. We must have giggled and fussed over our cracked lips.

My father did something then that sticks out in my mind as unprecedented. Our mother had not come along, and though we'd brought some food, Glen suddenly invited all of us to eat lunch in the cafe. That little outpost seemed so wonderful – with its thick white china cups and bowls, its chili con carne served with a little cellophane packet of saltines – a thing I found classy and amazing. The chili itself was delicious, thick, beautifully-spiced with cumin and coriander. We sat at the counter and spooned up the delicious stew, served by an enigmatic middle-aged woman. Who came here? How could it stay open? Who could live out here? And why?

Two Limericks

1)
A mouse with intentions oblique
Terrified a young girl with its squeak.
Her friend said, "Instead
Let's step on its head
And our mirth will inherit the eeek!"

2)
There once was a hairy old freak
Who was stoned every night of the week.
He said, when he found
He might never come round
"Is this heaven, or just Ca Ca Creek?"

What I've learned since: There are times – rare, I'll admit, very

Paul Winstanley and me, Islington, winter 1971

rare indeed – perhaps driving in a car with a few people, very tired, rather silly, you've stopped for a coffee break though and are feeling somewhat restored – when nothing does quite so well as a limerick. We don't know from what tucked-away recesses of the human so-called consciousness they come, peering and winking, like a spiny creature gawping from a rock-hole in the briny deep – but surely they do come, by and by, now and then. It is probably good they don't come oftener – but much much later one visited me in a triple-limerick, and here it is:

>There once was a girl in Nantucket
>who, seeing a thing, oft would suck it.
>In 2007
>she died, went to heaven,
>and her treatments made God kick the bucket!
>
>This unleashed tsunamis quite frantic
>pounding over Pacific, Atlantic,
>down and up to the Poles –
>galvanizing men's souls –
>it was all really rather romantic.
>
>This prompted that Nantucket girl
>to give reincarnation a whirl.
>She came back as a squid –
>perhaps we all did –
>as our lazy legs furl... and unfurl.

...and that is all I have to say on the matter!

From a letter to my mother
London, May 1972

Dear Mama,
I sometimes feel that my travels in the world are just somehow a search for my own origins; for the fatal links and sordid memories which glue the present me together. Sometimes I feel that you and

I are puzzling together over chains, years & summer days which molded and formed us/me/you.

I have just stumbled onto something which is so obvious that I don't know why I didn't think of it before. I'm sure I did think of it before, in fact, but forgot it, as the issue is a real and present pain more powerfully than it is any sequence of satisfying logics. But as logic is anyway just a picture of our own formations, this hypothesis continues to be satisfying, though not curative.

I think that my feelings about my body, and therefore *in* my body – namely,

a) Shame. "I am disgusting, repulsive (for thinking I am disgusting, repulsive); obsessed by the tiniest excreta; my mind, if not my body (for it is unfashionable to believe in this day and age that one's body is unclean) is unclean."

b) Fear. Of rejection: "everybody will see how my blubbery gut hangs out and will exclude me."

Of decay: "if I don't run a mile every day, do my stretches, eat at regularly timed intervals, never eat sweets, I will decay immediately into shipwrecked abandon."

c) Frigidity. "my cunt is filled with old torn-up newspapers and 30-year-old bubblegum. Little black ants stream busily in and out. The windows are never washed."

…these feelings are merely (merely!) obviously, a mirror image of Date St. House! To which I was ashamed to bring my friends home.

which was a greedy messy maw.

which, no matter how thoroughly or frequently cleaned, reacted with a veritable tide of newspapers, soup cans, stamp hinges, crud and dirty socks.

"everybody will hate me for my house (my body) (my mommy) loose-stomached, down at the heels, just basically wretched."

I'm very pleased to find such an explanation. Body = house. Body = earth. Body = city. Don't you think so? A fox's body is just as much his woods and copse, his leafy den and his chicken feasts, his sun and the fast leafbrown streams he slithers by, as is his own furred warmblooded little system. If the woods burns, fox moves on. If all woods are burned, fox burns. When he dies, his body is one cell dying into the big body – absorbed, re-used, gnawed maybe, or gently rotted.

Paul's daughter Anna at age four remarked on a snowy indoors foxden afternoon – "the wind is my thinking and the snow falling is my thinking."

Anyway. Just wanted to get this down.

May 8

[Paul] is much better today and even consistently cheerful, which is god! He's always joking about feeling terrible, but you can see he feels terrible just the same. In a way, it's a very likeable thing about him. He's a very sociable person, but, unlike others I have known, he's completely without powertripping & jealousy in a social situation. He says that's because he *knows* he's a heavy character anyway; and he's always (he didn't say this, but told me an incident from when he was five years old – he went up to his father and recited to him all the ways in which he knew his father sacrificed and economized to keep the family going – like re-using old bits of coal, etc. etc. and said "I know you think I don't appreciate you, but I do." His father was astounded.) had immense regard for other people's feelings; he also is very intuitive about them. His daughter Anna is the same way.

Commandment

You *are* one of us

says my father,
leaning down over me,
his cigarette burning.

This image of my father leaning over my crib, saying sadly, "Zelle, Zelle…" (he was the only person who has ever used my middle name) has stayed with me. He was expressing an almost chiding, helpless pity for my scratching and scratching with eczema (caused by the smoke, but in the 50's people didn't think that way).

What I've learned since: It's very useful to face these moments of memory – and any other, more obscure ones that arise when I go down In. Not trying to do *anything* to them – neither avoid, nor pump up – just observe, as clearly as possible. It is useful also to dance them; or to desert one's own form for a moment and enter into the form of the other – and even his cigarette. What is it made of?

It's useful too to notice and acknowledge, without hope or avoidance, the overwhelming power such an imprint has on our worldview, our body, our very way of seeing everything around us. I call this 'tacit atmospheres' – the combination of taken-for-granted factors that form into a sort of miasma of assumptions, smells, weights – and thus go on shaping us.

Awareness is all: and in this poem I'm expressing, even before I began to meditate, my understanding of the power of that conditioning.

Own it – and then it won't own you. Or – it will own you less; for whatever we see, we free. Some further shadow might come along, cast by that same scene – but it will be slightly different. We can get the nourishment of awareness out of each faced scenario.

∽

Paul and I traveled by oft-breaking-down Norton motorcycle through the gorgeous summer French countryside to Saint-Privat, in the Hérault, where he was to help an old journalist friend with some reconstruction on the ancient gatehouse in which the friend and his woman lived.

From a letter to my mother
St. Privat, July 1972

…This afternoon, which is turning out sunny, I am going to paint the large ex-paint can which is in the courtyard. Yesterday I filled it with rocks and rich soil (horseshit, chicken-shit, wood-ash, dirt) and planted some plump runner-beans. When I get back they should be well sprouted. It's very sultry today.

Yesterday I made onion tart. Wonderful. And we had fresh mackarel *[sic]*, and charcuterie with olives and pickles, and fresh homemade bread, and salad and cheese and wine. That is a normal supper. The night before we had fresh mussels cooked over an open fire; then small fish, nameless; and salad, bread, cheese, fruit,

On my Grand Tour, Trieste, Italy, August 1972

wine. The night before – Saucisson, grilled over the fire. Potatoes in cheese sauce. Fresh runner beans, cooked. Salad. Bread. Cheese. Olives. Humus. Wine. Etc. Butter, home-made fig jam. The wine befuddles me and makes me feel lousy and a bit plump in the morning, and it is also very difficult to resist, as I love it, and it's so good with food, and everybody else is getting jolly on it.

Ah, your letters. They were so good to get! That check from Sunset *[for a not-even-original recipe, I think $10]* was heartily amusing... Ted, who has friends in the local bank, is helping me to get it cashed.

...my possible plan to return to California... I would much rather descend unannounced, bearing boughs of dried rosemary and bay laurel and garlic so fresh the husks are wet... I don't want people to get used to me before I'm even there. And I may not come back. We'll see... I am apprehensive about going back. I am afraid I will find myself a California child once again, stuck, smogged. My plan – to work or somehow get money to travel again. England, or South America, or whatever happens. It seems a bit foolish to go all the way back home when for less money I could simply wait out the 6 months in Mediterranean sunshine somewhere; but I guess I want to see you and everybody...

...Guess what... there is terrible evidence that the hormones They inject in meat in America make people fat. Very fat very fast. Isn't that horrifying? It happened to Jo when she went to the U.S. She's very thin and had never changed size in her life. An American chick told her it was the meat, and she stopped eating it, and was okay.

Did I tell you that I asked MEN ONLY to send you a copy of the issue with my story? They said they would; I hope they do.

Love to Ian. Your letters are to me as water hyacinths are to a manatee. Paul sends regards. Love, love, Katy

Did you know that Renard's real name is Norman Goldstein?

~

And here, a list of all my worldly goods (except for the journals Mama was keeping for me at her house), carried in my knapsack across the seas back to the States...

Paul Winstanley, Saint-Privat, France

Possessions List
[inscribed on an Air France air-sick bag; front and back]
September 1972

...if indeed as the learned scientists say   our skin replenishes itself every 7 years, then I have acquired almost 1/3 of a body's worth of epidermal matter, gift
- 1 plastic bottle of inferior suntan lotion, 5F, Saint-Briac-sur-Mer
- 1 particularly typical string of unwashed hippie commie pinko beads, brown, Paris, gift
- 6 garments constructed, invented, executed, gaily worn by me, out of curtains, gifts, England, Switzerland, used
- 1 flour-sack, printed in English, Athens, 5 drachma
- 1 recipe for delicious, revitalizing meusli {sic}, London, gift
and what of the unseen generations of germs, riding me pick-a-back?

Saint-Privat, August 1972

And what of the things Europe acquired from me, what of those? worn-out old tie-dye shirt, much mended, gracing the back of some wandering freak? memories, imprinted irrevocably in the sweet brains and bodies of friends, or the perfunctory ones of busdrivers and waiters and glancers-in-the-street? What of the gifts I have left in Les Égouts of Paris, what of the meals dished heartily, greedily, smilingly, grinningly, dancingly, to the friends whose gifts gift me, what of my gifts, my aubergines, my cups of tea, my tears? Fallen on foreign soil, and thence undeclared to the sea.

1 vomit bag, found on Air France plane

1 ballpoint pen spring, unsprung, found on beach, or was it in the first floor of a dusty building? ...cut into two bits and twisted to resemble perfectly-serviceable earring wires, attaching...

2 brass stars acquired in an incredibly filthy shop in London for 2 pence each (used)

1 Swiss army rucksack, used, 2 Swiss Francs

1 backless t-shirt, trendy, the color of certain children's popsicles, London, 60p

1 t-shirt, remarkably green, Marseilles, 15 Francs

1 camembert box, crushed, containing embroidery thread and assorted needles for my humble mending; gift, London, used

710 nights, sleepless or joyful, indescribable, gift, used

1 Chinese ginger-jar, used, gift, St. Privat, the size of a small nectarine

1 rapidograph, Rome, 3000 lire

1 book, inscribed by giver, London, gift

1 absurd customs declaration, Air France, gift, which I unfortunately know how to read, better that I were an ignorant aborigine, knowledgeable only of my chapter of desert! my stretch of stars!

3 pairs knickers, grotty and clean (sort of) Italy, England, Greece, 10 drachma; flowered and polka-dotted, as is my girlish fancy

1 small stone, blue, white, and the color of sand, found on beach at Salerno, Italy and preserved lovingly

Back from tour, Saint-Privat, August 1972

San Francisco

September 1972 – December 1973

I do think there must have been a volume lost that would have belonged with the other twenty-eight volumes of diary from those teen years – because I remember writing a poem in a convent in Venice where I stayed a night on my Grand Tour, and I've never been able to find that poem since. I posted each diary to Mama when it was full – so it is possible one might have never arrived.

I'd left Paul working construction on Ted Simon's gatehouse, to take the train through Italy, Yugoslavia, Greece. Then, after being reunited with Paul the next month, back in that tiny village where the food was the best I had ever eaten or could imagine eating – I left him again, on the same stretch of road where I'd left David the year before.

I hitchhiked off to Paris, already brokenhearted. I had decided to go back to California and seek the Ultimate Encounter Group, to help with my OCD. I couldn't think where else to turn – and the compulsive thoughts were now driving me nuts. After many uncomfortable adventures I reached Riverside and persuaded

Santa Barbara, California, September 1972

Mama to leave her little Casa Naranjal and move to San Francisco with me and Ian, my little brother.

And so we did. Jim drove us – and we found the top-floor two-bedroom flat on Potrero Hill that became home (for $165 a month!)

languor

languor
soft afternoon
drone of freeway sea

breasts
all i draw
with black ink

two breasts
in my bed
mine
brownsoft edible

window
green plants stir
this:
later a lover
   my   breasts

This poem wasn't dated, and I've been trying to figure when it was written. The sexually-awakened tone and the suntan imply Poona, but the freeway implies California. Perhaps it was when I stayed in Santa Barbara briefly when I got back to California – I remember sunbathing nude, frolicking on the beach, with some handsome, hairy fellow with a handlebar mustache whose name I've forgotten, and with whom I had no chemistry.

Or, maybe it was written in 1972 or 1973 when I used to sunbathe on the spindly high back porch on Potrero Hill, looking out over

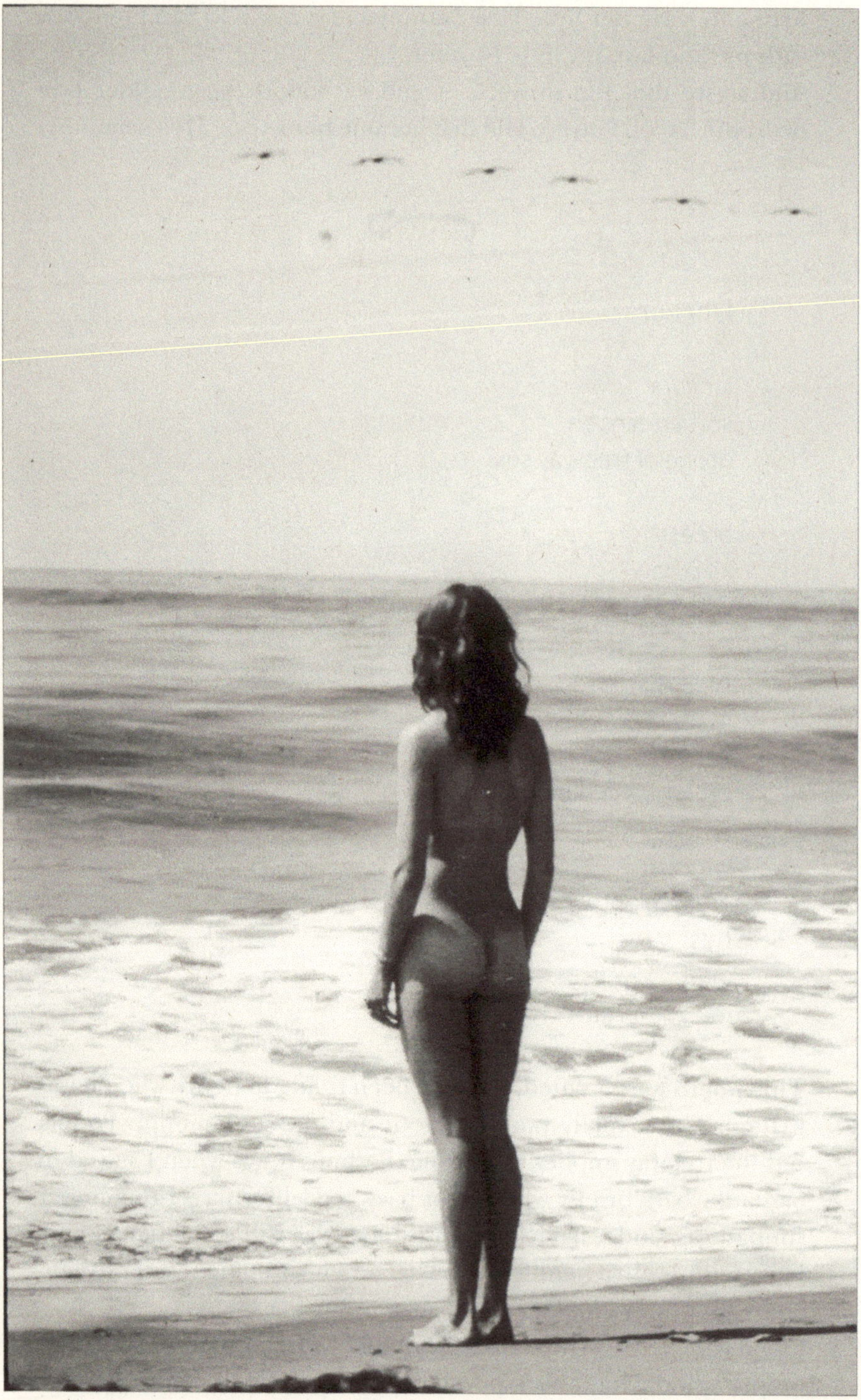

the Bay. Which lover? I don't know – Could it have been Herb, the wonderful daddy-man I was with next? (I never fell out of love with him, to this day – that big bluff chuckling fellow.) I tended to feel more aroused when away from the lover than when I was with him! But would I have heard a freeway from there? Possibly – an industrial area was nearby and there must have been broad roads. We could see the Bay Bridge from the balcony too. I did have green plants in my window and I did have leisure, which in Poona I mostly did not. And in Poona I rarely drew; while as a teen I drew a lot.

But I've included it because I found it among teenage poems, and because it is nice to address its topic.

What I've learned since: If they are little, and haven't been nursed from, they stay up always. And, after menopause they no longer yearn to be caressed.

The preciousness of them is so acute – the energetic truthfulness of their assertions – the subtlety of their responses – shrinking, expanding – they deserve all honor, all respect, all protection, all care.

They live from the inside out.

They are the 4th chakra: the positive pole of female lovingness. But they were hormonally driven, as the heart itself is not – the heart itself is just a vast space, universally open, unconditional. It reflects life in its amplitude of non-interference – and shines out spaciously. The breasts, though, used to demand much: hands, lips, mouth, eyes. No longer... peace now. Cessation. Jaunty adventure suits them now.

My opinion: Messing with breasts via implants, tight bras, squashing, wire-bolstered propping, is asking for trouble, and is a grievous insult to the Goddess. These actions show she is not seen, not heeded. Who should ignore the Mother of the World?

Oh, yes – they are for feeding babies. I know nothing about this, though no doubt I've felt something of that with a man. Blissful moments of strange caring; a head at my bosom.

What I've learned since: A padded bra keeps them from being hurt so much if elbowed in a crowd. Mine are just the right size.

My brother Ian in Riverside near Mom's house

If someone else doesn't or didn't think so, I don't care the *core of a cabbage.*

The right-size bra is really too tight. A size bigger is better (for me – I've not much to suspend).

Mostly, around the house, I don't wear one.

There's a huge gap in the market: somebody needs to create lacy, natural-fabric, no-underwire, padded, organic, colorful bras. But so-called cotton ones are nearly always athletic-looking. And so-called cotton ones often have cups lined with polyester (Victoria's Secret being a case in point) which undoes the purpose of the cotton – to cradle one's precious breasts in something other than a glorified plastic bag.

It's wonderful to be a woman, and have breasts, whatever stage of life you're at. Just remember – they live from the inside out!

true story

my 6-foot 2-inch 13-year-old little brother's
personal 6-lb. 12 oz. 80% empty can
of government-issue peanut butter is threaded with his
elbow-length hairs

Mom, Ian and I were very happy in our flat. We furnished it with wooden pallets dragged home from nearby factories. (I don't suppose I wasted a thought on wishing we had real furniture.) Mom painted her bay-window room white with a sky-blue floor. I cooked a lot. We had that great view from the spindly back porch – way out over the water, the ships, the bridge. Wonderful. We felt so free.

Ian read and drew comics all night and slept all day (his pattern still, though now computers are in it too). Mom went to liberal political meetings, and worked for $5 an hour at a home for wayward teenage boys. I did poetry readings, acted in blue movies, and wrote long letters to Paul.

Ian was always hungry. He'd come out to the kitchen at midnight

self a stack of twelve quesadillas or toasted cheese and take them back to his room (the repurposed living ~~room~~ ~~the c~~an of peanut butter here mentioned was from a box ~~of food~~ given out to poor people as ransom for Patty Hearst, who'd been kidnapped by the something-or-other Liberation Army: to free her, the Whatever-Liberation people demanded this distribution of groceries, and it was done. I went to claim a box, but Mom shuddered and said it was all creepy.
Ian's hair was very long, thick, and straight – and fell in the peanut butter.

What I've learned since: This too will pass. Ian's been quite bald for many years.

And: If you have lots of long hair, as I did for much of my life, it's practical to either comb it before you shower, or have a really good mesh thingie over the shower-drain. Unless you enjoy and can afford to call plumbers. If you have eleven amalgam fillings from a sugar-eating childhood, and later you get them all removed in India, by a dentist who waggles his head and says, "No problem, no problem, not necessary," when you ask about protection from the mercury shards and fumes; and you choose, out of laziness, to believe him – you will get very, very sick with mercury poisoning. This is horrible. You will feel pain everywhere, and throw up, and be unable to move for exhaustion. Eventually you'll get better, but six months later your long thick hair will start to appear all over the floor and in huge amounts in the shower in the ice-cold flat you're working out of in France. None of this is recommended. (The hair will grow back. The dentist, however, will die.)

What I've learned since: Peanut butter is demonized by some, and others it makes swell up and drop dead. But my kinesiologist tested it and said it's good for me. Organic, of course. I love a peanut-butter-and-pickle-and-vegan-mayo-and-miso sandwich on spelt sourdough bread. Yum!

Letting the Ghost Talk

I.

Ghost
who are you

I
I am the breathing one
who haunts your hallways
I am the man-shadow
the tormented fruit
of your postponement

I stalk you
the way a tree would
black and accidental
and then suddenly huge
at your elbow
in the night

I stalk you
to tell you
where this hallway goes.
You know there is a shadow-place
behind me
which gives me my power
my killing cold
too cruel to kill.
You and I are biding time
darling, fool.
My ice teeth
are sudden
and supernaturally long
into your bone shoulder
Sweetheart,
Shape for my shadow,
Gray blunder,

House for my hall.

II.

No wonder
they say the devil mocks.
I am elegant,
I am sweet
I plan your days.

I suck the pleasure from you
with a straw.

The little Japanese man stalks you.
Your doom is up your nose.
Mushrooms sprout
between your teeth
fungal terror overnight
And your armpits –
did you think them personal?
I've had my thin tongue in them
for years
I smack my little lips
all over you
in your sleep
Yes
I even rock you to sleep
licking your bottom
with the same thin
penetrating tongue

They say my saliva penetrates
the skin

I have bought your blankets
they are mine

I have given you love-licks

    in the musky wealth
    of your camembert rose
    I have been a spider
    made of Jupiter-stone
    sucking invisible at your asshole
    you are mine

    I wait for you
    I want you
    Demonia, anima,
    helpless breast-one;
    fearer of hallways –
    mate with me,
    suckle me,
    feel my teeth.

This is one of those poems that has lived in me since its inception, chanting at me now and then – the music of it remaining as the horror has left. It benefits by being read aloud in all its spookiness, with a ghostly emphatic tone.

How it came about: When we lived in Ferndale, in that colorfully-painted flat on Main Street, Taffy visited, and one night we played with a Ouija board. I had become inexplicably afraid of the hallway – a thing that had never happened to me before – and was convinced there was a ghost in it. I was terrified to come out of our bedroom into the hall. This made life complicated. Anyway, the Ouija board said a murder had happened near the house long ago and the ghost was a-roamin'. This news did not comfort me. We made inquiries and it turned out somebody said somebody said that this murder had indeed occurred, many decades before. I was terrified, and much embarrassed about my trembling. When we moved to the funky old house on the horse farm at the edge of town, the fear vanished.

Our flat on Potrero Hill was so lofty and airy - but there was a hallway in this flat too, and I became *afraid that I would be afraid of* a ghost. And then, it became so inconvenient to be unable to set foot in the hallway that connected the rooms! However, since I now had the tool of "stepping into a voice," here I "became" the ghost and let him talk.

What I've learned since: The 'ghost' was at least in part my obsessive-compulsiveness, and my unexamined Shadow. And yet maybe that Ferndale flat *was* haunted. And... in fact we're all haunted, by our pasts and the pasts of our families, and our friends too, and neighbors, and so on and on. It's called The Collective Unconscious, and it wanders freely right through our skins and ears and eyes, patterning our brains with tumults and tensions.

Meditation is the mysterious, effective door into the clean outer space we have inside; but also the way to look at the zillion-faceted beastie-ghost in all his shape-shifting sighing musculature. I heard Osho say, "All experiences are of the mind."

These days, if I would go into a house and find myself feeling terrible there, I would be able (I hope) to discern what was the house and its past, and what was me. And I would trust my body in its immediate desire to leave. And probably the discomfort would be the house, not me. But in San Francisco in 1972, that flat was fine – it was the accumulated sorrows of my twenty years that pressed on me; the unlived energies wanting space to howl and do backflips.

Shortly before I wrote this poem I'd had a nightmare about a spider made of some substance that was *so heavy* that the arachnid's very small body weighed as much as a whole planet. (I'd also dreamt of a little Japanese man who was dangerous too, so he appears in the poem.) There was a terrible, doom-laden feeling in this. The dream stuck with me, and when I went to India and began to meditate, it was as if the full weight of that spider had to unfurl and live and find its voice – in a thousand tears and expositions of sorrows; particularly those of my parents. Those pre-meditation dreams often contained symbols of great potency – and I am so very grateful that those energies have gotten to spread wide their arms and live in the open air. That is what transforms them; they become something else then – something delighted and graceful and freed; creative, innocent, optimistic; diluted hugely and inexorably by the sky.

My own experience: Osho's meditations *work* for this – because they are so lively and dynamic, and each contains silence too. And therapies are wonderful – and there are so many of them! Try them! In the beginning the pain being released can be crushingly tremendous – but then it *is* released, and the whole search becomes such fun; and, yes, each layer will feel grim as it confronts you – but the eagerness with which you approach it increases greatly. As Osho says, "Go on, go on."

Last night, now, in October 2015, I had a dream about an enormous, heavily moving, shining cobra draped up on the top of a bamboo screen between two row-houses in a terrace that managed to be both this Northern English town, and Poona. My friends were around. I wanted to flee the snake by going high into one of the buildings, taking with me a little girl who was nearby, so that she too could escape. I awoke frightened and oppressed-feeling, and it took minutes to calm down.

So just now I went into this dream, standing up and stepping into each symbol – the houses, the screen, the friends, the snake. And then the dream as a whole, asking the universe for its message.

And the meaning was: First, I had too many blankets on and thus felt heavy and oppressed! (Osho says most nightmares are caused by food, a similar sort of thing.)

Next, everything in the dream except the snake felt like the mundane trappings of everyday life, in all its blessedness and taken-for-grantedness. The little girl was my little-girl self.

The snake alone carried huge weight: he turns out to be realistic, grounded, earthy, visceral, *cold-hard-factitude*. He's masculine practicality – a thing I miss in my life, it is true! I used to be with such a man (practical, not reptilian! More bear-like – but in the dream the universe wanted to put that energy in reptilian terms, and who am I to argue?) And lord, have I missed the perfume of that particular male-armpit apocrine Newtonian reality! I've got so much fairy dragonfly butterflyhood myself, and that other thing quite escapes me much of the time. And the dream addressed some worrying I'd been doing before sleep, about upcoming loss of my dwelling, and not knowing where I was going to go. I was hoping, as I always hope, that something would come along to rescue me.

But my unconscious felt that on this occasion at least, this pie-in-the-sky-ness was out of balance, and sent the snake to pull me back into yin/yang groundedness.

When I look at my fear, it's that I might have to *do* something, to be

ld-eyed and calculating, and that thing called *realistic*.
uation, what would that be?

..., **2016**: Yes, it all happened like that: scary losing of home, uprootedness, wishing that snake's pragmatic roots would save me. Not saved yet... but gathering energy in the sun in Corfu for when I have to go back to England, to do battle (or not) with the Abyss.

And, 2021: Home is a Council flat all painted inside with clay paint with Tachyon Stardust in it, so that it is a healing box, and there are so many windows that all is light... My back window looks out on a green hillside, trees, no people. Bliss for two years now – though we are in Pandemic and urgent longings for going Elsewhere and Seeing People arise. But that Abyss had its time, and gave me a royal terror of homelessness. This might save me from rash unmoorings later.

To the Garden of Earthly Delights
(a funky bar-hotel on Potrero Hill)

    red bone
    junkie
    warpaint
    indian pain
    exile

    old whorehouse
    scene of my two orgasms
    the only ones
    since gentle France
    you called me out
    with ancestor wickedness
    pioneer city
    cheap love
    broken beer

works on floorboards,
dust and fingers,
quick body
slow black tongue.

I rose to you
shimmied in your slime
loved your
downhill
red victorian
warpaint corsetbone
women, men.

If I came out of the flat my mother had named the Missouri Compromise, on Missouri Street, and turned right; down one block, right again, and at the end of that block, on the left side of the street, I'd reach the bar called The Garden of Earthly Delights. There was good music, and I often went there to dance. Angry Vietnam veterans frequented it – many in wheelchairs. They roared and threw their beer glasses at the walls. Black folk went there, skinny white junkies went there. Ordinary hippies too, and even preppies out on the town. I went in my tight-flanked bell-bottoms and fur-collared, pinch-waisted jacket and platform shoes. I boogied over backwards till my hands could touch the seedy floor. In my dark mascara'd way, I showed off; but I was ecstatic in the funk, and my dance was true. I never drank anything but water. I just danced.

And twice I went upstairs with men: they were friends to each other, one white and one black; addicts. The black one was calm and kind, though distracted too because his wife was in hospital birthing an addicted baby. He was patient with my sexual shyness and, when I ultimately told him I was amazed and satisfied, he said in a deep drawl, "Ah'm glad Ah made yo' blood feel good."

The white youth was twitchy and excitable and no fun at all. I had to escape finally, his freaked-out, demanding shouts following me down the narrow stairs. I'd scared myself, going up there to those grubby, barely-furnished, spooky rooms – how low could I go? I rushed home in the dawn and wrote it all down in my diary.

What I've learned since: It's worth dancing anywhere, just about; maybe not precisely in a war zone (though if everybody in a war zone danced, including the soldiers, insurgents, rebels, what-have-you – the world would be the place we all truly long for it to be) but most other places. Supermarkets, sidewalks, your in-laws' parlor, strange bars, all are fine. There's no need to ingest any toxins to dance under either. Of course, if a place feels creepy, and you're not young enough to be forgiving, don't hang around.

Sex with weird strangers? Urgh. Then, it felt like pushing the walls back; a thing necessary as breathing. Now? Ack! It sounds like *germs* and *viruses* and *fungi* and *HIV* and other people's desolation being visited upon me. How *extremely* much more wonderful to cozy up in bed with myself alone, in clean flannel pajamas, on clean sheets, with a good book, my reading glasses, and a couple of hours during which most likely *nobody is going to bother me!* Teetering on stilty shoes up old wooden stairs to a dirty, bare apartment? *Quel horreur!* My current world has carpeted stairs, and warm, light, and clean interiors, and people in it who like meditation. I am so glad life has brought me this way, and let me only scratch 'n' sniff that other!

Writers speak of a time "between the wars" – 1918-1939, more or less. There was another "between the wars" – about 1964-1984 – after the Pill had been invented and antibiotics had become available for venereal diseases; and before HIV. In those twenty years, people could let loose and experiment wildly. And they did. And I did. And in a way I'm grateful – whatever idiocy I found it necessary to flail about in, I could do so without being killed by it or procreating. And by 'idiocy' I mean, *ignorant sex*: no guide, no help, no permission to trust my gift of instinct. No notion I could demand so much more than was being offered. No notion I could *wait in myself* instead of seizing so many poor wretched males in lieu of my father. No understanding of what really drives female orgasm and arousal. (Read *Vagina* by Naomi Wolf. Hints: Bonding. True relaxation. Feeling safe. Being given gifts! Being courted at a leisurely pace. Stroking. Compliments. Foreplay. Permission and space to go into cosmic, rather than just genital or even romantic, bliss-states.)

What I've learned since: Far across a vast sea from teetering San Francisco, a warm land of jungly leaves and plopping raindrops and hushy mornings where a stream of orange-robed meditators moved towards the lecture hall... was waiting in the near future. A place where one's freshly-showered body was all-of-a-flowing-piece beneath that loose robe; not bound or girdled anywhere. So that sitting and receiving amazing grace, happened all over. There was magic-land in the offing. I just didn't know it yet.

My Hermit Room

Seize the glow
The dying men with bitter lust for eyes
will try your back doors,
marching on cockroach hands and feet
with black hands and hair.
Seize the moment
where instinct runs like honey
under your tongue
Twirl beneath that clock
of stark anticipation –
lock your room.
That's what i want to do –

lock my room against the small dry voices –
What will they get from persuading me

this afternoon?
i am precious and sad.

I do believe this was written during the time – a period of about nine months – when I was acting in porno movies in San Francisco (and I do mean *acting*; no fun was had by all the bits and bobs of me). I still find it curious that I did not write about that time as I was living it – strange, and ominous – for I wrote about *everything*.

So I had to off-load the whole experience during that first celibate, shave-headed, wild wailing cathartic howling dynamic taking-responsibility-for-meeting-my-own-energies-face-to-face 24/7 meditation year in Poona.

The only time I'd ever seen any porn myself was in the flea market in Amsterdam, where there had been a stall with girly magazines on it, and one of them was open for the delectation of passersby. I was deeply shocked by it – not because it was porn – we all fancied ourselves liberated – but because the genitals on show looked to me so *animal* – furry! Red! Wild! And I'd thought, "*That's* what men like?" – with a kind of horror. For the only glimpse I'd ever had of my own was from above – a neat, chaste little V. I'd had *no idea* what was down there.

But when I finally experienced the industry myself it was not the least bit animal or wild.

Making those movies was icky, adventurous, well-paid (or so I thought at the time), boring, and silly. (What could be sillier than *acting* sexual excitement?) The men who directed and produced the films were as well-traveled sexually as the oldest, tiredest prostitute – like old tires with bald treads and a few weary leaks. They slept with new actresses as a matter of duty to their egos. Those men were greedy, kindly in a remote, exhausted way, careless and cynical. You could not really find the man in them, the soul, the Being, even. They were used-up, cloaked and covered.

But it was the 60's (the early 70's were still the 60's) and everything that hadn't been okay to do was okay now. We had antibiotics! We had birth control pills!

What we didn't have was awareness…

It is, I suppose, remotely possible that there are people who participate in those productions with delight and reward. I never saw this. The nearest I saw to such a phenomenon was a young woman who told me she'd had a convent education, and that her father had never allowed her to ride a bicycle. She seemed to have a very good time in the one film she made; if only physically. But for me, the satisfaction in that work was this: money (I could not discover how else to make any beyond minimum wage), variety: going to different areas of the city and its surrounds, different houses, meeting (sort of meeting) different people. And lastly, the

satisfaction of revenge: I was mad at sex, for I felt it had deserted and disappointed me, and so I thought I might as well make some money at it. (As I might have mentioned before, Osho says that pornography is ugly because women's genitalia are supposed to be in darkness, like the roots of a tree: roots should not be out in the light. It goes against nature.)
In this poem I'm crying out to find my inner nature – away from influences.

Rain Song San Francisco

It's raining, and all i want to do is rain.
My eyes have witch love,
and all i want to do
is shine them on your skin.

You are torn.
You are gone from me
back in zero time
You are spraddled in the black air
bleeding for my blood.

It will rain down into these rain streets
until January.
No wonder there are few flowers
and the soles of my feet
grow cushions of moss.
Do you feel moss?
Do you embrace the gasoline moss
of San Francisco?
My life is becoming a map

traced in tiny black footprints of pain.
The soles of my feet burst
with a red heart beating

cannot walk.
ant
ak to wanting,
climbing the slippery lichened reaches;
you are so far behind,
run,
climb the ugly grey arteries
to the chimneys. Stand on English tiles
and beckon me someplace.
i am so wavy, so undone,
i will see you in a drowned flash –.

Paul and I were writing to each other, with a plan, at first, that I would save up and go back to England and we'd live in the wild, cold Orkney Islands – he loved it up there. Somebody had given me Bob Dylan's telephone credit card number, and it worked, and I'd phone Paul weekly from the box on the corner and we'd talk for ages. The plan then changed – and poor Paul cashed in his life insurance to fly to me instead. The week before he arrived I went with Mama to a dream workshop in the Berkeley hills and met Herb, a tall, stocky, wealthy professor (Computer Engineering, Berkeley) and businessman. We started a relationship, which was delightful – Herb was a joyous character, and treated me with fond, affirmative appreciation. We were to stay together until July 1974, when I went off to India for good – and we'd remain friends after that too.
But during the first happy, horizon-broadening time with Herb, I didn't have the courage to tell Paul that I was falling in love with someone else! Oh god…
When Paul came through the Arrivals gate with his shoulder-length ring of grey hair newly shorn for Immigration, with his eager, toed-out walk, smiling his sheepish, full-lipped smile – I knew it was over. I'd gone off him. There was nothing I could do about it – I'd fallen out of love, and that was that.
There followed a few weeks of hell during which I went out on dates with Herb and often slept at Herb's place, whilst Paul had my tomato-soup-colored room at home, and spent his days drinking tea and talking with my commiserating mother. One morning I came home to find my room trashed – I had hung thrift-store hats

upside down from chains and filled them with soil and plants; these were all dumped out on top of my cut-up clothes, in a heap in the middle of the floor.

I didn't blame him. It certainly made sense.

I had also had sex with him – he patiently doing that-thing-that-worked, and which nice big Herb never got around to doing. We did this during my first attack of a-thing-I-did-not-understand, that was itching and burning like crazy Down There: the herpes I'd gotten from a teenage girl during the reluctant making of a porno movie I had tried very hard to get out of. The director, Jerry Abrams, was a toad-like smirking spreading sort of fellow who paid little and extracted much. He just pressed and pressed on me to come down and do the film – and I finally caved in. I was paid $35 to get herpes that afternoon. (The young girl, when I questioned the sore on her vulva, said, "Oh, it's nothing, it's not contagious!") And under the operating-theater lights I did to her what Paul did to me... Argh, argh... while director and cameraman, who must have known what that sore was all about, kept smugly mum.

The gay doctor at the free clinic gave me zinc oxide ointment to alleviate some of the discomfort, and simply said I'd have the virus forever. He must have told me I could pass it on – must have! But Paul knew I had it, and was also ignorant of its true awfulness. He got it first in his throat, then on his penis, and he suffered hideously with it thereafter. My own first attack lasted weeks, and was very painful – but after that it went underground and I forgot all about it, until five years later, when I had hepatitis A in India and it returned. Thereafter to haunt me.

Jerry Abrams the toad-weasel, by the way, once pressured and pressured me to push a huge black dildo up my bottom, under those bright lights. I refused, he insisted, I finally gave in, it hurt like hell, it was a horrible thing to do, to experience – *so much pain* – and afterwards I got an infection and the whole poor orifice swelled up and wept. The very word dildo makes me wince. There seems, down the ages, to be a very common species of beast which realizes the clueless un-self-worthiness of young girls, and slinks about getting them to do things they would never have dreamed of on their own, and do not actually want to do at all.

I stopped doing those movies when I'd been with Herb for a little while. He didn't want to be associated with such things. My income, of course, took a very steep dive, about which I felt indignant. Herb gave me odd jobs, like staining his deck, at which I did not excel; and the pay was as mediocre as my skills.

Paul: I gave him $200 from my ill-gotten gains and he set off to visit acquaintances in Missoula. He sent me angry letters for many years. He and my mother had a more amicable correspondence during all that time as well. I did see him once more: in 1987 I took a coach from London to Durham – a very pleasant journey, after the epic discomfort of Indian buses – and visited him in his spare, tidy little ex-miner's cottage. What was shocking for me was that he thought we might resume being lovers then!

It was with Herb, by the way – a lucky, golden man, very straight, who enjoyed the novelty of partaking of youthful counterculture-type things with me – that I had my last glimpse of David. We were at a Pointer Sisters concert, and there, a few rows away, was David Gancher, big as life. He saw me – but no words were exchanged. We had written to each other for a while, and when I'd told him how my sister and I had gotten into *The Primal Scream* by Arthur Janov, and had even been practicing screaming (my sister had passed through England on her way East) he had retorted, "Neurosis is cured by *willpower*, not by *slobbering caveman junk!*"

What I've learned since: Slobbering caveman junk is incredibly helpful for coming out of neurosis! Willpower is only helpful to *get you to* the meditations and therapies where the slobbering caveman junk can take over.

And: *Don't let people push you around!*

And: Distant love is just fine. We're not in control here – if somebody is far away, love them happily anyway, and don't bother life too much about it.

And in all that longing the young feel – poetry grows like moss. So what is the problem?

In Late Afternoon

in late afternoon
when the urgencies
draw back

i lie vivisected
on my bed
in the purity
of my mother's poetry,
its realized courage;

and i am glad
that i am letting
these thready magnets
draw me to paper again.

My mother wrote wonderful poetry. There is a YouTube vid of her, aged ninety-three, reading a string of them aloud. People who see it are amazed – the effect is dark and beautiful and stark and strong. What always impressed me was that she wrote for herself alone, never tried to publish her poetry – just her short stories were published. I suspect she didn't publish the poetry because it was so private – a thing that's never stopped me with my own, for in that way she and I were different.

She scribbled in notebooks, on backs of envelopes, bits of paper; and then pushed those into boxes or manila envelopes along with bills, old receipts, e-mail printouts, photos, junk mail, and other miscellany. I once asked her to will the poetry to me… it was all I wanted of what she might leave behind. As I remember, she gave a cryptic nod in response (she did not intend to leave, I think). When the time came, I wasn't able to get my hands on it.

My opinion: It is good to save the handwritten versions, even after the poem has been typed (I've not been terribly good about this as I love to throw things away. Just as Not Knowing is the Most Intimate, Throwing Away is the Wealthiest. Such a delicious feeling!) But yes, especially the early stuff I have kept. My mother's printing was lyrically curved and clear, and adds richly, in my eyes, to the value of the poems.

For Glen

father
body, old mule
my lit porch
shadows marble
onto funky street
waiting for men
my breasts are lit   tipped
drunken hills

my struggle
from you, from you

greybeard
weary hanged man
desertsand scraped
wind shoved

you away from me

you never saw me
did you
oh Papa
what use to rail
against your stomach
train to earth,
screech
to boughten placidity
of a thousand
stillbreathed desert years

My father read my first book, *Impassioned Cows by Moonlight*, published when I was twenty-one. This poem was in it. The expression on his face when I met him afterwards... said everything. A complex mixture of hurt, exposure, astonishment, horror, generation gap. Most of all, a muffled shutting-down of words. He said nothing – but all the pity I'd ever felt for him – and this was, and is, considerable and terrible – came flooding through me. I am supposing that in his world a person *just doesn't publish things like this*. I'm guessing he felt cataclysmically martyred by his duty-bound decades of providing for a family. I'm guessing he loved me, could not show it, and was shocked by the view of him I had; what, in other words, he got from me in return. I think he felt betrayed.

What I've learned since: My love for him is actually uncomplicated – pure, tender, fervent, and deep. And his love for me is the same – though he has been dead these many years.

What I've learned since: My brother recently told me that Glen held me on his lap when I was very small and read aloud to me from *The Scientific American!* So I was only partly ignored. (Though whenever I think of that, I wonder if he was trying to make me into a scientist already. Sorry, Glen!)

The Night Makes Bones

The night makes bones around my face.
Who is my intended,
my intended life?
The night makes blue bones.

When i was that boat
down in the harbor
of blue night
i had no power.

i have no power now.

When i was that boat
i was blue lines in a harbor.
The weight
of a squared shoulder   hurrying
on a wet street.
The power
of a heavy rodent
in a night cage.

i have no power now.

This poem is mysterious to me. I was surprised when I came across it in a box of old writing in my mother's attic. I took it with me on my travels then, like one might keep a little china frog or other talisman. I did not remember writing it, but I love its chant and channeled brevity. Our flat was near a district of factories and warehouses. I could see a night view of the Bay, with lights on ships, bridges, roads.

What I've learned since: In Human Design terms, I have a Profoundly Open Ego center – so it's not for me to be political, power-tripping, competitive, willful, pushy, aggressive; it's for me to become *wise* about these things. Therefore I can't take my place in the world as a contender. I have a different sort of power – of my own truth, my intuition. This is 'soft' power: it doesn't use muscle, but just some true-spoken words (or deftly just getting out of there, if I feel threatened. I like this idea but have often not managed it). The result is that I find power, as demonstrated by many people, amazing, shocking, daunting. I kind of want some and kind of don't. And in many situations the power of a true 'no' should be enough – but even that I often find *difficult*.
In this world, this slack wiring is a challenge.
I spent much of my life fighting all this, and trying to have Will. Running daily, forcing myself not to eat, meditating 8 hours a day – until I could finally no longer disengage from Will, and everywhere I went inside myself it was there, getting in the way – in

lovemaking, in meditation, even in illness, so that I shuffled real or imagined symptoms around inside myself like pieces in a board game, trying to dodge them, unable to let go the spurious control my imagination had over my body.

The day I climbed through the minuscule hole between two beats of Being and found my beyond-will surrender (Island of Mull, 2009, Cranio-Sacral retreat), was a wonderful day. Since then, I do my best to value and embrace the scary moments of giving up, of let-go; even when they make my arms vanish, my stomach fall like an elevator.

And anyway, who is this "I" who would have some sort of power?

To *what* does power belong? If it comes *through* me, as it does in Dynamic, or acting in a skit, or walking long and fast up and down hills with a friend – then it is not mine.

I have tasted an unutterable bliss in being at the mercy of everything… when I was homeless and one night, in my helplessness, felt a loving presence nearby, kissing my belly – and when I had brain surgery, and under the anaesthetic was helpless to the utmost – yet something in me reveled in this absolute beyond-the-power-of-my-hands situation. I saw it later in an inner picture: my spirit was like a clear stream running over smooth stones – joyful, so joyful, to have no control at all over whatever was going to happen.

And still another time, a few years ago, when I was in a distant country participating in a group I didn't like at all and could not reconcile myself to – as the charismatic leader hectored me to be different than I was, so that I was then full of anguished doubts about my own direction. And then in the night, alone in my little rented flat, I was woken by a sound, the sort of sound the spirit makes when it wants to get your attention – and was shown, for some bliss-buoyed hours, a vision of my life as a wide river, going on its path, a single hawk hanging in the air above it, off-center; and the river was so strong and so silent and so much its own thing… going towards death, inevitably but beautifully. And the very idea of controlling any of that was just… impossible, absurd. It was going where it was going; and in majestic beauty and silent, untouched, stately grace. No world there at all.

This is now my favorite thing, really – as D. H. Lawrence said in a poem, "Not I, but the wind."
I have no power now.

The Parent Experience

was mine too
blood in bed
thirst in the morning

the parents rose late
and snored before rising
from tall noses
and less married were the parents
than the beetles in the wall
and more married was I
to the soft god in the backyard
the mystery of shut blood nights
the guilt of priests
than were the parents married
to their consummations

and now
there is this to tell
I am restored
the backyard visits my hands
I cup immense places
in warm fingers

Agh... my parents' bed. A messy, tousled room, never cleaned (ever); the walls unfinished so that the struts showed. My mother's menstrual blood had inevitably leaked into the tousled, dirty bedding and the mattress, and was there for all to see. The room smelt of my father's old smoke, and of bodies, and general fug. We kids found it daunting and yet comforting – for the parents were *always there*.

When I think of this bed is when I can really understand my mother's despair most clearly: she was obliged by iron convention to sleep in the same bed with this other, all night every night; obliged to inhale his un-lived emotions, to pile them onto her own rampant and considerable ones. Obliged to breathe his smoke, and smell it coming off his body. Obliged to sleep in their same old clothes, for they had no nighties or pajamas. Helpless to acquire new bedding – there was no budget for it, ever, not once. And had there been any money, she would have bought blankets for the kids first.

She did make choices on how to allocate her available energy in the circumstances. She decided to read aloud to her children, and to hole up in that messy room and read and write alone, quite often. She decided to feed us, angrily or sometimes cheerfully, and do the laundry, sort of. She decided not to make us work around the house. She decided not to clean any more. She decided to scream at our father a lot, but not in such a way that any change occurred in our lives. And not to scream at us, though nag and chide and order us about, certainly.

My father hid his own unhappinesses in smoke and his beloved equations, and his hope that his Invention would make good. But it can't have been wonderful for him to have a raging wife who more and more as the years went by hissed nasty epithets at him and scorned his Southwest accent and his ways. Who didn't care about his Science and his Logic, and so wasn't especially supportive of what *he* loved best.

What I eventually heard from my oldest brother was that my mother was more interested in lovemaking than my father was, Mama said that Glen made love in his same old clothes; and that, when she cried after, he was angry and distressed. My mother was a spiritual wild-woman, and sex to her was Spirit through and through; my father didn't get this, and thought something was wrong with her. She too needed to create Beauty – not just children. She needed to have nice bedding, and an altar she could put pebbles and wildflowers on, next to her Kwan Yin statue, without some child destroying it.

But this is *their* pain I'm speaking of here, not mine.

As I've mentioned before, my understanding, from looking deep

into many hundreds of people, is that one thing prevents us from happiness: the recognition that our parents are as helpless and clueless as children; and the unconscious notion that if *we* are happy, we will be abandoning them on the roadside in the dust, thirsty and alone, to perish. We cannot bear this, for we love them; so we feel that the best way to keep them company is to squat down beside them and be as unhappy as they are. In this way they are not abandoned.
It takes enormous courage and awareness to stare this unconscious mandate in the face and not give in to it.

When Mama was in her seventies she and her next husband began buying old houses and, with Mexican labor, for she was fluent in Spanish, fixing them up and selling them. They did well, and could finally get a nice house for themselves, near the sea in Oregon; it was kept reasonably clean, and had a very pleasant atmosphere.

What I've learned since: Thank god for Human Design. it shows me my own way, my own difference. The ways I am not like my parents. This also gives me courage to have a life that is my own; not just a rote and faithful carrying of their old frustrations and sorrows.

the shoes

they gleam
snakes in twilight
turquoise amazons

selfish
cheek to cheek
they lean and shine

two sides
of one jungle woman

oiled as a monkey
self-adulating
magnificent
hissing
and slick

blue tongue silk
to your hard branch
cobrabelly
jungle decadent
from heated trees

Quite soon after Herb and I had met, I had cautiously taken $200 from my savings and gone down to Union Square. I had my thick, shapeless hair cut into a wavy shag, which suited my features well. Then I went shopping at a big department store and emerged with two pairs of softest narrow-wale corduroy trousers with wide legs, a coordinating sweater and two tops, plus a velvet jacket and a pair of platform boots.
That night I surprised Herb with my new look. He was delighted,

The all-woman theatre group I was in, invading the topless-dancing Carol Doda Condor Club

Herb at the Russian River

because, he said, it showed that I was flexible. And so I had veered away from the hippie, raggy look (though whenever I could I still shopped at thrift stores).

We were in Sausalito (a wealthy seaside village just North of San Francisco) on my 21st birthday. He offered to buy me a gift – whatever I might find in the boutiques thereabouts. In a window I saw a pair of astonishing shoes: bright turquoise, real cobra-skin, with high wedge heels, platforms, and a rhinestone buckle. They were very expensive. I wanted them! Herb bought them for me, though he was bemused by my choice! They were far and away the most luxurious, frivolous thing I had ever owned, or would own for a long time to come. They were so outrageous, in fact, that they demanded a poem in their honor. (I remember wearing them out to dinner once with a pair of dark brown velvet knickerbockers and a harmonizing lace blouse with a peplum and fishnet tights. And, no doubt, a turquoise ring, since I had a few. Wow!)

What I've learned since: What I already knew: we creative humans love to decorate our persons, just for the joy of it, as we decorate anything. And shoes... ah, shoes. Skyscrapers to view from! Polished vehicles! Swaying platforms from which to advertise our breasts and rumps! Borrowed power! Endless tweaking of outfits is supplied by a change of shoes! They can make or break a line, a harmony, a symphony of garments: present it loftily or neatly, or squash it flat as a Goodwill sneaker. And shoes can be humorous, and why shouldn't they? I love seeing a man in day-glo chartreuse trainers – lively!

It seems to me women love shoes and handbags because they are yin – like vaginas and wombs – and men love fast cars, rocket ships, and motorbikes because they are yang – and resemble themselves.

What I've learned since: The recklessness the 60's brought to fashion has never died. And thank god for that! We're all free to experiment.

Once I sat in front of Osho and told him I loved clothes, loved to be beautiful, and was worried this might not be spiritual? He

looked at me and replied, "Mmmm, Madhuri? Be beautiful! To be ugly is a violence to people."
Amen.

And, recently I read Veena's matchless *A Seam for the Master*, in which she describes making Osho's robes. He himself loved fabric and design and spent happy times choosing gorgeous fabrics!

About thirty-six years after the above shoe-buying day, I had lunch with Herb at an Italian restaurant in Mill Valley. He was still handsome and magnetic, tall, hulky and craggy, with a prognathous jaw; and he admired me, too, and we had a nice meal together. Then he said he wanted to buy me something… but I had to catch a plane, so he gave me some cash, and I thanked him and kissed his big warm cheek. And I flew to Texas, and in Galveston went shopping with Taffy, Karen and Mary Beth, and bought some shiny faux-snake turquoise Dr. Scholl's sandals. And thought of Herb. (The fact that I got food poisoning from the baby shrimp risotto I had at the restaurant is neither here nor there. What I learned from *that* was, don't eat shrimp in restaurants. Poor innocent evil farmed things!)

And later: Oh Herb. He died in April 2021 at his home in Berkeley, the same place we'd spent so many happy nights and weekends. He'd had dementia for two years, and had had very good care. I'm so glad we had lunch that day – for I never saw him again, though we did speak on the phone. Goodbye, dear man! You're flying again! (He'd had a pilot's license for many years.)

Crazy Rose

Sometimes i think i am a crazy rose
flying and tumbling
flapping my fine elbows.
When i smile into somebody's eyes
i am so afraid
of the teeth i might fly into
or the eyes i might not meet.

What I've learned since: It is very, very helpful to immerse oneself in therapy or meditation or dance groups, all sorts of groups congenial to one's interests. The sort of groups where the leader guides you gently to look into someone's eyes. So that then you are not responsible, in the beginning, for the initiating of this scary activity – someone else holds the door for you, watches the clock. And you gaze into the boundless realm. You are given back time and timelessness both – and the opportunity to fall into the mystery of another – and thus yourself.

If the spirit moves you, go to Poona, or Esalen, or Osho Leela, or Osho Miasto, or Osho Risk, or to whatever group you can find on the internet, or that a friend has recommended, that invites you into Tantra, Path of Love, art and meditation, emotional release, Awareness Intensive, Mystic Rose, women's empowerment, men's empowerment, Natsukashi the Original Face, or anything else you like (a group on restoring vintage cars might not help a lot with eye contact, but wouldn't hurt as an extra, if that's what you love). Once you get over any embarrassment, you'll have a wonderful, revelatory time; and feel like this is what life's all about!

I love a very special Japanese healer called Kohrogi-san, and when he leads a Natsukashi seminar, there is a thing he does: one by one, each participant lies down on a pallet before him, and he sits and gazes into the person's eyes. Whatever happens to you under that gaze, happens – for me it's different every time, but every time there is a sense of falling deeper and deeper, layer by layer, back inside myself, until I come to some amazing place – perhaps silent, perhaps laughing, who knows – and then Kohrogi closes his eyes, and that is the signal that it is complete. The person then gets up and crawls/staggers away, utterly zonked into the sky or the deep earth or sea – and probably has to lie down for a while, in the back of the room, to recover from all that gotten-to bliss.

I love it that one of his chiefest techniques, then, is so un-Japanese – for in that country eye contact is avoided.

During this long lockdown I once asked him, via email, if we could do this on Zoom. And, sitting facing each other across miles and oceans, we did. Just a few minutes – no words spoken – he looked into my eyes. Then, when I'd fallen into the hole behind the rainbow, he closed his eyes.

*pictures of the deity
the moon-faces*

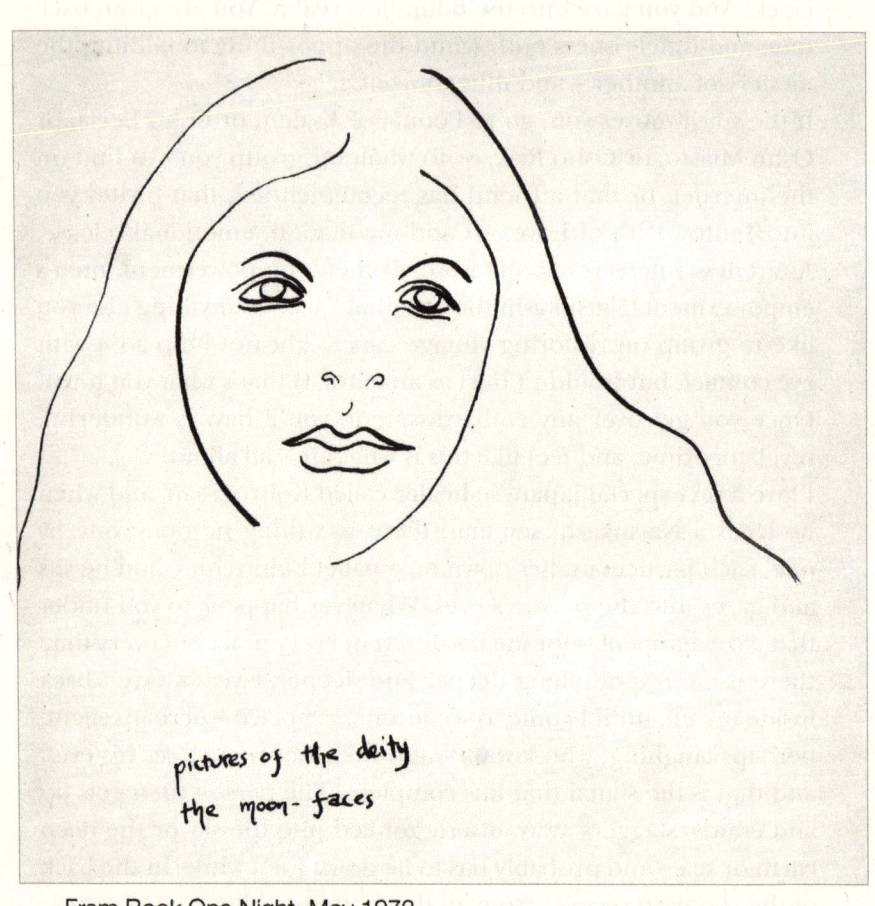

From Book One Night, May 1973

And I went to my bed and lay there all silent inside for a long time. It was a wonderful gift to myself.

Moon-Faces

What do you feel of her lips
when in the night she pretends she is a witch
and you are witches' food?

Would you flee across Canada with her
laughing on black roads
Afraid of mountain lions
Bedding in small cabins
where she brings you a black rose
and you, new from prison
put your tongue in all its petals
in worship of night
And she softens you the way the moon does
exactly that way –
But she is so near
Your tears would fall on her
if joyous tears came from you
in your paradox
and your pardon

Nobody ever told you
any different
...you only thought they did

Would you follow her
sipping from the night she has stored for you
Surrender
to the soft intelligence of stars
And when her moon
comes around again

you flee across canada with her
  on black roads
  of mountain lions
  in small cabins
  she brings you a black rose
  new from prison
  your tongue in all its petals
  black worship of night
  he softens you the way the moon does
  ly that way
  she is so near
  tears would fall on her
  joyous tears came from you
  our paradox
  pardon

and she cries out
Let her go to the other side of the earth
without you

The lips hung sideways over the earth
like a primitive moon
And there were reeds in a pond we have not seen yet
where frogs croak like magicians
and fireflies mate
and we would hide there,
and we do

You have never seen her asleep before.
She is satiated, she wants to dream.
You have never seen a beautiful black
planet asleep. You were so watchful.
You are still thirsty, you see that you
will always be thirsty –
The window is like a glass of water.
You become glad you are not younger.
You are alone.
The moon sleeps on your pillow.

One night, in that flat in San Francisco, in May 1973, I sat down, did some pen-and-ink drawings, wrote this, and then bound it all in colored construction paper. I called it *Book One Night.*
I am rather astonished at this poem, for it took me many many years to stop Doing, chasing, and running after men. Yet this poem is female all the way through.

What I've learned since: Once, in Poona, I did a meditation for twenty-one days: being a man. I told nobody, just went into the persona of a particular German weight-lifter I wanted, who didn't want me; and stayed there. I rode my bicycle like it was a motorbike. I made a tattoo on my arm with a ballpoint pen. I walked like a panther. I lifted weights. My period didn't come. It was wonderful. Simple. I enjoyed it all so much. But after twenty-one days I was lying on the floor in Buddha Hall listening to Osho's voice, and I noticed

lips hung sideways over the earth
like a primitive moon
and there were reeds in a pond we have not seen yet
where frogs croak like magicians   and fireflies mate   and we could hide there,
and we do

that I did not *melt*. I did not give up, surrender, float. So I decided I must be in a woman's body for a reason; and I came back to mine.

What I've learned since: It is lovely to be pursued, spoilt, honored by a man. But even to feel this I had first to learn to let go of chasing. I was terrified no man would see me, want me. How many years I wasted chasing them, driving them away! Some would have come for me, if only I'd given them a chance. Maybe some right ones. Maybe.

Month Nightmare

The secret places of me
i love to have them fill with blood
red dawn to darkness
the primitive
to his mother's own sweet wine

take time, take time.

Oh no
shrieks the sun princess
for her dreams are upon her
take them away,
take them away
put them down in the cellar
where they belong

But madam
the cellar is filled with blood
even the gopher holes are ruined
you grow small and large before my eyes

Periods *are* surreal; we go into a space outside the workaday world. Such a strange business, too, to bleed each month; each girl has to

what do you feel of the lips
the lips of her
when in the night she pretends she is a witch
and you are witches food

by Katy Akin

encounter the almost sci-fi oddness of this. And then, something is calling from inside... some atavistic process of death, cleansing, renewal. If we ignore this and get on with life, we're missing something very valuable – an *ingoing* time. A down-deep time.

What I've learned since: One day they go away forever, those demanding, inconvenient, messy periods. They take their horniness, their misanthropy, their irritation, their cramps, their bloody cotton and their ripe, metallic, stuffy smell – and they pack up and leave. And, after a time of somewhat-grueling readjustment, a new life begins – freer, calmer, more independent, more steadily, strongly creative, more altruistic, more benign. (Did I say *radically* freer?)

And so, I would advise each woman, however her cycle takes her (for we're all different) to make the most of it while it lasts. Go sexually *wild* if that's how it affects you! Be profoundly a hermit if that's how you feel! (I used to go from the former to the latter in the space of a minute once the bleeding actually began.) Howl the house down – and then hole up and refuse all visitors! Unplug (or turn off) the phone! Take a shower, put on your period panties, grab a blindfold, and go to bed!

I've read that over the course of a month, a woman has a taste for two different sorts of men: a wild, bad one at ovulation, and a steady, husbandy sort the rest of the time. Life isn't very interested in our moralities. It also doesn't care that idiotic male bossy sorts have seen women's periods as somehow 'unclean' (what does *he* know about it?) Life dishes them out anyway. (And I feel happy for a woman who gets a monthly holiday from that sort of guy.) Nature *likes* all that messy stuff.

Towards the latter part of my menstruating years I stopped using tampons and went to pads. Mildly more gruesome, but I felt I could breathe better – bleed freer – not plugging myself up. Tampons seemed sometimes to be too rough in there.

I support each woman having her period ritual – doing exactly what feels good to her for that time. The world can do without you for a couple of days. If you have kids, hire help. If you can't afford that, why have kids?

…Or trade childcare with another mom, turn and turn about (not that I know anything about this!) Or let Dad do it. (A Slovakian husband is the best bet for this, I've read; a Danish one next-best; an Indian the worst.) Or, if you're very lucky, there's Granny and Grandpa, and the other Granny and Grandpa, and maybe some aunties and uncles too (though maybe beware some of the uncles).

Book, Book

Book, book
when you are not with me
i sing for you

Dieseled with coffee
as futile as ever a poet
was
Weeping into the clouds
where the sun casts energy
like a net

And it is every day
i ever sang from the throat of

And singing is seldom,
usually
i am a thorough dog
scouring the ground for bones

Oh, I love this! It's just so true of me then; writing was what pulled me through. Inside me a desperation was brewing, though in my quest for wonderful eating experiences (Herb took me out to fancy restaurants, and I'd starve myself all day beforehand) I'd push it aside. But I never stopped writing in a current diary, generally cloth-covered by me, perhaps embroidered too. This poem probably referred to a gap of days.

In December of that same year I flew with my mother to Bombay, to meet my sister again and to meet Osho for the first time. The world split open then, with a *crack* much louder than anything I'd ever heard; and life began.

What I've learned since: These moments, when you suddenly see how futile are your daily scribblings, are beautiful and precious. Celebrate then well… a pen and paper will do, or a dance.

The Dwarf Talks

I am in my center.
The picket fence rises around me.
This little dwarf comes in and
sits on my lap.
He bites my neck and says

*Listen, helpless breast-one.
Mount Rubidoux
in afternoon sun
is your home
The still fullness here
Your body grows strange.
There are the peaceful towers
and inside, shit and graffiti.
Creased road curving down the mountain
to the riverbottom*

the sage, the rock you sit on.

*The mountain is your cocoon,
pupa! And inside is where
you crouch
folded and immense*

School portrait, age seven

*Where you lure your brothers
and count their bones*

*Look
the airplane
vanishing in haze over Rubidoux*

*Look
your dwarf birth
shattering and shaking
the stones
and fists of old mud
down onto Riverside*

*Onto the schoolyards
Onto teachers   like the hands of violent lovers
the children never see
Onto the lab where your father
does scuba agriculture
in huge tanks of formaldehyde
twining lazy ivy
in ambiotic languor
for all those hours
every day*

Riverside, flat and semi-desert, was surrounded by distant mountains. Closer in, there were the Box Springs mountains behind the University – high, completely dry hills, really – and, across the city, Mt. Rubidoux. There were rich houses at that end of town, as the land rose – and gardens surrounded them, lush with California abundance – olive, loquat, lemon, orange, apple, plum; pyracantha and avocado and pomegranate and cypress and trumpet vine and wisteria and magnolia. Then, at some distance from all that but still in the lee of the mountain, there was an isolated stucco house, two stories, stout, square, with a tall set of concrete steps up to the entrance. This sturdy building was surrounded by fenced-off plots of garden in which agricultural experiments were being done. For this was an outpost of the U.S. Dept. of Agriculture, and here my father toiled, day in and day out, year in and year out, for nearly all his working career.

He was famous among his colleagues for being able to solve any scientific problem; he was dedicated, thorough – yet operating so far below his capacity that it was a terrible frustration for him. He *lived* in scientific methodology – scrubbed beakers, chemical pongs, drying racks, cleanliness and order; yet at home all was disorder, chaos and dirt. He tried to create orderly labs on home territory over the years – a front bedroom, a converted garage – but these never really took. He would devotedly do fruit-fly experiments, and cache colorful bottled chemicals, and teach us about them; but his great scientific creativity went mostly into his equations and the Invention which consumed his life for so long.

Sometimes on a Saturday we'd hike all the way to his lab, miles and miles in the heat, for we had no car yet – and climb those stairs to get inside the cool, thick-walled building, and pull out from the dispenser the fabulous, ice-cold manna of a Nehi orange soda-pop in a curvy thick-glass bottle. Oh, the fizz, the *orangeness* taste, the icy cold! Heaven!

Mt. Rubidoux itself was dry, eroded with gullies. Some eccentric rich man had caused a tower to be built up on its flanks – the same man who'd built the Spanish-style Mission Inn, a grandiose landmark in the middle of town, as well as some rich houses here and there. The tower could be climbed inside via steps. Of course teenagers did awful things in there – how could they not? So it was a sort of smelly privy-folly.

What I've learned since: The deserts of childhood are our playing fields for the inner work. There is a way to see things, feel them wholly – avoiding nothing that you see – and then letting them stay or go as they please. If wholly seen, they go – but you can't be ambitious for that, or the energy diverted into ambition puts the brakes on the going.

I wanted to say in this poem that despite all my escapes – to Europe, particularly, and to San Francisco – there was no use pretending I was not still in ghastly old Riverside. One is *always* still in ghastly old Riverside, as long as one is afraid of it.

And yet... even Riverside is an imposed landscape; it was visited upon me at birth; I did not originate there, in my essence, my being. If my essence was of it, I would never have longed to leave.

And so one can sit anywhere, and go Inside, and face the various landscapes that arise; and every one is as temporary as any other. And every one lifts off when seen – though there are magical landscapes that one may or may not have actually been in, which carry an inner Truth, an echo of a place or quality within; and those deepen with our regard.

The childhood landscape is the stickiest, for the architecture of our identification is built here, containing, most of all, atmospheres the parents carried. So these scenes go the deepest. And past life pictures can underlie even these. All to be watched, tasted, drowned into; yet rigorously observed. For one is not there, but Here. Now.

Dusk Like a Flower

Dusk begins, huge & wide & sweet as a flower.
Sun behind clouds that have sped all day between buildings,
huge as brave cobras with turquoise eyes
...is seized with a last burning heartfelt shine
Red & pink & deepening in-the-curl-of-the-ear blue;
dark seizing buildings, final earth-surrender

Dusk spans softly out, like rolling ink-presses,
gentle as mouths chanting, chanting
Construction pipes glow while dusk deepens to shining
Superman, insect, inside-the-closing-fist blue
Weeds, luminously clean as cornflakes –

Clouds slide back, turning, parting, sun-eyed –
i'm lost among buildings, careless as flowers,
run over by evening like airy dreaming trains –

My mother and me, Potrero Hill, early 1973

Is there ever a time when our consciousness cannot perceive the beauty of our earth, our skies, our Outer Space? This impossible gift we've been given by some sleight of magic? Does death get in the way of this perception? Is consciousness itself beauty?
I don't know... but for this poem,

Have I learned something since? is not relevant.

Lucid Dream

you have to listen
way down there
green meteor
in the wake of a folded cloud.

bring something back with you.
you know the grey cruel forces?
I want to wear them under my fingernails
like bruises.

My mother used to read pop-psych books and then wax very enthusiastic about each of them. She was very interested in Lucid Dreaming. So I watched it too: that space before sleep, or on just awaking; a place you can also go to on purpose, by relaxing and staying alert at the same time. Pictures from the unconscious drift by, and might help you.
"You have to listen / Way down there..." Just two days ago I spent not quite three hours in-swimming – way down in, where the humming field vibrates, comprising all of me – and I can be a still observer of the lush material that rises, is apprehended by my gaze, is felt clearly, and then makes its own exit, its life and purpose done. I call this "Self-Healing."
"You know the grey cruel forces?" Yes, they rise too – and are seen for what they are – some child-sorrow, primate-wiring, hopeful/

My sister mock-fighting in Turkey, on her way overland to India, late 1972

hopeless little assumption of 'how things are', gifted me by others, long ago – and they rise too, and are gone. I need not "wear them under my fingernails / like bruises." That was before I learnt meditation.

What I've learned since: The endless riches of our lives in this universe confer the privilege of being and participating in the Material. The fact that there is a watcher to this confers Consciousness. The former is to be embraced with wonder. The latter is the key to this.

Perhaps matter and consciousness are not separate. I've heard that Material arises from Consciousness (scientists are still trying unsuccessfully to prove the opposite).

I love the sense of freedom in this view of things.

Letter from my sister, 1973. Destiny calling!

Entering India

Flying into the specter
of my own mystery
Moon, old woman on the wing

Below, pools of silver
flash tropical,
go black.

Nobody out there.
Sadness, and sadness
too whored a word
for the piano keys
it plays

There was old Mrs. Swain
lived down at the corner
in a yellow frame house
with stiff doeskin dresses
with noose-small, beaded necks
hanging on the wall, from a long-ago job
at the reservation.

And with the ghost of her husband
in stiff bib overalls
who'd died on the toilet.
To us she was television
and two circles of red
on wrinkled cheeks.
Mrs. Swain can I have some candy?
Can I have a bowl of money?
Can I have a bowl of god?

i was born
asking for candy
and for a long time
i will ask, and ask

till i am dead of asking,
till i am dead of asking,
and awake.

My little sister had hitchhiked across Asia to India, and there had met Osho, a luminous mystic. She immediately summoned Mama and me. Nine months after receiving the first aerogram, we were in the air... (What happened next is recounted in *Mistakes on the Path*.)
I well remember writing this in my diary, sitting on the plane as we came down over India. It was night; lights below were curiously weak, yellowy, blurred. It was December 9, 1973, and I really was poised on the very brink of a new world, a new life – one in which I would live far more intensely than ever before.
For some reason a scene from childhood came back to me then – the old lady with circles of rouge on her cheeks who let us come and watch her black-and-white TV – the only TV we saw, allowed by our mother in ten-minute doses only: "It'll rot your brain!"
Mrs. Swain and her husband had worked on an Indian reservation

Me in San Francisco, early 1973. I don't remember who the guy was

when they were younger, and beaded dresses with strangely tiny neck-openings hung on her wall.

What I've learned since: Yes, Desire has been an enormous theme for me. We kids could not have most of the things we passionately wanted. We wore hand-me-downs, were given toys only at Christmas and birthdays. There was candy on payday only, or if we could collect enough soda-pop bottles out of the bushes around town to redeem for nickels to buy candy bars.

For some reason the advent of meditation in my life brought desires into sharp relief. I craved childhood foods and candy, wrote endless aerograms to our mother (who was then back in San Francisco) with lists of what I wanted her to send: undies, chocolate, ballpoint pens, Fritos, etc etc (almost all of which didn't get sent, and if it had, would have been extracted in Customs). Later I desired Men with that same horrible passion. And clothes. And shoes. Osho said to me, in January 1974, "All desires are innocent."

Things soften, drop away. I can now shop with a budget and keep to it, more or less. Desire is energy; life singing to life. It's not a problem.

In my Human Design, Desire is something I'm here to become wise about. I've done my best: meditating on it for twenty-four days once, in Missouri, when I really wanted to leave and had no graceful way to, and was determined to wait to be invited someplace. All I could do then was turn around and *face* the passionate longing to be elsewhere. Dance it, observe it, throw my arms up into the air and howl it, allow and celebrate it.

And then the invitation did come, and I moved to England.

I've discovered that when I desire something, things can stand in for other things: fruit stands in for sugar. Remodeling a garment I have, stands in for buying new ones. Dancing stands in for all sorts of things. But I do treat myself as much as I am able.

Then… asking for a bowl of god? Ask away – this is particularly good for you. Nothing has to stand in for a bowl of god. And the asking itself might just be the goodies in the bowl, if examined well enough.

Two Poems by my Mother

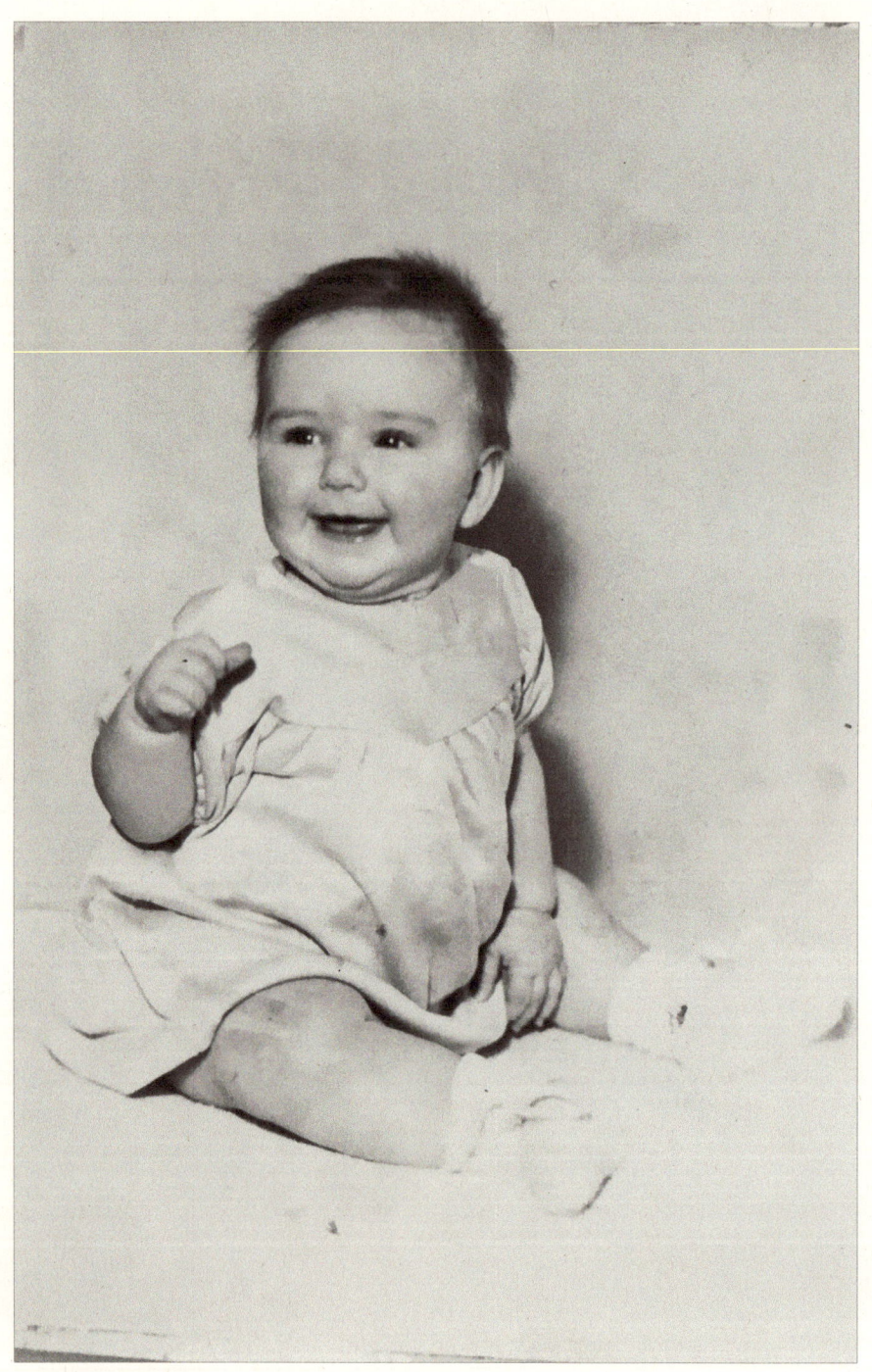

Me as a baby

The first one she wrote in the early 70's, when the hippie revolution was starting to fray at the seams and 'the look' we all had then – shaggy, windblown, relaxed – was beginning more and more to be commercialized. Mom was *really* a free spirit, and apparently she didn't approve of whatever it was she was seeing.

A Mother Laments

What have you done with your eyes?
My children what have you done with
Your eyes?

What have you done with
Your hair
Beads
Boots
Reefers
Hash pipes
Children, what have you done?

Your eyes have been painted
By a commercial artist
Who did not bother to fill in
The water
Ferns
And deepnesses of fucked-in woods

You have traded your decorations
And who knows what else
For Penney mannequins
Children   what
       Have
          You
             Done?

My mother Virginia/Devadasi, France 2013

...And I can't resist adding in this one:

For Katy

Beautiful child with sea-grey eyes
Daughter with mermaid hair
Never in the years I dreamed of you
Did I dream you half so fair.

"Bendita sea tu madre"
So many a one will bless
My Katelin's grace and beauty
I have known since you came to me
Tu madre bendita es.

And to conclude – and further celebrate the era this book covers, I'm concluding with a story I wrote in 1996, while I was working in Tokyo.

Mom as a teen

The Two Princesses

Once upon a time, in a faraway land, in a middling-poor town, in the middle of a vast desert, two little Princesses were born, not entirely by mistake, into a very poor family. In fact, their mother was a Queen and their father a King, but all were under an enchantment and did not know that they were Royal. So the father toiled for little money, walking miles to his work each day, and the mother went nearly mad with worry for her seven children.

One day a visitor came to the little house in its small and unkempt garden – an old friend of the King's, from his brief university days. The friend had been to far-off, marvelous lands, and he had brought with him a magic box in which he put small representations of scenes from these lands; which were then broadcast by means of a lamp behind, onto the dingy wall.

So all the family gathered and watched, open-mouthed, while the wall came alive with strange and marvelous things – bullock carts, and a red castle, and thick jungle coming down to the sea – this was in a place called "India." And high mountain meadows, and a million flowers, and cows with bells, and wooden houses with peaked roofs and intricately carved decorations. This place was called 'Switzerland'.

And the youngest Princess said, all to herself, inside her little tummy – *"I* am going to India!" And the older Princess said to *her*self inside, "And *I* am going to Switzerland!"

The Princesses grew up lithe and graceful, and they danced all the time; until one day, holding hands, they danced right out of that desert town and left forever. Their mother, the Queen who did not know she was a Queen, helped them to catch a ride in a carriage, making sure the driver was not one of the dangerous maniacs so prevalent in that country. They went to seek their fortunes, and to find a better place to be... and to follow those tugging sensations in their bellies which told them in which direction to go. They were seventeen and fifteen, and they were very brave.

Now it must be remembered that this was a strange and wondrous time in the history of the world – a brief time but well-remembered – called 'the Sixties'. As if the decade itself were the Pied Piper, it led millions of children out of their houses into the streets to dance and play. A kind of madness had overtaken the young people – divine madness – and they were frolicking in the meadows, decking each other with flowers; playing music, wandering the roads of that large and various land. And everywhere they went they hailed each other as if they were old friends.

After many adventures, including a perilous climb up a wild mountain called 'Storm King' in a vast range called 'the Rocky Mountains' (they stood at the top at evening, and the rain began to come; they ran down the back of the peak, leaping from boulder to house-sized boulder, as if in a tumbled, tilted landscape of the moon – and found their tarpaulin by its plastic shine in the dark, and crouched there 'til dawn) – they came upon a curious sight.

In a wide plain of waving yellow grasses under the lee of mountains, in a place called Colorado, a large wooden stage had been constructed, and upon it a man with very black skin, and lips like soft black bananas, was singing. *Young girls they get weary – ooh they do get weary – wearing that same old worn-out dress...* he sang. The little Princesses looked around, and then looked at each other. All about them young people flitted like so many multicolored butterflies, in tie-dye gauzes, velvet skirts with handkerchief hems, embroidered headbands. The hair on each and every one of them was big and dramatic – fluffed, crinkled, brushed out from their heads and dotted with flowers. They had haughty looks on their faces, as the glorious often do.

The little Princesses could not help but notice that they themselves were wearing only old trousers, much stained with travel, and boots for hiking; and a little thin blouse without sleeves called a 'tank top', each. For that is all the clothes they had in the world, save for one change each in their rucksacks. So they hastily ducked behind a bush and changed their clothes. The elder Princess put on a white lace dress which the old lady who'd sold it to them for a pittance at a rummage sale had told them was a hundred years old; the younger wore a long gown they had made from a patterned bedspread, from that faraway place called 'India'. Their long hair had been braided in dozens of little braids to keep it out of their way while traveling; they now unbraided it and combed it out, and lo! – it stood out around their heads as glorious and mane-like as any 'hippie's' from San Francisco – for such were the people of this caravan they had encountered.

As they walked out from behind the bush a curious thing happened.

A man was walking towards them. He looked exactly like Prince Valiant, except that he was older – and had somewhat lighter hair and rather a different face – and he had a wild light in his eye. He wore only a pair of chamois trousers with wide, belled bottoms in the fashion of the day; and no shirt. He came straight up to the elder sister and, looking her in the eyes said in a purring voice with foreign intonations, "You arrrre a devil! And an angel! And a devil! And an angel!"

For he was flying in some inner stratosphere, peopled by his own deities and devils, in the thrall of a certain mushroom the people ate in those days, when they could find it.

Well, what with one thing and another, while on the wooden stage the music continued, with skirling violins and famous singers of ballads and thin young men with white faces grinding their nether regions about in the air – the fates of the two young Princesses moved towards their inevitable directions. They were destined to part for three long years... and to meet again in a far-off, miraculous land.

These two Princesses – how shocked and sad they were to say goodbye when they had been each other's sole support for all their journey! But the elder had been invited by the Chamois Prince to join the traveling show – where music, made and danced to, was recorded on flat little strips of stuff made from boiled trees, and preserved so that it could be shone large again, with a light behind, in theaters for people to watch. The younger Princess, he said, was too young to go. So she, tearful and fledgling, was left in the care of a group of friendly people called 'The Hog Farm', which was about as elegant, perhaps, as it sounds – their spokesperson, called 'Wavy Gravy', did speak very eloquently though; and I hope that they were kind. And quite soon, the Princess' mother, the Queen who did not know she was one, hitched rides in many carriages to go and take her to a vast city called 'New York', where the young Princess took work as a governess, and continued to study dance.

The elder Princess felt worried about leaving her sister, and guilty, too, for deserting her. But the opportunity to travel, and see strange new sights, and feel new skies open before her – was more temptation than she could resist.

The band of wandering minstrels slept in teepees tie-dyed in many colors; they traveled in large yellow painted vehicles which had been formerly used to take children to school; they dressed themselves very fancily, and read picture-books all day, about 'Fat Freddy's Cat', and 'Mr. Natural'; they ate mushrooms and cactus buds which gave them strange visions, and they were seldom without their hand-rolled, strange-smelling cigarettes. They looked a bit sleepy all day, and spoke a strange patois which has now passed, largely, into history. All this the elder Princess absorbed whilst she rode with the Chamois Prince, who treated her very nicely and with respect for the most part, though when he ate the cactus buttons he behaved a little oddly.

The men who were recording the scene onto the thin flat strips of boiled trees were entirely foreign. They too began to eat of the mushrooms and cactus buttons, and then for hours they would direct their cameras (for that was the name of the strange devices they used to imprint the pictures on the stuff) at the sky, and murmur to themselves, *Très bien, très bien! Très, très,* très *bien!* This caused the Chamois Prince, who spoke their tongue, to snicker and guffaw.

One day the group, perhaps a hundred of them, reached a vast and dangerous city, at the very edge of the continent; they slept in a large, unfinished hostel there, and many members of the group were accosted by thieves; and one evening while a red sun went down through the poisonous fumes which blew about the city, the Chamois Prince (who had been wont to twirl a rodent's skull about on a leather thong whilst intoxicated, and the like) repaired with the elder Princess to the room they shared, and took out from a small leather case a little, braided whip, like a tiny rattlesnake.

"I weel not hurrrrt you," he reassured her, and, commanding her to lie down, raised her dress up and began to stroke the whip over her young backside. He did not hurt her, as he had promised; but she was very much confused. In fact, she was confused mightily, almost all of the time. (The only time she didn't feel confused was when she had risen early one morning, in a place called 'Iowa', and crept out in the dawn and gathered field-flowers, an armload, and strewed them in the bed so that the Chamois Prince saw them when he awoke; that was a thing she knew about, though she did not know how… perhaps in the century she came from, these things were done.)

That same evening she discovered that the Chamois Prince was far more than twice her age, and she was shocked. Being so unused to the world, she had not been able to see it.

Next day they all flew in the belly of a big silver bird to an island kingdom across a great water. The Princess was agog and could barely eat the lunch brought her by smiling attendants.

In the island kingdom she felt even more strange, for though the people spoke her language, it was not really the same at all, and so many things were different that she felt off-balance and very stupid. And she was cold. Oh, she was so cold! Her few clothes, left over from the desert, were thin, and she was always shivering.

The Chamois Prince had friends in this land, and he compelled her to do such things as sleep in a wide bed with another man – like himself, a university professor – *and* his wife; the wife turned grumpily away while the two men quickly had their way with the little Princess. The little Princess did not enjoy this at all, and felt deeply embarrassed and ashamed; but, she thought, she herself did not understand the ways of things, and grown men must. So she submitted, not to have them feel that she was not – a high accolade of the day – 'groovy'.

Soon the Chamois Prince had to leave that island to return home, and he left the Princess there, at her own request. For she was determined to continue on her travels. There was one last minstrel show, with lights streaming from the stage while trees blew in the wind, and the Princess' boy-scout hat flew off her head to disappear forever into the crowd. The musicians were called 'Pink Floyd', and the mushrooms the Princess had been fed caused her to see an endless procession of twining lovers in the trees and clouds.

Well, after this the Princess had many adventures, and traveled to many lands. She fell tenderly in love with a Prince who did not know he was a Prince, but left him in a land called Provence, because the voice tugging at her belly told her she must go on alone; she fell desperately in love with a Prince who thought he *was* a Prince but didn't have it quite right just how; she fell in love with mummers and minstrels and mimes, and she wandered and was sometimes alone, and she wrote and bound and illustrated little books of her poetry, embroidering the covers with her own hair, to amuse herself and to give as gifts; and she was often mightily confused about the ways of the world.

So often did our Princess suffer, wondering who she was.

So many sights she saw – so many moods she felt – so many people she met – but what was *she* in all this? She felt no center in it save when she wrote. And even in the flowery meadows and high snows of the land called 'Switzerland', which she did reach, she felt that a veil stood between herself and the world.

One morning quite early in her onward journey she was adrift in a vegetable market in a great and famous city. She was accompanied by the Prince-who-thought-he-was-one-but-didn't-have-it-right-just-how; and his brother, who was young and envious. They were in a crush of people all buying and selling cabbages, and skinned hares, and oranges, and pears. All the night long the black-haired minstrel Prince, for it was he whom she thought she loved, had done to her what is called 'making love'. And perhaps he was, making love; but the mushrooms he had eaten, and fed to her, had not this time given her any flight into anywhere, but only served to remind her coldly and soberly that 'making love' was still unknown to her.

Suddenly out of the crowd there stepped a tiny lady. She was about four-and-a-half feet tall; she had eyes like brown egg yolks; she wore a brown coat buttoned up against the frigid morning. She came right up to the Princess and looked her in the eyes. A great love seemed to flow from her; her eyes had a melted, runny look.

"*You!*" she said to the Princess. "You're a *beautiful* girl. You're going to have a wonderful life! You'll have a hard time for a while yet, but then it's going to be all right – it's going to be very, very beautiful." The Princess, in her flame-pink satin and net skirt and her witch's boots and too-thin blouse, gazed at the little lady, heard her thick Cockney brogue; and looked, questioningly, first at the black-haired Prince on her right side; then at his brother, on her left, as if to say: "But what about *them*? What about my black-haired Prince, the hippest, the most brilliant, the most groovy in all the world?"

The old woman glanced cursorily at each brother and then back, eyes brimful of love, to the little Princess. "*You*", she said. "*You* are a beautiful girl. You're going to have a *wonderful* life. *I see these things!*" And she melted back into the crowd and was gone.

One day long after, when many adventures – sad, absurd, frightening, tender, bizarre – had proceeded past the Princess's untutored, often bewildered eyes and heart, she found herself in a pretty, rather anarchic city, back at the very western edge of the continent of her birth. She was with her mother, the ageing Queen-who-didn't-know-she-was-a-Queen; but who, having finally left the poor, oblivious old King, was just beginning to lay the groundwork to finding it out. The Princess had rescued her mother from the desert town far to the south and they had rented cheap lodgings together on a hill high above the sometimes-foggy, sometimes-sparkling bay.

One foggy day, the postman came and brought them a letter from a faraway land called 'India'. For the littlest, youngest Princess, being very brave and having followed the tuggings in her belly, had hitchhiked alone, armed with a knife, her hair in dozens of little braids, wearing the gown made from a bedspread, over the vast and scary continents to get to India. She too had had many adventures, and flown in the belly of a huge silver bird over the water; she too had been in love with a Prince who was definitely a little bit confused about the issue.

In the letter from the littlest Princess there was a miniature portrait, and it fell out and fluttered to the pavement as the elder Princess unfolded the thin blue paper. She bent and picked it up. It was of a man – but was it a man? No – it was a *spirit* – but more than a spirit. He was laughing. The elder Princess felt a strange sensation in her stomach. *He's* laughing! she thought. *Why – I haven't laughed in a year!* And she was filled with a terrible regret. And yet, she was afraid to look at the portrait again – for it seemed to be reminding her of something, deep inside her backbone and deeper, even, than her vitals. Something she already knew, and yet which it would upset her entire life to remember. (And yet, what had she to lose?)

Her mother, the Queen-who-did-not-know-it, took one look at the portrait and said, "I'm going." For she, too, was brave. And she, too, had nothing to lose. But she was older, and she *knew* she had nothing to lose. The Princess her daughter still trembled and held back.

But as inevitable as the sunrise, they went. Through a strange and unusual coincidence, they both had exactly enough money to pay the fare in the silver bird; and so it happened that around noon on a day which smelt, as all days smell in India, of frangipani, and spices, and excrement and urine and damp, like an old wet washcloth slapped across the face, they got out of the belly of the silver bird and greeted with glad cries the youngest Princess. But the eldest Princess stood a little aback, for her sister had changed.

Still long-tressed and slender and beautiful of countenance she was, but lit by a flower of passion and inner sustenance… a maturity had settled in her, though she was just eighteen; a beauty and joy glowed out of her and surrounded her as she stood on the warm earth in her long orange skirt and short Indian blouse, and she smelled of spices and oriental musks.

Osho as he looked when I met him in December 1973, in Bombay

em to a dwelling-place she had found for them all, ıt wooden house with carved window-shutters, where ught strange fruits for them to eat; and there they changed their garments.

And then she took them to meet the man in the portrait.

First they went in a rickshaw to a large, plain building with a flat face; climbed many stairs; went into an apartment high up; and there, in the hallway, met the fierce gargoyle which referred to itself as 'Laxmi', which guarded Him. It gazed at them in ferocity and said a disparaging thing or two, but it let them pass.

They went down another corridor and, knocking first, opened a door. First the youngest Princess, then the Queen (who was just this moment stepping over the threshold into her Queenliness) stepped in; the eldest Princess stepped – and was hit by a wall of bliss so strong she fell to her knees. A perfume enveloped her, as of pines and intimate, primeval forest mysteries; but the intensity of the *consciousness* in the room was so strong that those primeval smells had been transformed into light. She was blasted by it. She felt like a beetle suddenly transfixed in the vivid daylight of an open door. She could barely breathe, and yet all there was to breathe was ecstasy. She didn't know what to do.

As she managed to rise and step forward, as if on a stage before a thousand people (but all were light, and only her own fears were played back to her instantaneously) one single thought came in the calm bright empty space, and sat startled in her mind: *Why, he's not an Indian – He's an everything!"*

And so it started.

My sister and me in Riverside, 1969

I'M GRATEFUL TO....

Peggy Sands, book designer extraordinaire, for your creative flair that always takes me much further than I knew it was possible to go; for your loving supportiveness; your labors WAY above and beyond the call of friendship, and for believing in my work.

Surahbhi, Jenny Harpur, and *Julia Farrants,* for the loving, careful, intuitive editing – each of you has her own style, and each had valuable input. (I was particularly grateful since two prospective editors had already refused the project: one because she thought the idea of publishing one's teenage poems was *absolutely terrible* {and she could be right, but I felt I had to do it anyway}, and the other because she was freaked out by photos from the sixties showing naked people frolicking {innocently!} in the woods. {As it happened, those photos were unfortunately deemed too incendiary to print}).

Punya, for your Swiss-standard tech help and overview, and for being there in such a consistent way through the travails of this and my previous book. You cannot know how essential this is to the birthing – it gives me courage. In those last fraught weeks, you hung in as, quite simply, a hero.

My late mother, Devadasi, for storing my every scribble through the decades. And for giving me nothing but praise and encouragement from the toddler day I began to make up poems.

Alexander Akin, my nephew, for storing boxes of journals and photos.

Wai Lun Lee, from Easy PC, for giving tech help, even from faraway Japan.

Lamberts Print Shop, Hebden Bridge, for always being there to print more editing copies, and for the professional scans of pictures. You even deliver!

Hanging Loose Press, in Brooklyn, for publishing my poems for so long, and for inviting me to submit the manuscript for *Impassioned Cows by Moonlight.* This was so encouraging, and such a delight!

Professor Dennis Saleh – I don't know if you're even still with us – but as my first poetry teacher, you were superb: knowledgeable, enthusiastic, helpful, and unafraid to give praise if you liked something.

The late Denise Levertov, for mentoring an unknown teen.

The late Jacques J. Vidal, for the adventure, and for being such a sweet, alive, and hearty man

The late David Gancher: We loved, we struggled, and poems and songs came out. Glory Hallelujah! I feel very appreciative towards you, despite the gulf that emerged between us.

Carl Gancher, for your sensitivity, grace, and compassion during our phone talks about those long-ago times.

The late Paul Winstanley: You were good to me – better than I was, finally, to you. I'm very sorry.

The late Herb Baskin, for the little island of stability during that time, and for being you: inimitable, jovian, joyful – someone I've never stopped loving.

And to the few scoundrels and perps in these pages: I'm grateful you can't keep me from telling my story, including your part in it! I'm sure you had your reasons, and I would love to hear about them sometime. I guess we are all, in our own ways, both idiots and angels…

Audiences in coffeehouses and open mikes in California and Britain, who listened to some of these poems and expressed warm appreciation. I love to read aloud, and your presence there made it all so juicy and rewarding.

ABOUT THE AUTHOR

Madhuri was born in 1952 in California. She spent 30 years in Osho's communes, and now lives in the English Pennines, where she loves to go on long walks. She is a poet, memoirist, Human Design reader, Metaphysical Therapist, and artist, and is a frequent contributor to Osho News. This is her 7th book.

For more information or to buy her books:
madhurijewel.com/books